Teachers Organizing for Change

Teachers Organizing for Change

Making Literacy Learning Everybody's Business

Cathy Fleischer
Eastern Michigan University

National Council of Teachers of English
1111 W. Kenyon Road, Urbana, Illinois 61801-1096

Manuscript and Production Editor: Tom Tiller

Interior Design: Doug Burnett

Cover Design: Pat Mayer

Cover Photograph ©1998–1999 Tony Stone Images. All rights reserved.

NCTE Stock Number: 49995-3050

Library of Congress Cataloging-in-Publication Data

Fleischer, Cathy.
   Teachers organizing for change : making literacy learning everybody's
   business / Cathy Fleischer.
        p. cm.
   Includes bibliographical references and index.
   "NCTE stock number: 49995"—T.p. verso.
   ISBN 0-8141-4999-5 (pbk.)
   1. Literacy programs—United States—Case studies. 2. Parent-teacher
   relationships—United States—Case studies. 3. Teachers and community
   —United States—Case studies. 4. Language arts teachers—United
   States—Case studies. I. Title.

LC151.F59 2000
428'.007—dc21

00-020044

Contents

Foreword

In 1988, the Modern Language Association, with support from the Ohio State University, the Ohio Humanities Council, and the Federation of State Humanities Councils, sponsored *The Right to Literacy* conference in which "teachers of reading and writing in classes from first grade through graduate school, as well as teachers without institutional affiliations in rural communities and in urban centers"(Lunsford, Moglen, and Slevin 1), came together in Columbus, Ohio, to better understand the dimensions of their work. Sessions at this conference identified a range of issues and questions that became the focus of a follow-up conference, The Responsibilities of Literacy, held in Pittsburgh in 1990. Milbrey W. McLaughlin, professor of education at Stanford University, visited as many sessions of this conference as possible, listening, taking notes, and drawing conclusions that informed remarks she made during the conference's final plenary session.

A decade removed, I recall McLaughlin expressing appreciation for the range, quality, and effectiveness of the literacy work that conference participants shared with one another. I also hear her saying something like this: It is dramatically clear from the work and ideas you are sharing with one another here that the public's definition of literacy and how it is learned is different from the definition of literacy that underlies your effective efforts to teach reading and writing in and outside of schools across the country. We need to better inform the public about the nature of literacy and how it is best learned. We need to get new definitions of literacy and literacy learning abroad in the land.

All heads nodded agreement. McLaughlin's charge was right on. Even as she said the words, McLaughlin knew, of course, that half of what she was saying would not come as news to any one of the literacy workers gathered in Pittsburgh in 1990. Research has demonstrated beyond question that literacy is not simply a matter of decoding the words of already-composed texts, nor is it a matter of learning letters and then learning how to string them together into words, and words into sentences, as one might string beads into necklaces. Literacy is instead "the ability to use language in order to become an active participant in all forms of public discourse" (MLA, 1988). Literacy is the ability to use written language to claim meaning for experience and understanding, and to establish relations with others. It is not surprising, then, that when we understand literacy for what it is, we want it to be learned not in rote drills or decontextualized exercises but rather in purposeful, functional activities undertaken in socially meaningful contexts.

McLaughlin also knew that while her audience realized that public understandings of literacy and how it is best learned were inadequate, few if any in that audience knew how to help the general public become better informed. Participants in the Responsibilities of Literacy conference were for the most part teachers, not policy makers nor even policy advisors. How might teachers take up the work of political activism and still responsibly fulfill their work as professional teachers? How might they work to enlighten public understandings and still devote the time and energy it takes to prepare for, teach, and assess their students' learning in our overcrowded classrooms?

During the decade that has passed since the Responsibilities of Literacy conference, it may well be argued that public policy and public understandings of the nature of literacy have regressed rather than progressed toward enlightenment. Tests constructed to assess the measurable if not the meaningful have proliferated, and in too many cases, sadly, they have driven competent and creative teachers to set aside instructional practices that promise to prepare students to become lifelong readers, writers, and learners. In too many cases teachers have replaced these practices with test-preparation drills that enable students to reproduce tomorrow what they will forget the following day. A focus on short-term results has replaced long-term goals, hardly the foundation for educating a citizenry prepared to thrive in an information era and in the global economy that policy makers appropriately remind us are shaping the world in which our students will live and work.

It is not that dedicated, accomplished teachers of literacy—like the author of this book, Cathy Fleischer, who is already well known to us for her influential work in teacher research—have not labored diligently to develop, disseminate for critique, and use theoretically sound and research-tested practices for teaching literacy. NCTE's journals, books, and conferences testify to those efforts. Nor is it as if dedicated teachers of literacy have not worked in the public arena to develop and write standards for teaching and learning at local, state, and national levels and to put in place teaching practices designed to prepare students to achieve those standards. In fact, it was at the conclusion of three years of teachers' work on just such a project that Cathy Fleischer tells us she decided to undertake the study that led her to write the book you are about to read.

At a meeting of the state board of education in Michigan, Fleischer watched policy makers dismiss arguments for English language arts content standards when those arguments were made by well-informed, experienced teachers and then turn around to embrace the same arguments when they were made by concerned parents. Following that meeting, Fleischer tells us, she decided to immerse herself in research that would allow her to offer practicing teachers a variety of ways in which they might proactively gain public support for forms of literacy education that best serve students' learning. *Teachers Organizing for Change: Making Literacy Learning Everybody's Business* is the product of that work. In it, Fleischer introduces us to imaginative, effective teachers like Cathy Gwizdala, Julie King, Kathleen Hayes-Parvin, Carolyn Berge, Rhonda Meier, and Amy Pace and the specific ways in which they have successfully informed their students' parents about how literacy is best taught, and in the process, how they have engaged parents in their children's literacy learning. If these rich case studies were all that Fleischer offers us in *Teachers Organizing for Change*, this book would be most valuable reading and would take its rightful place among a growing number of inspiring books that report on parent outreach projects. But their work is not all that Fleischer presents us.

In addition to sharing with us detailed case studies of teachers who have developed and are successfully using a variety of practices to do what Milbrey McLaughlin urged all literacy workers to do a decade ago—to exercise our hard earned authority to enrich and extend public understandings of literacy and how it is learned—Cathy Fleischer does two other things that recommend this book to readers. First, she relates the voices and accomplishments of teachers working for change to the voices and accomplishments of activists working for change in other fields of general social importance, among them, urban neighborhood organizers like Saul Alinsky, community health and social workers like Bill Berkowitz, water quality and environmental advocates like Andy Buchsbaum, hazardous waste activists like Lois Gibbs, and public health workers like Barbara Israel, to name a few. Second, she discusses the work of teacher activists and social activists in other fields in terms of theories and principles found in the literature of community organizing. In so doing, Fleischer not only introduces us to a rich body of literature with which we may be unfamiliar but also creates a dialogue between this literature and educational literature with which readers will be familiar. Grounding her discussions of community organizing in examples from the fields of environmental and public health and her discussions of teachers working for change in parent outreach, Fleischer focuses readers' attention on the truth of Ernesto Cortes's observation: Organizing is teaching.

As she introduces us to concepts (e.g., communities, not individuals, are the unit of practice) and strategies (e.g., the gossip factor) that underlie the work of community organizers, Fleischer demonstrates how the time teachers spend in parent outreach is, in effect, time spent developing and realizing effective instruction for their students and time saved in working through misunderstandings and handling problems. As she focuses our attention on the work of social activists in the fields of environmental and public health, Fleischer extends the repertoire of practices that we may use to inform and enlist public support for sound teaching practices. And as she introduces us to community organizing literature written from a variety of perspectives, Fleischer provides us with a theoretical basis and principles that can guide us in the development of additional practices for use in settings like and unlike the illustrative ones we read about in *Teachers Organizing for Change*. Whether she is describing orientations to change that community organizers assume or the model for teacher organizing that she has developed, Fleischer illustrates her descriptions with examples of work that teachers are already doing or with work that teachers will recognize as doable and worth doing.

An imaginative researcher and theorist, Fleischer does two additional things that make *Teachers Organizing for Change* required reading. Reminding us that she is the teacher and teacher educator we have come to know in her earlier writings, she provides us with a set of hypothetical scenarios—scenarios featuring teachers like us, teachers we have known, teachers facing the challenges that surround us—and in discussions of these scenarios she demonstrates the range of community organizing orientations and strategies that we may use to convert problematic situations into productive occasions for teaching and learning. In addition, she provides us with workshop materials we may use to prepare groups of inservice and preservice colleagues to reach out to parents—and by extension to the public at large—to create more accurate understandings of our work. In effect, she leaves us with means to do what Milbrey McLaughlin called upon us to do a decade ago: Provide the public with theoretically sound, research-tested information about the nature of literacy and how it is best taught and learned in order that we who teach in and outside schools may engage the nation's boys and girls, men and women, in equally sound, equally well-tested literacy education.

Cathy Fleischer is a graceful writer whose conversational style makes readers feel as if they are sitting there with her as she interviews activists—and reading over her shoulder as she discovers resources for teachers in the community organizing literature—and thus reading *Teachers Organizing for Change* is as pleasurable an experience as it is educational and necessary. *Teachers Organizing for Change* is a book for which we have been waiting. And it comes not a moment too soon.

Works Cited

Lunsford, Andrea A., Helene Moglen, and James Slevin, Eds. *The Right to Literacy*. New York: MLA, 1990.

Modern Language Association, Ohio State University, and the Federation of State Humanities Councils. "Call for Papers." The Right to Literacy Conference in Columbus, OH. September 1988.

Patricia Lambert Stock
Michigan State University

Acknowledgments

When I began doing research for this book, I saw myself as mildly politically active but embarrassingly unaware of the nitty-gritty of true activism. Thus the organizers who jump-started my education by sending me toward particular books, authors, Web sites, and other organizers were a true gift. I'd like to thank those whose names you'll read in the pages that follow for their time and for their patience with me as I learned: Renee Bayer, Dan Cantor, Tracey Easthope, and Barbara Israel.

I am also grateful to the teachers who have shared ideas with me about parent and community outreach over the past decade. Several of the teachers whom I interviewed for this book have worked together for a number of years. We all feel, I know, immense respect and gratitude for each other for the amazing learning that has taken place: Carolyn Berge, Cathy Gwizdala, Kathleen Hayes-Parvin, and Julie King. Others whom I interviewed and who helped inform my thinking in important ways include Jennifer Walsh, Sue Kohfeldt, Ronda Meier, and Amy Pace.

Another group of teachers, those in the Eastern Michigan Writing Project Teacher Research Group, nudged me toward thinking about the next steps that teacher-researchers can take toward becoming teacher-organizers: Jennifer Buehler, Cari Gittleson, Sarah Lorenz, Mary Martzolf, Jennifer Nicholson, Terry Stout, Dawn Putnam, Tesha Thomas, Karen Watts, and Paige Webster.

Several colleagues and friends either read drafts and offered specific advice or just talked with me about my ideas; I'd like to thank them for their honesty of response, which continually pushes my thinking. Specifically, thanks to Bill Tucker and Becky Sipe, my colleagues at Eastern Michigan University; Dana Fox at the University of Arizona; Laura Roop of the Oakland Writing Project; and Patti Stock and Janet Swenson at Michigan State University. Thanks to Patti also for both writing the Foreword and helping me with the title. Michael Greer, formerly at NCTE, is integral to this list, too, as he encouraged my writing this book from the moment when it was just an idea. Also at NCTE are Tom Tiller and Zarina Hock, who guided this book to completion with great attention and grace.

For this particular book, the traditional "thanks to the spouse" line takes on new meaning. My husband, Andy Buchsbaum, is its inspiration—as the person who first introduced me to community organizing and who for the last seventeen years has talked to me about the connections between his work and mine. Andy is a longtime organizer and advocate, and his everyday work has demonstrated for me the power that a community of committed people can direct toward creating change. I thank him for his patience—and for the work he does which has helped change the lives of countless others.

And to my sons Seth and Jesse—budding community organizers and activists already—thanks for sharing the computer with me!

1 Entering the Conversation

Our national discussion about public schools is despairing and dismissive, and it is shutting down our civic imagination.

Mike Rose, *Possible Lives*

Today, unreasonable voices outside our profession are clamoring to tell us how and what to teach. People who have little idea how children learn to read and write are speaking out loudly, bombarding the media with simplistic "quick fixes" and loud criticism of sound educational practices. And we are letting them do it.

Regie Routman, *Literacy at the Crossroads*

L et me begin with a story which will, I hope, illustrate how the words of Mike Rose and Regie Routman quoted above became real for me—and have, in fact, sounded a battle cry in my own work and life. A few years ago I attended a meeting when new English language arts content standards were being considered for adoption by the state board of education. These standards had been in the works for three years (see Wixson, Peters, and Potter; Fleischer et al.). K–12 classroom teachers and English educators had labored over the exacting thought and writing of these standards, spending hours and hours after school and on weekends, to produce a document which reflected current theory and research about how best to teach reading, writing, speaking, and listening to all the various kinds of kids we see in our classrooms. These teachers studied hard, argued hard, and wrote and revised in hopes of coming up with a document that reflected the best of what we know about how to teach the language arts. At this particular meeting, teacher after teacher stood up to defend the document to the board of education, many of whose members were dismissive of their arguments, letting the teachers know quite clearly that they believed the document was too progressive, out-of-sync with the kind of teaching the board thought should be going on. Teachers watched these board members in disbelief, disheartened by the fact that a number of them had decided the best methods for teaching English without having spent even a fraction of the time these teachers had spent in classrooms, without having read even a quarter of the material these teachers had diligently studied in order to prepare the curriculum statement. The teachers were frustrated, aware that their voices were coming through to certain board members in muffled tones at best, their message blocked despite their knowledge and passion.

After a somber lunch break in which the teachers shared their despair at the tone of the meeting, we met again in the imposing auditorium in order to hear open testimony from those attending. A number of parents rose to speak, their strong voices filling the room, and, as they did, I could feel a palpable shift in the tone of the proceedings. As parent after parent began to testify, forcefully defending these content standards as important for their own children, illustrating their defense through specific classroom examples, I sat back, amazed at the knowledge and understanding of these parents, wondering how they knew so much about the issues that so occupy the hearts and minds of language arts teachers everywhere. As the last parent got up to speak, identifying both herself and the school her children attended, I recognized the location and even knew the teacher of one of her children: a school that many would define as "challenged" for a number of reasons (from its low socioeconomic status to the many parents who hadn't themselves graduated from high school and were often suspicious of schooling in general), a teacher whose commitment to whole language principles was well known to many of us in English education around the state (based on her participation in Writing Projects, TAWL groups, and other reform movements). This parent began to speak, slowly at first but gathering momentum as she went— and articulately defended the whole language program her child was a part of, explaining why it worked well, how her child had grown, how her child had learned how to learn. All the time she was speaking, she had clutched in her hands a pink booklet, a booklet I recognized even across the crowded room as one written for parents by her child's teacher, Cathy Gwizdala. In this booklet, Cathy had carefully laid out for parents her whole language philosophy, focusing specifically on spelling growth and documenting carefully how certain students developed their spelling over the course of the year within a whole language classroom (see the Appendix to this chapter for excerpts from Cathy's booklet). This particular parent, now that she understood why whole language was used in her child's class, was not only support- ive—she was impassioned. The room was silent except for her voice, with the board members leaning forward in their chairs to catch her words.

This incident has stayed with me over the past few years as I've thought hard about what actually occurred that day. We all know that the voices of teachers, even knowledgeable and caring teachers, have been very nearly dismissed in the public discussion of our nation's schools. What became clear for me that day is that the voices of parents, especially those who have been educated and informed by teachers about the issues that matter most, can help us reenter the conversation.[1] Parents—and other community members—can help set the terms of the discussion that's held about public education, in part because, as "the voting public," their voices carry a certain weight with legislators and school board members, and in part because their increased understanding of the issues allows them to be informed consumers of media hype and hysterical talk. These two roles for parents are intertwined, one dependent on the other, and are vital if we have any hopes both for changing the tenor of the conversation and for expanding participation in the conversation to include the voices of teachers.

When I think about the response to teachers by the state board of education that day, I recognize it as typical of what I've come to see and to despair of as I have tried to make sense of the contrast between, on one hand, the hard work that knowledgeable teachers do to make their classrooms places of hope and learning for the students they teach and, on the other hand, how such teaching is often depicted by others. I pick up the newspaper day after day to hear these good, informed ways of teaching attacked by reporters who aren't always clear on the issues; I go to local board meetings to hear certain board members lambaste these ways of teaching as unproductive for kids; I even find myself at my son's soccer games listening to parents complain about certain teachers for teaching whole language or writing workshop or any of a variety of approaches that informed educators in our field know work for kids but that have somehow become negative buzz words for the English language arts classroom. And it has become more serious than just talk; we read in NCTE's *Council Chronicle* about a twenty-year veteran teacher in the St. Louis area fired for violation of the student discipline code because she did not censor a student's language in first draft writing; we hear about a principal suspended for over two years (at an estimated cost of $1 million) because of her advocacy of whole language and learner centered curriculum in her school (Flanagan, "Myers to Be" and "Beleaguered Principal"). We read newspaper after newspaper and listen to radio and television commentary, only to hear whole language attacked as "a simple way to prepare a nation for a godless world system" (Duff) or process writing reduced as "the notion that standards, grammar, grades, and judgment are bad. Self-expression, self-esteem and personal rules are good" (Leo). These ideas somehow take on a life of their own and become a version of truth for those who read and listen to them; suddenly, these "facts" then carry over to state and national legislators. We need look no further than the recent furor in Congress over the Reading Excellence Act to see this process in action: legislators began to make decisions based on impartial understandings marketed by certain individuals and groups whose characterizations of reading instruction were taken as the sole truth.[2] Or we might look instead to the amazingly circuitous journey of the recent Ebonics debate, in which loud and adamant voices protested the use of Ebonics in the Oakland, California, schools, fueled by a wire service report that teachers there were going to "train teachers to conduct classes in the nonstandard English speech familiar to many African-Americans" (Chiles A15). This misleading media report, later acknowledged to be "inaccurate," led "the rest of the country initially to believe the Oakland school system was going to 'teach' ebonics"— rather than train teachers to recognize patterns of speech common to African Americans and use that understanding as a way to nudge these students into standard English (Chiles A15). This inaccurate version nonetheless became the version of truth believed by both ordinary and prominent citizens around the country, encouraging everyone, it seemed, to voice an opinion—but an opinion based on misinformation. In fact, in a recent front page story in my local Michigan newspaper (from the Newhouse News Service), the reporter takes the stance of surprise when he claims, "The smoke has thinned, the spotlight dimmed, and some intriguing news has trickled out of Prescott Elementary School on the west side of this struggling city: Ebonics might actually work" (Chiles A1).

I learn about these attacks, these mischaracterizations, many of which (not all, I know) are done by fair-minded people who simply don't understand the issues, and I wonder where we have gone wrong. How is it that the national characterization of some of these sound educational ideas has become so reductive, so simplistic, and so dismissive? How is it that so many ordinary people, predisposed to believe in schools and teachers, have been influenced so strongly against certain ways of teaching? I realize, of course, that a number of attacks emerge from the work of well-orchestrated and well-funded groups whose tactics for undermining certain educational practices are sophisticated. My concern here is that teachers too often hold back from explaining their methodologies because of both the real and the imagined influence of these groups, conflating mere questions by parents who could be swayed either way with the well-formed attacks by those who are not willing to listen to anyone. A case in point concerns two sets of my friends, both of whom have school-aged children. One couple is very liberal; both the husband and wife are strong activists who work for social justice issues in their professional work and personal lives. The other is a more middle of the road, slightly conservative couple. All four of these people are educated, intelligent, and concerned about schooling issues. All have, on several occasions, questioned me, sometimes vehemently, about their children's respective classrooms, the second set of parents in particular becoming incensed at certain practices (such as inventive spelling or young adult literature or the perceived lack of grammar instruction), the first set of parents merely wondering why things are done in particular ways. Usually during our conversations, I spend about five minutes explaining some of the theory behind such practices and the kinds of pedagogy they might look for in their children's classrooms. And every time, each of them responds with relief: "Oh, I get it now," they tell me. "That makes sense."

As I think about their reactions, I realize that as English educators and teachers, we've not done nearly enough of this kind of explanation in order to relieve the anxiety of parents like these—the vast number of people who may never have heard of whole language or process writing until they read an article in *The Atlantic* or hear a commentary on their local talk radio show. After hearing certain practices maligned over and over, they naturally are suspicious if their child's teacher seems to use the particular practices named in these reports. Thus by our silence, we are contributing to the tension that seems to be on the increase between teachers using these best practices and parents who are rightly concerned about the education of their children. And so, a cycle begins and even escalates: Many teachers teach quite separately from their surrounding communities, certain individuals and groups raise objections, the media jumps on the controversy, school boards respond and issue edicts . . . and teachers go on teaching, the more informed ones continuing in the practices they are convinced work, the less certain changing practices to satisfy these edicts. What seems to be lacking in this scenario is the teacher-professional seeing as part of her or his job the task of informing and educating others, a necessary part of any professional's job (as Schön and others tell us). Vito Perrone puts it succinctly: "Only when teachers themselves assume the dominant position in regard to issues of teaching and learning in their classrooms, and begin to speak more broadly and authoritatively on matters of education, will we see significant improvement" (qtd. in Routman 169).

Rose reminds us of the danger of this dismissive attitude toward teachers that seems integral to the public discussion, lamenting that it is "shutting down our civic imagination." Routman brings it closer to home, stating that many outsiders to education who don't understand the issues behind progressive teaching practices, who haven't immersed themselves in either the theory or the practice of such teaching, are often the loudest voices in this one-sided debate. She challenges us to become more vocal: "We are letting them do it," she insists; we are letting these others set the debate, and it has thus become too often a simple-minded debate presented in either/ors which ignore the complexities and complications of real classrooms. As I read Routman and Rose and Perrone, as I sit in more and more board meetings like the one described above, as I attend PTO meetings and overhear conversations in grocery stores and airports and movie theaters, I know that it's time for the voices of teachers to be heard in this public debate. As classroom teachers and English educators, we cannot sit back any longer and let those who are not knowledgeable about classrooms and kids and the complex contexts that are our schools set the tone and the language for the public discussion. We must become leaders in informing the public about the complexity and the reality of public education; we must become political. Routman again helps us by defining what she thinks it means for teachers to become political:

> actively and thoughtfully entering the educational conversation . . . , having the language and the knowledge to move beyond our classrooms and schools into the wider public arena to state our case, . . . carefully listening with an open mind and being responsive to the public's concerns and questions, . . . knowing how and when to communicate and who to seek out for support, . . . using research and reason instead of emotion and extremist views, . . . being professional in the highest sense (xvi–xvii).

To this wonderful list, I would add one more: beginning our activism with the group that not only desires knowledge the most, but which can be our best advocates in the public debate—parents. What we learn from the anecdote which begins this chapter, and what I've learned from observation in my various roles as former high school teacher, as English educator, and as parent, is that when a teacher explains and translates to a concerned parent and includes that parent in some of the actual practice of his or her theory, the parent can become a strong advocate who can promote changes in ways that a teacher cannot. The parent can then take the lead in educating others—not only in formal ways such as speaking at a board of education meeting, but also in the casual conversations that take place every day.

Merely exhorting teachers to become political is not enough, of course. Convincing teachers who are already busy and overwhelmed to take on what seems to be just one more task is not easy. But I wondered, when I first began to think hard about this issue of advocacy, if lack of time is the only barrier standing in the way of educators entering a more public conversation about their teaching. And so I asked: Over the course of two intensive workshops on teachers and advocacy attended by about one hundred teachers, my colleague Laura Roop and I invited teachers to write about their reasons for shying away from this role (Fleischer and Roop, "Reaching Out" and "Taking It"). Time issues, as you may imagine, cropped up again and again, but variations on two other responses appeared almost as often. The first was that many of these teachers felt they had a lack of articulated knowledge of why they teach in the ways they do, i.e., a lack of a clear theoretical understanding of the issues behind certain practices. So, for example, while these teachers might know that certain practices are successful with their kids, they aren't really certain about *why* that is the case. They have learned about such practices in a workshop or in college, and they have tried them and adapted them and made them their own, but they seem to have a hard time articulating to themselves why these practices fit in so well with their own stances in teaching.

The next most common answer was this: Most of the teachers we surveyed feel they have no idea how to communicate their beliefs to others, especially others they suspect might be opposed to their stances. They imagine the forces that object to their work as so strong and organized that they don't even know where to begin to respond. And they feel uncomfortable being put in the position of conflict. At a workshop I recently attended, one teacher pushed this even farther. "As teachers, we are trained to be nurturers," she told us, "to see all sides of the issues, to see things with all the shades of gray. That way of thinking and talking doesn't make for a very good response in a public forum where everyone's looking for sound bites."

But teachers can do it. We all know teachers, like Cathy Gwizdala, who have been able to educate their own parent communities about best practices in English language arts. As we see from the story above, her choice to become more outspoken about her beliefs made a difference. As she felt more in command of her own knowledge, she was able to write a booklet for parents; in turn, after they read the booklet, her parents felt more knowledgeable and were thus better equipped to communicate with others—a broadening circle, beginning with the teacher.

And there are other teachers who also do an impressive job of helping parents and surrounding communities understand the curricular issues underlying our best practices. We have incidental, anecdotal accounts of what has worked in specific communities, anecdotes which help as we consider how what others have done might be transferred to our own situation. When I've shared Cathy's story, for example, with various groups of teachers, everyone wants a copy of her booklet; everyone wants to know, "How can I do that?" Convinced that other teachers would have equally interesting ways of parent outreach, I began asking teachers I knew about how they educated the parents of the children in their classrooms. The teachers I spoke with came from a wide variety of classroom circumstances: different grade levels, different kinds of schools (suburban, urban, rural), different parental backgrounds (wealthy, poor, middle class; working parents, stay-at-home parents; single parent, dual parent, grandparents, and so on). This variety came to be important to me as I realized the means of outreach are not necessarily universal: The local circumstances of the school, the parents, and the students dictate, in large part, what kinds of approaches will be successful. A few of us began to talk in some depth, coming to realize more and more how important this kind of education was if we wanted to have our voices impact the public conversation, and, as we shared approaches, we began to learn from each other's practice. Eventually, we developed some workshops about both our rationale for this work and approaches that have worked (we led workshops nationally at NCTE spring conferences in Charlotte and Albuquerque, and regionally at Michigan Reading Association and for a Goals 2000 group in Midland, Michigan). Responses to our workshops were extremely positive; other teachers seemed to be grasping for ideas on how to work with parents and took away a number of specific strategies that had been successful for the teachers with whom I was working.

As you read the chapter which follows this introduction, you will meet five of these teachers and hear some of the ways in which they have expanded and integrated their teaching programs to try to include the education of parents. Their stories certainly are not the only stories out there; neither are their strategies the only ones that can be successful in reaching out to parents. What I find intriguing about their words, though, is how a conscientious approach to informing parents plays out for them in some very different settings. What is also useful, I think, is what their experiences might trigger in another teacher's mind about what might work in *her or his* particular circumstances. When Kathleen, for example, talks about how she uses "teaching letters" to help educate the parents of middle school children about the language of poetry, another teacher might be inspired to try out the concept of a teaching letter, but in a very different way. When Carolyn speaks of an introductory picnic for all the children and parents in her multiage elementary classroom of fifty students, a high school teacher might be inspired to try another kind of introductory activity for the families of just one of his or her classes.

What inspires me in their work is the way in which each teacher's attempts at outreach have led to parents' increased understanding of why these teachers teach in the ways they do—and, in many circumstances, to the parents' verbal expression of that understanding to other parents, to other teachers and administrators, and to others out in the community. I'm not talking about an all-out revolution here, but rather a quiet one, characterized by talk among parents and others that is beginning to counteract some of the other messages about education that they receive on an almost daily basis. I've come to believe—quite strongly—that a quiet revolution is where we need to begin.

But I also wonder if this kind of quiet revolution is enough. While I remain exhilarated by the fine work these teachers are doing with parents, and while I believe it is a start toward the kind of change that needs to take place, two concerns have stayed with me. First, I worry that while the teachers profiled in Chapter 2 are experiencing success with their parents because of the individual strategies they are adopting, these strategies might be seen by others as just that: a group of isolated exercises which results in other teachers acquiring a laundry list of ideas rather than a consistent outreach program. This lack of a consistent program leads to my second concern: Without a sustained, consistent approach to parent outreach, how can we effect the kind of long-term change we need—from the necessity of including teacher voices in *all* the conversations about educational issues to the specific information that needs to be part of the present conversations about reform? My fear is that while English educators and teachers are starting to learn a lot about parent outreach, we generally don't know how to expand from the incidental, anecdotal accounts of how to work with particular parents in order to create a more sustained program of parent outreach that will help in creating a new mindset. And that's what we really have to do: create a new mindset for people—about teachers, about the curriculum, about best practices.

Creating this new mindset in any significant, long-term way is no easy task, especially once we move beyond the level of the individual to consider changing the minds of a group at large, such as a school board or a legislative body or even "the public." And it becomes even more difficult to effect this kind of change when we feel under siege, as teachers have rightly felt in recent days when the attacks on English educators and language arts instruction in general have reached a crisis point, when our only option seems to be *reacting* to a way of thinking that seems pervasive. The Reading Excellence Act serves as a ready example of this. As Congress sat poised to pass a law that would limit, even disallow, approaches to staff development and reading instruction of the whole language variety, teachers were urged from all sides to react: to call and write their representatives, to write letters-to-the-editor, to publish press releases, all in the name of taking a strong stand against this legislation. NCTE became actively involved, starting a Web site with updated information as well as providing sample letters and responses for calling a legislator and producing the NCTE *Action Handbook* (which later evolved into a packet titled *Shaping the Future of Education: A Guide to Political Advocacy for Educators and Administrators*), with many examples of how to understand the legislative process and contact legislators on current issues affecting education. Numerous sessions at recent NCTE and other conferences have devoted themselves to this topic, such as Regie Routman and Donald Graves's presentation "If Not Us, Then Who?" and Denny Taylor's address to the Conference on English Education, both at the November 1997 NCTE Convention in Detroit.

The strategies that have been impressed upon teachers through these various forums are necessary and important ones. When under immediate attack, as teachers all over the country were with this proposed legislation, one needs to *react*, and to react quickly and strongly, with as many voices as possible. But relying on these reactive strategies alone to bring about long-term change is a bit like shutting the barn door after the cow is gone—i.e., responding after the battle lines are set and the terms of the discussion are defined. What we miss in this approach is the opportunity for teachers to be the ones who are actively setting the parameters of the conversation, helping to create public opinion—rather than being placed in a defensive position all the time.

What we need, I believe, is to find a way to balance this kind of reactive response with a more proactive one—reaching out to inform the communities around us *before* the crisis occurs, and as an everyday part of the work we do. The anecdote cited in the first pages of this chapter is a perfect example of what I mean by a proactive response:

Cathy Gwizdala took the time to inform the parents in her classroom about her pedagogy—before they even raised questions—as a way of helping them understand why they might see certain practices in her classroom. Then, when those practices came under attack by an outside force, the parents felt compelled to speak out—with knowledge, with vehemence, with conviction. Rather than being placed in a defensive position, struggling to explain to parents the rationale for inventive spelling, for example, *after* their hackles were raised by articles they had read or stories they had heard, Cathy was able to anticipate their questions and head off many of their concerns. What would happen if we could create a cadre of educators who approach parent outreach in this kind of ongoing, proactive way: seeing part of their role as one of constant education of parents, even when things seem to be going smoothly and parents are not raising any questions and complaints. Could a proactive approach of providing information and listening to concerns in a serious way head off problems down the road? Could a consistent program of proactive work make those moments when we need to be reactive a little easier, lessening the siege mentality that has pervaded and overwhelmed our work for the past few years?

Most teachers do not see this charge of parent and community outreach as part of their role at present. Ooms's 1992 survey of first-year teachers indicates the amazing statistic that 70 percent of them felt parents were their adversaries (qtd. in Swap 156), a feeling I dramatically recall from my own first year of teaching when my voice quavered every time I had to call a parent, a task I avoided as much as I possibly could. And it's no wonder. Teachers generally have little or no instruction in working with parents, other than some sessions in how to run a parent/teacher conference or how to get more parent volunteers in their class. And if we start thinking of the role in even more expansive ways, moving toward teachers working with parents in a consistent, proactive way, a way that will create long-term change with the goal of changing the public's mind, we're left, I fear, with few models of how to proceed.[3]

If so many teachers feel they don't know how to take the kinds of stances that need to be taken in order to help change public perceptions of education, I began to ask myself, then who does? Are there other groups or individuals, outside of the world of education, who have been successful in this goal of creating new mindsets, who have been responsible for creating a shift in people's perceptions? As a place to begin searching for models, I started thinking of all the shifts I know—grassroots changes in perspectives on social issues that have happened in my lifetime—and two immediately came to mind.

The first is the change in how people think about drinking and driving, brought about largely by the creation of MADD (Mothers Against Drunk Driving). In 1980 Candy Lightner's thirteen-year-old daughter was killed by a drunk driver as the young woman walked down the street. As Lightner explains in her book *Giving Sorrow Words* (co-authored with Nancy Hathaway), she was shocked when she was told that although the man who committed this crime had had four prior arrests for drunk driving, he would probably get off with a slap on the wrist: "Lady, you'll be lucky if he sees any jail time at all, much less prison. That's the way the system works" (9). In part to assuage her grief, she began to talk to everyone she could think of about the horror of this response—to other parents whose children had been killed by drunk drivers, to various community groups—raising questions as to how such an action could be condoned, both by the public at large and in the legal system. Gaining the support of others through her vehemence and compassion, she gathered together with people to talk to legislators and ask them why they allowed such light penalties for such a heinous act. She thus began a public campaign both to change the public's perception about drunk driving and to change the laws which governed such conduct: to make citizens recognize the reprehensible nature of such an act and to feel a moral responsibility to have a designated driver, to make the legislators realize that citizens would no longer put up with this conduct. "Today, most people understand that it's not something to joke about," she says, "it's not macho; it's not cool; it's not funny. It's a crime" (12). She, who describes herself as naive and unknowledgeable about mounting a campaign about anything, created what is known by many standards as the most successful grassroots initiative of the 1980s: Through her organizing campaign, she and her group, Mothers Against Drunk Driving, actually changed the general public's response to drinking and driving.

About the same time that Candy Lightner was starting her campaign, a group of neighbors outside Buffalo found that they and their children were developing rare and serious diseases. As they searched for reasons for these illnesses, they discovered that their homes and their children's school were built on an old toxic dump, which was oozing poison into groundwater. Relieved that they had discovered what they believed was causing the sickness, and convinced that once city officials had heard their pleas something would be done, they brought their concerns to the proper authorities—who refused to recognize the problem and refused to take any action.

One of the moms in the neighborhood was a woman named Lois Gibbs. Shocked by the lack of concern on the part of the city officials, she felt she didn't have any choice but to do something—what, she didn't know. Relying on what she later called "motherly instinct" (qtd. in Berkowitz, *Local Heroes* 109), Gibbs sought out respected scientists to help her understand the problem, garnered the support of her neighbors and friends, told her story to the media, and began to do her own research. She explains that she knew nothing about how to organize when she started but insists that once people recognize something is wrong, they "have a responsibility": "You know more than most people," she insists, "and you have the responsibility to share that, and you have the responsibility to pull these people together. . . . And every time you say you can't do it, you go over and look your kid in the eye" (qtd. in Berkowitz, *Local Heroes* 115). As she convinced more and more people to join with her and spread the word about the hazardous waste in her community, the story began to take on a life of its own. Soon the national media camped on her doorstep for months at a time, and legislators began to take notice. Eventually the state of New York paid to relocate many of the families, a coalition of the state and federal governments and the original owners of the site paid for cleanup, and the most comprehensive cleanup law in the world, the so-called Superfund law, was passed by the United States Congress. Lois Gibbs has gone on to create her own organization, the Center for Health, Environment and Justice (formerly called the Citizens Clearinghouse for Hazardous Waste), to help other neighborhoods faced with the same problems. And "toxic waste dump" has become a household word.

What Lois Gibbs, Candy Lightner, and a host of others have done in order to effect change is known as *community organizing*, simply defined as "people working together to get things done" (Kahn 1). Community organizing generally takes place as a group of people come together initially because of a shared response to an injustice, a fear, an issue, a cause; as a group, they figure out how to make changes in the status quo. They learn to work together, to listen and set goals, and to discover the power within their numbers to make changes in ways that individuals just cannot.

As the spouse of an environmental activist who relies on community organizing techniques on a daily basis, I knew something about the subject. I had heard of Saul Alinsky and ACORN; I had a friend in the field of public health who talked about organizing in her work in prenatal care in downtown Detroit; my husband had for years worked at organizing various communities to rally around certain environmental issues. Over and over, as I complained about press coverage of educational issues, I had heard him say, "What you should do is mount a campaign," "What you need is the gossip factor," "Why don't you create a press strategy?" I would always nod, assuring him he was right, but that neither I nor the teachers I worked with had time to do something like that. But, really, I had no idea what he meant, or how to even go about doing any of these things. I watched him in awe, campaign after campaign, as a certain group would get swayed to the way of thinking he was promoting, but I had no clear vision for how he did it or for how community organizers do their jobs every day: how their work differs in different communities or what circumstances can make or break a campaign. Nor could I really imagine how that work might connect with the work of teachers. I only knew about the success of his work and that the images that kept cropping up for me about how people actually go out in a community and create changed attitudes were gleaned from these strong examples to which I had assigned this vague name of community organizing.

Lately, though, as I continue to be frustrated by the work of state and national legislatures and the articles I read in the newspaper, I've been coming back to the ideas my husband had impressed upon me. Could a look at community organizing help me think about outreach differently? Could we learn something from community organizing theory and practice that could translate to teachers? If we had a model of community organizing techniques, could we adapt it and use it regularly so that our outreach to parents would no longer be anecdotal and sporadic but rather consistent and sustained across various communities? Would it help us learn proactive measures, so that we didn't always have to rely on reactive responses? Could it help us stop the band-aid approach we're using now in order to prevent the kinds of crises in which we seem to be currently embroiled? What would change if teachers started to view themselves as community organizers?

Organizer Ernesto Cortes believes that teachers and organizers already have much in common:

> Organizing is teaching. Like any organizer, a teacher stirs curiosity and imagination, connects to people and what's important to them, and teaches them how to acquire the capacity to pursue their inclinations and their imagination. Organizing is getting people to understand the meaning of things and how the world works—and then acting cooperatively on that understanding. (Cortes 7)

I agree. I think that teachers are natural organizers. Think what we do every day to create and sustain communities in our classrooms. We take a bunch of disparate individuals, sometimes up to thirty-five or forty at a time, who bring diverse backgrounds, experiences, socioeconomic factors, race, gender, interest, reading level, skills, strengths, and motivations, and somehow—at our best—manage to form a cohesive group. We use rites, rituals, and ceremonies (according to Ralph Peterson in *Life in a Crowded Place*); we coax and cajole, we help them find a common purpose, and we call upon a host of other strategies to create—in a few short months—a cohesive learning community. If we teachers can do this—at least with our students—we must have great knowledge about community organizing and a host of strategies of which we are often unaware. As Bill Berkowitz, a community organizer from the world of community health and social work, tells us, community organizing is "more than a matter of technical skill . . . effective community work is also a matter of *mindset* and particularly of the feeling that you can, should and will use the skills you already own to help others, to build supports, and to create desired change" (*Community Impact* 21–22).

Certainly, the teachers with whom I have worked and whom you will meet in this book have that mindset. They know that parents who are knowledgeable are the first line of defense against attacks and can become the voices of reason in a time of unreasonableness. They know that working *with* parents is just that: a two-way street in which people listen to each other and learn together. And they already own a number of the technical skills necessary to help others, to build support, to create change, although none of them, I am sure, would term their techniques "community organizing." What I hope to show in this book is how teachers might be able to build upon this mindset and knowledge, expanding their ways of parent outreach by drawing upon the lessons of community organizing. Learning about community organizing, I believe, might strengthen our ability to enter the public conversation and change commonly held perceptions; it might help us consistently, thoroughly, and, most important, proactively create a new way of thinking about education.

To learn something about community organizing, I immersed myself in disciplines that were totally new to me and, I assume, to large numbers of my readers. And while I cannot claim to be an expert about the intricacies of community organizing, I have learned a lot—enough, I hope, to be able to explain some of the basic underpinnings of and motivations for this kind of approach to the teachers and English educators who read this book, in hopes that they will see its potential as a tool for our work. Starting in Chapter 3, as I lay out the parameters of a community organizing approach, you will discover that it finds a home in a number of disciplines: in social work, in public health, in political science, and in natural resources, to name a few. As I searched for answers to my questions about this way of thinking, then, I found myself on floors of the main university library where I'd never been before; in other locations of the university library, often tucked away in the basements of buildings far across campus; in the city's public library. I found myself reading unfamiliar authors, who were writing for unfamiliar presses, in words that took on new meanings. (*Strategy*, for example, is a word that carries very specific meanings in a community organizing world—and not the meanings I have given it thus far in this chapter; the word is further complicated by the different nuances it's assigned depending on which strand of community organizing is using it.) To further my knowledge, I conducted interviews with community organizers. As their stories brought to life the words I'd been reading, I found myself fascinated by their commitment and knowledge, their imagination, and, most of all, their stamina. Among those whose words and stories inhabit this book:

- Dan Cantor, Executive Director of the New Party, a vital third party trying to make its way in mainstream U.S. politics, and a former organizer for ACORN;

- Renee Bayer, Community Academic Liaison Coordinator for the School of Public Health at the University of Michigan, and a longtime community activist whose work has ranged from environmental issues (cofounding the organization Recycle Ann Arbor) to social justice issues (cofounding the Nicaragua Medical Aide Project) to public health issues (organizing women on public assistance in one Detroit neighborhood in an education program about maternal child health issues);

- Tracey Easthope, a community organizer with the Ecology Center, a large environmental advocacy and education center in Ann Arbor, whose work ranges from organizing medical personnel against medical waste incinerators in local hospitals to stopping toxic waste dumps from being built in communities;

- Barbara Israel, a professor and chair of Health Behavior and Health Education at the School of Public Health at the University of Michigan whose work has ranged from her own community organizing projects in a number of settings (including auto plants) to teaching community organizing strategies and techniques to public health professionals;

- Andy Buchsbaum, Water Quality Project Manager for the Great Lakes Natural Resource Center of the National Wildlife Federation, a former attorney with the National Environmental Law Project (the litigation arm of the environmental and consumer advocacy organization Public Interest Research Group), and a former campus organizer for PIRG, who has also worked closely with Ralph Nader and his organizations.

These individuals' different perspectives on the work they do and their understandings of how community organizing becomes a reality in various contexts and from various starting points helped me to think about community organizing from five different orientations, which I explain in some depth in Chapter 3: an education orientation, a planning/development orientation, a mobilizing orientation, a social action orientation, and an advocacy orientation.

Scribbled in the margins of my interview transcripts and reading notes are messages like this: "How do inservice nights for parents compare to neighborhood meetings for organizers?" "How are the characteristics of a good organizer like that of a good teacher?" "What about house parties? How could we use these?" and "Are teachers comparable to organizers? and parents to leaders? how do we 'train' parents like organizers train leaders?" These scribblings are indications, I think, of the immediate connections I consistently found between what community organizers do as a matter of course and what teachers might do. In Chapter 4, I try to make these connections clear, beginning with my vision of a community organizing model for teaching, a model that both brings together and remains true to what community organizers in their various approaches might consider common to their practice. The intent of this chapter is not to mandate a step-by-step process for community organizing, but rather to suggest some general components that teachers might consider for their own parent outreach programs if they recognize the rationale of wearing the hat of a community organizer. Just as Rothman refers to the "mixing and phasing" that real organizers use in their movement in and out of the various orientations toward community organizing ("Approaches"), in this chapter I connect how the individual attempts on the part of the teachers mentioned in Chapter 2 might fit into a model like this, giving the flavor of what a community organizing approach to outreach might look like.

If teachers are to take on the community organizing approach to their community outreach—to become, as I suggest in this text, *teacher-organizers*—they must learn how. In Chapter 5 I lay out some ideas to help teachers get started: from ways teacher educators might introduce the concept of advocacy in their methods courses to an approach teacher leaders might try out in their professional development for practicing teachers. Utilizing one of community organizing's standard training approaches—scenario development and enactment—I demonstrate in that chapter how the model of Chapter 4 might work in real settings. Beginning with scenarios I created (based on true stories shared with me by teachers), I suggest how a community organizing model might work in practice; I further suggest how to turn this scenario work into a process for teachers to think through their own situations and contexts.

Finally, a footnote to my process of discovery comes to mind. One lesson has been brought home to me over and over in my research into community organizing. Folks who, like me, have done extensive work in composition studies and English education pride ourselves on the interdisciplinarity of our fields—on the fact that our work truly has become a "blurred genre." We look to such disciplines as women's studies, anthropology, and psychology on a regular basis in order to stretch our understandings. As I began this research project and moved into fields of study beyond the margins of our normally wide range, I was struck by how the conversations which consume my colleagues and me are echoed in these other disciplines of political science, public health, social work, and environmental studies. Skimming through articles in their journals, I hear questions raised about the ethics of research and the various responsibilities researchers have for telling the stories of others. I read Israel and her colleagues as they identify key principles of community-based research, including in their concerns how the research must mutually benefit all parties in order to be ethical, how change in the community must be a primary concern of all research. I read Bryant's *Environmental Advocacy* and am struck by the connections he finds between environmental advocacy and action research. As I read on and on, John Dewey's name crops up often, as does Paulo Freire's. My point is this: My immersion in these new disciplines not only opened my eyes to some new ways of thinking that will forever inform my world view, but also showed me the strong connections we need to continue to forge across buildings and libraries and thinkers. We have much to learn from each other—and many more conversations to share.

Notes

1. Although I use the term *parents* throughout this book, I—and the teachers with whom I have worked—are very sensitive to the fact that not all children live in either a one- or a two-parent household. For many of these children, the term *parents* might mean stepparents, aunts and uncles, grandparents, or other caring adults.

2. For a fuller exposé of this issue, see Denny Taylor's *Beginning to Read and the Spin Doctors of Science*; for more on the general mischaracterization of educational issues in the popular press, see Berliner and Biddle's *The Manufactured Crisis*.

3. Jim Vopat, for example, creates a wonderful model for parent outreach in his book *The Parent Project*, a model that meets many of the criteria I would set for a sustained program that goes far enough in effecting changed perspectives. The problem with this program, I have heard from a number of teachers, is that it seems too "big"—requiring more time and energy than many of them believe they can actually put forth.

Appendix

The following pages contain selected passages from Cathy A. Gwiz-dala's pamphlet *Spelling Development of First-graders in a Whole Language Classroom*.

Spelling Development of First-graders in a Whole Language Classroom

by
Cathy A. Gwizdala

Table of Contents

Introduction

Note: *Literacy is a word that I will use often in this booklet. To me, it means reading, writing, listening, speaking thinking and viewing, all developing in the same child, each at its own rate, with each part's growth enhancing the other parts. A literate person is an effective communicator, and is able to enjoy, as well as understand ideas, whether through reading, writing, listening, speaking or viewing.*

Dear Parents,

You may have noticed that our classroom last year was different from most first grade classrooms that you had seen or knew about. We used no "reading books", spelling workbooks, phonics workbooks, no skill sheets, etc. In the absence of all these things, you may have wondered just *how* or *if* reading, spelling and phonics were taught at all.

Well, I am one of a growing number of teachers from all over the world who believes in the whole language philosophy. In a nutshell, this means that I believe that literacy development is natural, and develops in much the same way as your child's abilities to speak and walk. All these skills become more and more refined as your child grows older and has more chances to practice. (It's just like when they first learned to talk. You were thrilled at the first "Ma-ma-ma-ma-ma-ma" or "Da-da-da-da-da-da" that came out, and accepted it as the beginning of talk. In a whole language classroom, we're thrilled with the beginnings of writing where the spelling is "inventive" or "temporary", because we know that, as the children grow, the spelling will also mature, just as those "mama's and dada's" became clearer with more practice.)

As a teacher who believes in the whole language philosophy,

* I do not believe that reading and writing and spelling should be taught separately.

* I do believe that all the parts of literacy develop together, each enhancing the growth of the others.

* I do not believe that all children can or should learn the same skill of reading or writing at the same time, or that each small reading, writing or spelling skill must be learned before the next, supposedly more difficult one may be introduced by the teacher.

* I do believe that, when children are given the opportunity and tools to practice reading and writing in their classrooms and at home, they will naturally learn the skills necessary to be good at both, without completing workbook pages for practice.

*I do not believe that partial stories in the basal readers give the children a love for fine literature that will last them a lifetime.

* I do believe that, after enjoying fine literature by listening as it's read by others, personally reading, and participating in extension activities, children will develop a lifelong love of good literature.

* I do not believe that children are empty vessels, just waiting in their seats for the teachers to "Fill them up" with knowledge.

* I do believe that children can handle much of the responsibility for their own learning, and that, with guidance, they can and will seek information using resources such as encyclopedias, storybooks, videos, television programs and other people.

6

In order to teach in a way that supports these beliefs, I tried to create a classroom full of real literacy experiences. These real situations, coupled with the students taking so much responsibility for their own learning, made our classroom look and run very differently from traditional classrooms. Our classroom was often noisy, cluttered, and full of groups of students everywhere but in their seats.

A quick peek into our classroom door may have made you think that the kids were just having a good time while I sat around watching them. Let me assure you, those kids learned a great deal last year. (and I stayed very busy) Their literacy development went through the roof! As you know, your children kept journals all year. While they kept theirs, I also kept a journal on the computer. Throughout each day, during most of the school year, I typed in specific examples of things I'd seen or heard the kids do for the singular purpose of illustrating the literacy development of the children. I'd like.to share just a few of those examples with you now. Remember, these are *real* examples from *your* children throughout the 1993-94 schoolyear. I hope you enjoy them, and see how much they really were learning.

What Can Parents Do to Support the Whole Language Process?

You may be wondering what you can do to further your child's literacy development at home.

*When your child takes down the turning rod from the mini-blinds to point at words as she reads, as Kayla did, *encourage her*! That's very literate behavior, and we want to encourage that in all our children all the time.

*When your child wants to write all the time -- that's great! Provide as much paper as he needs, and encourage letter-writing, grocery-list writing, sign-making, etc., then really send the letters, take the lists to the store during shopping trips, and hang up the signs, so he can see the usefulness of his writing.

*Take frequent trips to the library. Your children love to read, and the books are all free!

*Listen to your child read as often as possible. While listening, try to concentrate more on making sure she gets the meaning of the entire selection, instead of focusing on perfect word-calling. It's okay for your child to make a little mistake once in a while.

*Let your child see *you* reading and writing as often as possible! While that may not *seem* very important, it's one of the best ways for you to show your child how much you value reading and writing.

*Try to provide a quiet time and place for your child to read and write. Every once in a while, turn off the TV., VCR, video games and stereos, and set aside the time for reading and writing

*Come into the classroom anytime, and watch what wonderful things go on! You'll be as amazed as I was, I promise!

11

Parent Response Sheet
Please return to Mrs. Gwizdala

Dear Parents,
  Now that you've finished reading this booklet about spelling development in our first grade classroom, please let me know what you think about it.

_____
_____
_____
_____
_____
_____
_____
_____
_____
_____
_____

Do you think I should continue compiling these booklets for parents? _____

What should I include or how can I change them to make them
better?_____

_____
_____
_____
_____
_____
_____
_____
_____
_____

13

Thanks!
Cathy Gwizdala

2 The Quiet Revolution: Teachers Reaching Out to Parents

Teachers cannot suddenly redefine themselves as political creatures whose goal is to convince parents to think in certain ways. Not only would such a heavy-handed approach fail miserably, but also it would be inappropriate for a number of reasons. Above all, our priority as teachers remains to teach the children. This is a charge that, when done well, takes an inordinate amount of time and leaves us with little energy to become the next Norma Rae or Ralph Nader. Thus, any attempt to work with parents must integrate somehow with the job teachers already do, so that instead of being perceived as an "add-on," it's seen as a "part of." Equally important, our relationship with parents is always a precarious one. It's become almost a cliché to talk of parents as their children's first, best teachers, but there is much truth in that statement. Parents know so much about their children's needs, strengths, desires, and interests; we have an obligation to open our minds and hearts to listen hard to what they tell us about their children, even as we balance that with the knowledge we hold about literacy and language arts instruction. While we have a lot of information to share with parents about how to teach their children, we must always remember that this can't be a one-way agenda, carved in stone and unresponsive to individual needs. We can't become preachy, standing on our soapboxes and informing those "uninformed" parents how they must think about our pedagogy.

Working with parents, then, needs to be more of a quiet revolution, the kind of revolution that depends on talking and listening, on teachable moments, on stolen time. It becomes a balancing act which factors in the needs of parents and students, the knowledge of all parties, in a time frame that can be carved out of busy lives.

Parts of this chapter were previously published as "Advocating for Change: A New Education for New Teachers" in *English Education* 30 (May 1998): 78–100.

Over the past few years, I've worked with a number of teachers who are creating this quiet revolution in amazing ways. These are teachers who are well grounded in and strongly committed to certain beliefs about teaching; they have studied and thought hard about the best ways to teach kids to read and write, and they have definite agendas for language arts pedagogy. But these are also teachers who are listeners, welcoming the words of parents and students in order to learn more about how to be effective with individual kids. These teachers are gracious and interested, and they welcome parents into a community of learning in which everyone has something to offer, everyone has something to learn. Perhaps it is this kind of attitude, coupled with a number of specific strategies, that allows these teachers to be so successful in their parent outreach.

These are also busy teachers. Each of them is involved in numerous activities outside of their regular teaching (some related to education and some not). All of them figured out a way to make this parent outreach an important part of their practice, rather than merely an add-on, and assured me that the time spent working with parents in these ways was a curious thing: when they spent the time to reach out to parents in proactive ways, they reduced the amount of time they had to spend responding to concerns and problems. Was parent outreach then a time-saver? Maybe not, but at least, as it became integral to their teaching, it became an important use of their time.

Most of the teachers I've worked with did not initiate ways of parent outreach because of complaints or problems in the classrooms, but rather as a preventive measure, realizing that their ways of teaching might seem unusual to parents schooled in another era. Neither did these teachers consciously start this work so that their parents would become active respondents to the misinformation and half-truths out there about language arts instruction, but, in most cases, parents took on that role when it seemed appropriate.

The teachers you will meet here are quite different from each other: They have differing amounts of experience as teachers, they teach in very different kinds of communities, and they teach different grade levels. The kinds of strategies they use for parent outreach, then, vary, depending on their context and comfort level, although, as you'll see in the conclusion to this chapter, there are some important commonalities in their approaches. What's important to take from these brief narrative portraits, I think, is less the specific strategies than their overall approaches and the factors that influence their choice of certain approaches. What Julie does in her classroom, because of the context and her comfort level, will be quite different from what another teacher can do in her locality. In other words, these stories are not meant as a source of how-to lists of the very best ideas about how to work with parents, but rather as a way to get other teachers to start thinking of appropriate ways to reach out to parents in their own situations.

Julie King: "Clarifying My Own Theory and Communicating It to Others"

Julie is a relatively new teacher, untenured, but determined to put best practices in English language arts instruction into her eighth-grade classes in a suburban middle school. Julie's district is a fairly wealthy and homogeneous one, a very grade-conscious district in which parents regularly call to see their child's numerical grade on any given day. When I first met Julie three years ago, after she had taught for just two years, she was struggling with her practice. "I had no plan, no kind of scope and sequence for the year," she explains. "There was a curriculum, although it was more like a list of skills, a thirty-page list. Hundreds and hundreds of isolated things . . . [I knew] there was no way I could teach every isolated skill in that book. [And] no matter what I did, the kids didn't like reading . . . the kids didn't like writing [and] they weren't writing anything interesting." Julie, like many new teachers, turned to familiar sources to figure out what to do: her memories of her own teachers and the practices of the teachers around her—what she now sees as rigid, teacher-centered lessons involving teaching skills out of context. She tried to adapt those kinds of lessons into experiences that were more student-centered: having them write lessons out of their spelling words or using a five-paragraph essay format to write about their bedrooms—lessons which resulted, as she says, in "meaningless babble." Frustrated, Julie enrolled in a National Writing Project summer institute. She read volumes of professional material, she met and talked with other teachers who had tried reading and writing workshops in their own classrooms, and she began to reflect seriously about what she believed most about how to teach English—what her personal goals were and how she thought kids could best learn to read and write. "Now," she says, "it just seems like second nature to me. . . . If you're going to learn to read and write, you have to read and write. . . . Kids can come in [the classroom] and they can . . . learn how to read and write by reading and writing. What a concept! I just had never experienced that at all."

Julie continues: "At a certain point I decided I can't go back and do this the same way anymore." But she worried: "Everybody's going to hate me if I do this and everybody's going to say I'm wrong . . . teachers, kids, parents, administrators, everybody." Julie responded to that fear by spending hours carefully studying her district's mandated curriculum and trying to see how workshop strategies might fit into what she originally thought were fairly rigid requirements. "I really studied it, read it page by page and thought really hard about it: 'If I teach this way, am I still meeting the needs and expectations of this curriculum book?' My answer was yes, I can defend this; I can pick up a kid's piece of writing and the curriculum guide and say it's here. The kid is going to get [the skill]. It's just going to be in a different way."

Julie went back to the classroom with a whole new approach to teaching. She immediately approached her principal and department chair, talking to them about the changes she planned to incorporate, inviting them to visit and help her think through these changes. But she worried about how the parents would react. "Either I was just going to go in and teach the [new] way . . . and field questions if they came up, or I was going to be proactive. I decided to go the proactive route and really back up what I was doing." Julie began that year by sending a letter home to parents before school even started, laying out for them what the class was going to look like, what parents should expect to see their children doing at home, what their children would be doing in her class on a day-to-day basis (see Appendix A for this and other selected materials developed by Julie). Personalizing the letter by using a "mail merge program," Julie was able to address each parent individually and explain, for example, what "Sarah's writing folder" would look like.

Julie followed up that welcome letter by putting together a newsletter for parents about reading and writing workshop, collaboratively written by the kids. The newsletter explained many aspects of her workshop format, with articles on topics such as peer response groups, process writing, revision strategies, and individual-ized reading programs. In kid language, the students explained their own views on what these aspects meant. Julie explains that having the students understand the language of the workshop is not only empow-ering for the students but also a key to helping parents understand: "Our language is not the same as . . .what literature teachers in college might use. But [the students] have language for writing: they know what portfolios are, they know what a rubric is, they know what assessment is, they know what writers' tricks are. I know that understanding this language gives you power and I'm trying to do that for my kids." She continues: "I think that if I can provide the parents with a definition that they can understand, . . . then they can talk intelligently about what is going on in school. They don't have to say, 'Oh, this teacher is doing this weird thing.'"

Providing parents with the language and the strategies behind her teaching continues to occupy Julie's attempts at proactive teaching. For example, Julie's students regularly record their responses to their reading in a writer's log, using one entry a week to write a letter to someone about the books they are reading. One week they write to a peer, one week they write to Julie, and the third week they write to their parents. Parents are asked to write back, just as the teacher and peers do, and Julie includes some instructions to the parents on appropriate kinds of responses. Although some parents do the minimum, many parents "are so geeked!" Parents write about their excitement that their kids are reading at home and recommend other books to their children. Other examples of Julie's outreach to parents: She regularly asks parents to read and respond to their child's portfolio, and she develops teaching units which include the parents—such as her recent Generations Unit, in which students worked with their parents and extended families to research and eventually to write pieces collected in a book about elderly relatives. For Julie, getting more and more of the writing and reading her students do into the hands of the parents is key—once they see the amount and quality of the work their kids are producing, many of their fears are allayed—while at the same time she constantly tries to find strategies to help the parents understand why the students are approaching literacy learning in these ways. This project, in particular, has had a positive impact on parents, especially in helping them understand and become involved in their own children's learning. According to Julie, "I think I realized [from doing this project] that if you involve the family in . . . part of the work, it helps. . . . It got families together" to talk about school.

Julie has also found herself seeking new ways to explain her pedagogy to parents within a system that sometimes seems unfriendly to it. Recently, she found herself sleepless on a Sunday night after spending the weekend estimating grades and filling in the forty-five multiple choice bubbles required for her school's midterm progress report—questions that "don't fit any kid." She explains:

> They're not true grades, they're not true comments, but I have eighty-six Language Arts students and thirty-two Reading for Pleasure Students. I can't write all those [individual] notes; I just

can't. So I got up at eleven on Sunday night and I sat at the computer and typed a two-page letter [to parents]: "I just finished doing progress reports, but I feel that with the format . . . I couldn't tell you enough about what we're doing in Language Arts, so here's an update."

She formatted the note to parents as a newsletter and the next day stuffed them into envelopes which the kids addressed ("a little mini-lesson on addressing envelopes!"), and, she said, "it made me feel much better."

The most ambitious project Julie has taken on is the creation of a booklet for parents, entitled *Seeing Common Ground: A Parent's Guide to Process Writing Instruction and Assessment.* In this booklet, Julie starts with definitions for the terms *process writing, authentic assessment,* and *portfolios* and illustrates those terms through specific examples taken from her students' writing. In the section on process writing, for example, Julie interweaves the writing of one student through the various stages, pointing out how particular strategies helped the student move through a piece of writing from its conception to publication. Julie describes the booklet as "an argument for what I do and how I teach" so that parents will be more informed in a nonthreatening way not only about what their children are doing, but also about what is considered best practice in English language arts. She explains:

> [Many parents] were taught very traditionally and so . . . it is hard for them to understand what I am doing. . . . So I'm hoping by providing definitions for some of these things, they will be able to understand what they are and help their kids . . . , and talk about it in an intelligent way to somebody else. I just think that if you have the language you have the power. . . . I think it's easy to [help kids] study for a spelling test. Not quite as easy to do a writing critique when your kid brings home a paper. If I help explain to parents what process writing is, how you respond . . . then they can feel more useful and they will be more useful.

As Julie's knowledge about teaching has increased, so has her confidence. Once scared even to call parents, she is now a vocal proponent of what she believes language arts education should be. She is vocal at PTA meetings, especially on the subject of assessment; she is part of the districtwide writing team; she's been given released time in her school to work on writing-to-learn initiatives; and she regularly speaks at workshops and conferences about her teaching. She concludes: "I wouldn't say that I'm real political . . . , but I see how I've grown. . . . I feel . . . because I am able to explain myself . . . that if someone were going to throw stones at the way I teach, I'd have somebody to back me up."

Kathleen Hayes-Parvin: Extending Multiple Invitations, Especially to the Disenfranchised

Kathleen teaches sixth grade in an extremely diverse middle school, filled with students of many nationalities and backgrounds—African American and Chaldean children, most prominently. Formerly a special education teacher, Kathleen turned to language arts instruction just five years ago. As with Julie, it was a summer with the National Writing Project which

> changed my life. . . . [I] ended up with some people who were such professionals, who regarded their profession like lawyers and doctors regard theirs. This was so different for me. . . . I hooked up with some people who were so incredibly powerful in terms of their conviction about what they did, why they did it, . . . finding out the theory behind what [they're] doing.

Kathleen began immersing herself in professional materials, talking to others about their own classrooms, thinking hard about her own beliefs. She took advantage of other professional opportunities, attending conferences and joining the Michigan English Language Arts Frameworks (MELAF), a three-year professional development project to study best practices in English. She explains how this immersion increased her confidence: "I knew I did good things for good reasons before, but when you can say you have the theory behind you and you have the books that empower you, that convinces people that . . . you do have something to say worth listening to."

Kathleen has worked particularly hard at developing a strong relation with the families of the students she teaches, a time-consuming task but one she says is "well worth it. It's just time well spent." Her job, as she sees it, is to extend multiple invitations to families, invitations so varied that she eventually finds a way to hook every parent, even those reluctant to participate in school events. "I grew up in a house in which my parents weren't particularly school congruent," she explains. "They were both dropouts at sixth grade to support their families, so school was scary. Part of my goal is to try to include parents who weren't particularly enfranchised . . . in their school life." She begins the year in August with a phone call or letter to every parent in her classes, inviting them to a brief beginning-of-the-year conference, to introduce herself and to learn from the parent about the child as a learner. She sees this contact as "unbelievably important. Because the next time you call . . . you don't feel threatened by, 'Here I've never met this person and I'm calling to say something terribly negative about their child.' You feel like, 'Hey, I've called this mom or dad, I've welcomed them to our team, and now I'm calling for their help,' and they're much more likely to do that for me." She notes that she gets 100 percent participation from parents: about 80 percent come in for a conference and the rest respond to her through a letter or phone call. "The parent you can't get to come in [at first] is the parent you need most to get. . . . I take it personally, like a personal affront if they don't [respond]," she laughs. "I make it my business to keep going."

Once she gets the families of students in her room, either through these initial conferences or through a later open house, she demonstrates to them the rich literacy in the room, exposing them to the kind of environment that surrounds the children. There are books everywhere: picture books for children, adolescent literature, classic literature, student-produced books, and professional books. She also introduces the parents to her lending library, a collection of books about literacy that she has found useful and which she invites parents to borrow. "It's another invitation," Kathleen explains. "No one's ever borrowed a book from it . . . but it helps them know that I'm confident about what I'm doing, that I have theory behind what I'm doing, and that they're welcome to share in that."

Later in the year, Kathleen begins her parent education program in earnest. She starts with the poetry anthology produced by kids: a collection of poems the kids have written, placed in a three-ring binder. In the front of the binder, Kathleen includes a "teaching letter," a letter to parents which talks about the poetry in the binder, carefully explaining to them what the students have been working on, what they should look for when they read through the poems, and asking them to write a response to what they've read (see Appendix B for this and other selected materials from Kathleen). She then sends the book home with a different child each night, beginning with a parent whom she knows will set a tone of support and care for the writing so that subsequent parents will get good ideas for how to respond. Parents have responded by writing their own poetry, by writing in different languages (which the kids then translate and put into the book), and by writing carefully worded responses, such as, "These poems are a delight. The art of words is a valuable tool in communication." Kids feel they have real audiences; parents have a real sense of what their kids are learning, not only through the poems themselves but through the teaching letter.

Kathleen then begins a series of invitations to parents, urging them to compose pieces for the next class anthology, usually devised around a theme (such as heroes) or a genre (such as memoir). Again, she includes teaching letters in her invitations, explaining, for example, that

36   *Teachers Organizing for Change*

"Memoir is a literary genre that helps us find meaning in the events of our lives. Unlike autobiography, memoir does not attempt a complete timeline of life experiences. Instead, it focuses on a few select moments in our past that, together, reflect larger truths about our existence." A number of parents begin to write, although many of them feel a bit apprehensive about it. Kathleen urges her students every year to help the parents through this process, using the strategies they've been taught: peer conferences with nonjudgmental comments or writers' tricks to stimulate revision. Kathleen shares the story of a student asking the class one day if her mom could come in for a peer conference because she was stuck in her writing. The class agreed and the mother came in to read her piece! She received helpful advice and continued to send in subsequent drafts with her daughter for more response from the class until she felt her piece was ready for publication. This same mother told Kathleen about the peer conference her daughter and husband held for her one evening, all of them sitting around on the bed and talking about writing. Kathleen explains, "She told me later she could tell . . . all that her daughter had learned about writing and how impressive that was."

Again, writing in different languages is celebrated and translated for the book; for those who just can't write, Kathleen urges them to come in and share something else. One year a parent who was a filmmaker brought in a documentary he had made, and explained about composing, rehearsing, and publishing in the film genre.

Kathleen expands upon these ways of encouraging parent involvement and understanding through a number of other projects: student-led conferencing in which parents spend an evening at school as their child takes them through her portfolio of writing; an elders project similar to Julie's but which invites older community members into the classroom for a day of interviews and learning; a group project with some at-risk girls and their parents to try to help the girls begin to think about their own connection to schooling and literacy. For Kathleen, each of these experiences expands the community's understanding of the education of its children. She explains:

> It's like this Amish Friendship bread [her class recently received].
> We squeeze the bag every day, and at the end of ten days we add
> another cup of milk and another cup of flour and another cup of
> sugar, and we squeeze it all together, and then we ladle out 4 new
> starter packages and we give them away. And as they mature,
> these people give them to four other people.

The results of this expanded understanding are becoming clear. The parents in Kathleen's class not only become intimately involved in the workings of the class; they also begin to understand in some detail the kind of literacy environment in which their children are taught. Terms like *reading workshop* or *writing workshop* or *process approaches* are no longer words on a page. Parents now have firsthand knowledge of what those terms mean, and thus they are more inclined to reject the arguments of a newspaper article lambasting this approach to teaching or to explain to other parents what is happening in this particular class.

> I've seen parents from this school go speak on our behalf at school board meetings in Lansing. I've seen parents at this school talk to different people about the best practices they've seen at the sixth grade. . . . They've come to expect that's what should happen, that kids would write real stories and not diagram sentences or work on things in an isolated fashion. . . .

For Kathleen, this is evidence of the impact her approaches are having on the families of the children she teaches.

Carolyn Berge: Creating Conversation and Community

Carolyn Berge is a multiage primary school teacher who has been in the profession for over twenty years. Carolyn was recently certified by the National Board for Professional Teaching Standards, and her reputation as a master teacher precedes her. Parents vie to get their children in her class. "It's like winning the lottery if your son or daughter gets into her class," one parent told me. "Other parents come up to you on the street and offer congratulations." Carolyn has worked with students in a number of settings—private and public, working class and upper class, from preschool to middle school—and explains that it was her experiences in a school that had large numbers of at-risk kids that helped her begin to learn how to do parent outreach. She explains: "There were so many different types of parents . . . and even for the kids who were the most at risk and had the hardest family lives, their parents always cared . . . . I was just really curious about them without judgment. Otherwise the defenses happen and [then] of course teachers can't communicate—with good reason."

Carolyn has taken this approach to parent outreach into every setting, believing that one has to find ways to establish communication and create a community wherever one is. It's the atmosphere one establishes that's most important, she insists, an atmosphere of "truly wanting" parent involvement and not merely paying it lip service. "I do lots of *things* [to promote parent participation], but I think the biggest thing is to create a trust." Her current assignment, a mostly upper-middle class setting with a large population of children of professors, doctors, and researchers, presents its own challenges. She describes the parents as "very visible," parents who place "a high value on education," parents who are concerned that even their very young children have the kind of preparation that will help them get into good colleges.

Carolyn works from the very beginning of the year to establish a real community with the parents and children in her classroom. She always offers some kind of getting-to-know-you activity, usually a potluck picnic, which she describes as one of the most important activities she sponsors. Caroline sends out invitations to all the families in her class, asking them to come to the picnic on the Saturday before school begins: "have people bring food, sit down, and get to know each other. . . . Parents love it, kids have a blast, and it's a nice relaxed way for me to look like a real person. . . . [By the time they leave], they have already a feeling that they are a community, . . . a community of learners."

Continuing this message of becoming a community of learners, Carolyn hands out a long list of possible ways parents can volunteer for the classroom: from sharing occupations and hobbies to donating supplies to coordinating the classroom newsletter, "a big array of things that says 'I really care about your input.'" As a result, three to four parents a day regularly help in her classroom; many more are involved outside the confines of the school day. This year, one parent created portfolios for all the students; another comes in every other week and writes a newsletter with kids. Parents who are involved in these ways are exposed to the kinds of teaching and learning that go on in the class; they have firsthand knowledge of how Carolyn conducts writing and math clubs, how she uses learning logs for six- and seven-year-olds, how she promotes student choice; as participants in the classroom community, these parents learn how to respond appropriately to students involved in those activities.

Carolyn also designs her classroom schedule so that "the beginning of the day is really flexible." Kids come in and right away choose one of her many "Smart Choice" offerings: writing in their journals or learning logs, working on calendar math, or reading a book. When the parents come in to drop off their children, the kids are busy, giving Carolyn a chance both to talk with parents and to invite them in to see their children making choices, reading and writing on their own, pursuing their own literacy in appropriate and productive ways.

Carolyn also offers other venues for parents to learn more about these ways of teaching and learning. Every year she offers a series of inservice nights for parents, in addition to the regular Curriculum Night (see Appendix C for a parent workshop survey and other selected materials from Carolyn). One of her most successful has been her language arts inservice, in which she tries to present whole language "in a tactile way." As parents enter the room, they are surrounded by evidence of literacy on the wall: kids' writing and a chart of how children's writing develops. As parents take their seats, each is handed a piece from a jigsaw puzzle. Carolyn invites them to sit down at a table and look at their puzzle pieces to see if they can determine what the entire picture might look like, first by themselves and then with the small group at their table. As Carolyn explains,

> Of course, nobody can. . . . And the analogy I make . . . is that this is what whole language is to me. I then show them the picture [on the cover of the jigsaw puzzle] and they all say, 'Wow, that's it.' And I say, "Well, in our whole language classroom, what we're dealing with is looking at the whole first and trying to gain meaning . . . before you learn the pieces. Now you look at your piece and say, 'Oh, it fits there.' When I do that, it is . . . a revelation to them, why I don't do isolated phonetic skills. It's because the meaning has to be first for kids and for all learners.

As the inservice continues, Carolyn invites parents to write a description of a classroom they remember from their childhood, leading them into a discussion of how classrooms have changed. After she shares with them similar descriptive writing their children have done about their own rooms, she asks them to bring home their writing, show it to their children, and have their children run a peer conference with them, with the kids offering them two pluses and a wish.

In this inservice Carolyn meets a number of her goals: helping the parents to understand the terms involved in whole language (like *process writing* and *peer conferences*) and how those terms play out in her classroom; showing parents the kinds of writing and response that six- and seven-years-olds can do; and having them experience what it means to write themselves. She says most parents, initially skeptical about whole language, experience "this huge 'aha.'"

Carolyn continues to run inservice nights, this year offering parents a list of possible topics at Curriculum Night. Based on the needs and questions of her particular parents each year, she creates inservice opportunities which help them understand more clearly her approaches to teaching.

Like Kathleen, Carolyn has developed a parent lending library, but it serves a different purpose in this community. Carolyn recalls that during her first year at the school, before her reputation as a whole language teacher was established, "the parents really felt a need for it, because they didn't trust invented spelling, and they didn't trust process writing. . . . They wanted to read about [the whole language debate]. There are some people here who [read the books] cover to cover, underline if they could!" Now she finds parents don't check books out quite as much. Carolyn uses the library, though, to help parents who have specific questions and to encourage their participation in the classroom. This year, a parent who is a mathematician and felt the math program was not enriching enough took Carolyn's advice to borrow a book; she now comes in regularly to work with small groups of kids in the ways she learned from her reading.

Carolyn uses a number of other strategies to help educate her parents about her approaches, such as newsletters which include student writing and portfolios that travel home for comments. Her newest addition is the Walking Journal, which she describes to parents in this way:

> We call it that because every day, a different student will walk home with it, share it with his or her family members and write a little something on one of the empty pages. . . . Whoever wants to write is welcome to do so—children, parents, grandparents, even pets (with some human translation please). . . . [T]he purpose of the Walking Journal is simply to model and encourage written communication. But mostly, it is fun for all of us to learn more about our extended family of learners.

So far, the response has been wonderful; parents and students are writing and sharing.

Carolyn knows that her work with parents has led to some changes in their views about how children learn and how schools might function. One incident captures this change well. In accordance with a mandate put forth by the school district, Carolyn's school was attempting to create an enrichment program for gifted and talented kids, one which was antithetical to her beliefs about how children learn but which she was reluctant to criticize. After hearing about the new plan, her parents—who had had the benefit of the inservice night on whole language, multiple newsletters which featured kid writing, the lending library, and many individual conversations with Carolyn—immediately came to her and said, "This isn't like your classroom. This isn't like anything you've talked about or shown us." The parents then organized and went to the principal and various committees to express their displeasure with the proposed program and to suggest an alternate approach. Their ability to articulate how they believed kids best learn was convincing; their approach was adopted by the whole school.

For Carolyn, the bottom line is helping parents to see themselves as part of the learning community that she and the children create each year. As someone who is constantly reading and thinking hard about her practice, Carolyn wants to share her ideas and knowledge with others, even as she celebrates the ideas and knowledge they can contribute.

Ronda Meier and Amy Pace: Reading and Learning with Parents

Ronda and Amy are in their second year of a shared teaching program of developmentally appropriate practices for fifty third- and fourth-grade students in a school they describe as "the parochial school" of their district: a school filled with middle- and upper-middle-class children in a district which boasts an unusual mix of rural, neighborhood, and city schools, with a large percentage of Title 1–eligible students. Relatively new teachers, both talk with amazement at the changes in their teaching in the five years they've been in the classroom: Ronda speaks for them both when she says, "I had never heard of whole language" when she entered the classroom; now the two rely on reading and writing workshops, inquiry projects with topics chosen by the students, student-led conferencing, and a host of other practices. Why the changes? The two credit a number of sources, from their own positive and empowering experiences when they were students to the support they've received in their own district: strong and active language arts consultants, a support group of K–12 teachers who have worked together on curriculum development over the past four years through the MELAF project, and participation in various whole language groups and the National Writing Project. Mostly, Amy says, "we had support. We had people who thought like us and would support us . . . what knowledge they had they would share with us." Now, Ronda adds, they "feel empowered and respected" by other teachers and administrators, a feeling that helps them continue in their work.

But this feeling of respect has not always transferred to the parents in the community. While their administrators and other teachers and even some of us in English education around the state have been increasingly impressed by the practices Amy and Ronda use in their classrooms and the high level of literacy produced by their students, parents have not always been aware or understanding of their pedagogy. Amy explains, "Ronda and I had several conversations [over the years] about how our philosophy was different [from some of the more traditional teachers] and why we were having problems with parents, not attacking us, but really questioning us. We were tired of always feeling we had to defend ourselves." Ronda adds, "I knew there was a lot that [parents] just didn't understand" about some of their practices, such as hands-on math instruction, inventive spelling, inquiry projects, and student-chosen real books rather than basals. Last year, this lack of understanding reached a peak. Until that time, each was teaching in her own classroom, with Amy in a different school. When they decided to teach together in a shared teaching classroom, Amy transferred to Ronda's school, and the school administration assigned them to adjoining rooms with a connecting doorway, in order to turn two classrooms into one, and ordered new, round tables in keeping with the classroom design Amy and Ronda desired. But as Ronda describes the first day of that experience,

> There's no furniture [the newly ordered tables hadn't come in yet], there's fifty kids in the room and a new teacher [the parents] had never seen before. . . . There was panic! [Parents were saying] "What are you doing? I strictly said I did not want my child in a split! Is this going to be a split?"

Both Amy and Ronda realized that the parents' panic was understandable: they were unprepared for changes that they didn't understand. So, the two decided to do something both to help the parents and to help themselves; specifically, they decided to start a parent study group, inviting parents to join with them to read and talk about some current issues in education, focusing on why they were using certain strategies in their teaching. "We knew that we wanted it to be a discussion with parents; we didn't want to be preaching toward them," explains Amy. "Small and intimate and comfortable," adds Ronda, "not a debate, more a discussion." When Open House came around in the third week of school, they invited parents to join in a parent study group—and were "heartbroken" when only a few parents signed up.

Because they believed strongly in the parent study group concept, they continued to press forward, realizing that perhaps they needed to explain more clearly what they meant by a parent study group, "because parents didn't know what we were asking them to do." They began to reinvite parents through a series of humorous and serious requests, including the "Top Ten Reasons" parents should join (from "An excuse to leave the house without the kids for a change" to "It can count as a date" to "Score brownie points with your child's teacher") and "Defining A Parent Study Group" ("It is a group of people who gather together to read, share and discuss topics and issues in raising literate children"). Even after the group got off the ground, Ronda and Amy continued each month to reinvite any additional parents who wanted to join in—about seventeen parents came regularly to the six meetings they held over the course of the school year. (See Appendix D for selected materials used by Ronda and Amy in conducting the parent study group.)

What would motivate parents to take time out of their busy schedules to participate in this kind of group? Answers from the participating parents varied. One parent explained: "I wanted to understand the way of teaching and the terms used in the classroom, thus making it easier to help my child at home." Another said, "I had concerns about my nine-year-old's reading." And a third participated in order "to demonstrate to my children my deep concern with their education. Their education is a top priority in my household."

For Amy and Ronda, a parent study group needed to answer both these stated concerns and the unstated ones they knew lurked in some parents' minds. It was important to them that the design of the group allow for reading and discussion, but also that it mirror the approaches they use in their classrooms. So, for example, parent choice—of topics, of meeting times, of the size of the group—was a key component. Parents decided to meet one evening a month, from 7 to 8:30, although, as Amy remembers, "We rarely got out of there at 8:30." Ronda adds, "9, 9:30, one night it was close to 10." Parents also decided to limit the group membership to parents in the Meier-Pace classroom. More problematic was convincing the parents that they should decide the topics of study because, as Amy explains, "They didn't have enough background knowledge. [They would say] 'Just tell us about reading.' [We'd want to know] 'Well, what about reading do you want to know?' And they didn't know what to ask."

Eventually, the parents agreed that what they wanted to know was "what you do in your classrooms, so that when our kids come home at the end of the day, we can understand what they're talking about." For Amy and Ronda, this meant a combination of discussion and hands-on demonstration as they helped the parents understand the language, the terminology, of the classroom. The topics they raised in the monthly meetings were multiple intelligences, reading, math, spelling, inquiry, and the MEAP Tests (Michigan Educational Assessment Program, a series of statewide tests in reading, writing, science, and social studies given at various points in a child's schooling).

Each month, Ronda and Amy sent home to the parents of all fifty kids an article focusing on the topic of the month, "so it was always an invitation. It wasn't one elite group every time." Articles were chosen carefully, beginning with one from *Newsweek* entitled "Your Child's Brain" (see Appendix for Ronda and Amy's list of suggested articles for parent study groups), which they hoped would not only prove accessible to all parents but also hook them into expanding their ways of thinking about education; the discussion that night was as rich as they had hoped. Amy explains, "It got across the idea of a variety of learning experiences . . . hands-on kinds of things as important for children's development." Ronda laughs, "They came out saying, basically, our educational system is screwed up!" As the meetings progressed, Ronda and Amy chose articles that were specific to the topics at hand but accessible to educators and noneducators alike.

On the nights of the meetings, parents would gather with the two teachers in their classroom, sitting around in a circle on the comfortable couches and chairs, eating the snacks provided by Amy and Ronda, and taking advantage of the child care they had arranged. At the first meeting, the two initiated an icebreaker in which parents recalled their own elementary learning experiences, thus setting a context for their discussion of the *Newsweek* article. The teachers then gave parents a few minutes to review the article they had read, asking them to write a journal response to their reading, which led the way into discussion. As the meetings progressed, this general format continued. At future meetings, Amy and Ronda added a second-half activity in which they demonstrated the connections between the article and their own classroom practice, using as many hands-on examples as possible, so that the parents might, as Amy said, "experience as much of [what we do in the classroom] as they actually can." Parents took a spelling test on the night of the spelling meeting, for example, experimented with math manipulatives for the math meeting, and sharpened their "#2" pencils to attempt a section of the MEAP reading test for the assessment session.

For Amy and Ronda the Parent Study Group had unbelievable benefits: they developed friendships with a number of the parents, they noticed more parental involvement in all kinds of classroom activities, and they gained new insights into the needs of many of their students. Perhaps most important, the parents became "wonderful PR people," spreading the word among other parents about the benefits of the kinds of learning that were ongoing in the Meier-Pace classroom. One parent, for example, after hearing from her peers about the kinds of reading, writing, and math activities happening in the classroom, had her daughter transferred in. Amy recalls that at the beginning of the year, "She was very strongly against us, not personally . . . , but our type of classroom environment." Ronda adds, "She said, 'I strictly requested the other teacher, because I did not want my daughter to have this type of classroom . . . split, multiage, free-for-all . . . chaos.'" As the year progressed and she began learning more specifics, she changed her mind, Amy remembers: "She even said . . . 'Had I know what was going on in your room, what was *really* going on, I would have moved my daughter in a long time ago.'"

The public relations factor also showed up at a meeting that Amy and Ronda's administration set up to explore with all parents the possibility of beginning the multiage program in the school. The parents in the Parent Study Group attended in full force, stepping forward to answer the questions posed by other parents, based on their new understanding of what really happens in a multiage classroom. Amy remembers, "Our parents were able to articulate that their children were being challenged. The [other] parents had this under-standing that [a whole language multiage classroom] was a free-for-all, that there was a lot of downtime or playtime. These parents were able to say, 'No, these kids are working hard."

According to a number of parents, this experience was extremely enlightening for them as well. Parents' responses indicate not only their newfound acceptance of the pedagogy Amy and Ronda use ("I have discovered that what I 'thought' was going on in my daughter's class was really *not* what was going on. I've learned so much about her methods of learning in the classroom. I know now she's on the right track"), but also an increased understanding of how to use that newfound knowledge to help their children in their homework ("I felt confident of the classroom and confident when I worked with my child"). For many, this new understanding transfers beyond the confines of this one multiage classroom, to a more general acceptance of current pedagogies ("The most important outcome of the Parent Study Group is the development of a community of understanding that promises to move pedagogy in a positive direction; i.e., for new methods to be accepted, this process is necessary.")

Amy and Ronda explain that for the last several years, people in their district have been talking about the fact that all teachers need to be able to communicate better with parents. Instead of waiting for the district to come up with the plan, these two young teachers just took the plunge. In Amy's words, "We just said, we'll do it ourselves, just start small."

Learning from Teachers

As I examine these teachers' approaches to informing parents, I notice some striking similarities, similarities that are echoed in the voices of many other teachers I have interviewed and observed over the past two years. Despite differences in the communities in which they work, the grade levels they teach, and their own levels of experience and background in English language arts, these teachers' specific approaches seem to group themselves into some broad categories—what I would call general advocacy strategies for informing parents. Briefly, let me describe these advocacy strategies.

Extending Multiple Invitations

These teachers all find a variety of ways to invite and reinvite and reinvite parents to become part of the classroom enterprise. They understand that not all ways of entering the classroom conversation are equally comfortable to people, so they seek multiple approaches to reach out to their constituencies, such as inviting parents to write about their children's learning and asking them to help out in the classroom in any way they can—coming to an open house or a parent inservice or study group, writing for a class book, or talking to the class about another kind of endeavor. These teachers also find ways of outreach which speak to the needs and character of an individual community. In some communities, a parent lending library may work because people in that community are voracious readers; in other communities, a parent lending library serves the purpose of adding authority to the teacher's voice merely because it's there. Some parents will never walk into the classroom, will never write for a class book, will never gain knowledge of the curriculum by participating in the academic structure—but they will learn about the curriculum by talking with the teacher on their way to a field trip. In short, teachers need to know their communities and learn the best ways of outreach for that community.

Initiating Early, Proactive Contact with Parents

All teachers have stressed to me the importance of some form of "getting to know you and your child," whether that takes the form of home visits, picnics, surveys, or another activity. The time spent in that task (and, not to underestimate that time, it is enormous) seems to pay off for every teacher I know: Parents are more receptive because they've made a connection with the teacher early on and are more likely to continue their involvement in the classroom; teachers feel more comfortable talking to the parents on subsequent occasions. Many teachers also use this early contact to explain their approaches to teaching reading and writing, especially if their methods might be different from what the parents are accustomed to. Newsletters, for example, which help the parents understand what their child will be doing in class and what they should expect to see at home help set a tone: The teacher has considered carefully this way of teaching and is helping to provide parents with the language necessary to understand its parameters.

Empowering Student Voices

All these teachers take time to help their students understand the language that writers—and teachers of writing—use. Once the students can use terms like *process writing*, *portfolios*, or *revision* comfortably and correctly, they can help educate their parents—whether it's through a peer conference on the bed one night or through a collaboratively composed student newsletter about the workshop classroom. When children speak naturally about writers' tricks to aid in revision or literary logs to improve their reading, that language becomes part of the family's understanding of what constitutes school—even if it's a different language from that of their prior experiences.

Immersing Parents in Their Children's Reading and Writing

For all these teachers, getting examples of their children's reading and writing into parents' hands was vital. Then, in more than a "check-your-child's-homework-and-initial-it" approach, these teachers found ways to guide parents into how to respond to their child's learning—ways which then educated them about best practices: hosting an inservice in which parents write and respond to what their children are writing, or sending home students' work in an individual portfolio or a class poetry anthology, prefaced by a teaching letter on how to respond. Clearly, not all parents will feel comfortable in this role at first, but the more teachers help them learn how to respond, the more knowledgeable they—and their children—will be about how people become more literate individuals.

Becoming Knowledgeable and Articulate Themselves

Underlying all these strategies is this last one: that all the teachers bring a deep understanding of language arts instruction that was not arrived at easily or quickly. They all have worked hard to come to know their own beliefs about children's learning, to understand how their beliefs connect to the published writings of those conversant in "best practices," and to feel comfortable in expressing those beliefs to others. Teachers who use these advocacy strategies almost always name the support groups which have helped them on this journey: National Writing Project groups, TAWL chapters, and study groups or teacher research groups. They often talk also about that moment when they finally read published authors whose beliefs express so clearly the ways they've been thinking about their own teaching. For these teachers, this support in coming to understand where they stand has been vital. Once they feel more knowledgeable, they have been able to articulate that knowledge to others, drawing upon the specific strategies mentioned above.

When I look at the fine work these teachers are doing, and I think about the other exciting examples of parent outreach I've come across as I've talked with teachers over the last several years, I know this: Teachers already do a lot to inform their parent communities about the practices which inform their pedagogies. Good teachers all over the country are taking the time and developing the expertise to reach out to parents, and many parents, in turn, are beginning to reach some new understandings about the multiple reasons teacher professionals embrace certain practices. And, as a result of this action, a number of parents are taking action of their own, whether it's disagreeing with another parent who lambastes whole language on the sidelines of the soccer game or going forward to testify in front of a school board. Teachers who recognize that one of their professional roles is to do outreach in their community of parents and other adults are setting the stage for some changes in how the public views the education of its children.

I am aware that many teachers reading this chapter will find some of these outreach strategies familiar or even be reminded of other means of outreach they employ that aren't mentioned here. This fact alone strengthens my rationale for this chapter and for this book: Individual teachers seem to know innately that this kind of outreach is both necessary and, when done well, extremely effective. Individual teachers even do this kind of outreach, some more often than others. But what

I've found in my conversations with scores of teachers is that for most busy professionals, their approach to parent outreach is sporadic at best—generally spontaneous, often forgotten from year to year, and too many times done merely in response to a problem. In essence, such outreach is rarely part of a sustained program and is certainly not a universal among teachers across the country. And as a result, what we learn about outreach from our colleagues and peers arises from a remark shared in the staff room or over a cup of coffee after school. It is not the stuff of teacher training programs or staff development sessions. And when that chance remark strikes a chord, we try out something here or there, but rarely in a sustained, organized way: rarely, that is, in the kind of habitual approach to a conscientious program of parent outreach that I believe is necessary in order for it to become a regular and effective part of our practice and in order for a proactive approach to parent involvement to become a matter of course in our lives.

What I want to suggest from this chapter and in the rest of this book, is that we begin to think about our jobs differently. If we want to be able to do our jobs effectively, to be allowed to continue to teach in ways that we know work with students, then we must find ways to push to the forefront of our jobs this task of parent outreach. We have to discover the means to work with parents regularly and consistently, in ways that have proven to be effective. We have to find strategies that work, strategies that fit into our practice and into our time constraints, yes, but also strategies that allow us to reach out to parents as a matter of course—before a problem sets in. We have to become proactive . . . so that we don't always have to be reactive. In the current climate, it's no longer a luxury; it's a necessity.

I believe we can learn from the lessons of others about how to do this, specifically from the work of community organizers who, for the last century, have explored how to go about working with others in order to change minds and create new ways of viewing the world. Community organizers, who come from a variety of disciplines and see their work and commitments in a variety of ways, have certain commonalities in their approaches—and a track record that is truly inspiring. Teachers, perhaps, can learn from what these organizers do in order to create a sustained model for creating new understandings.

In the chapters that follow, I will try to lay out my argument about community organizing more fully by, first, giving an overview of community organizing theory and practice, referring often to the work and lives of the organizers whom I interviewed over the past year. Community organizing, as you will see, is an umbrella term, one which encompasses widely diverse ways of thinking, but which comes down to some very basic commonalities. In subsequent chapters, I will suggest some components which seem to be at the heart of any approach to community organizing, specifically suggesting how these components might connect to the needs and commitments of teachers.

Am I suggesting that teachers take on a whole new job and become community organizers, too? No, but what I am suggesting is that if teachers begin to view their jobs through the lens of community organization, we might see some vital changes in how the public views our role—and, maybe, in how the public views its role—in the education of children. Maybe it's worth a try.

Appendix A

This appendix contains the following materials developed by Julie King:

- Welcome letter to parents
- *The Student Times*
- *Seeing Common Ground: A Parent's Guide to Process Writing Instruction and Assessment* (selected pages)

Language Arts
Ms. King
Holmes Middle School
Conference (fourth hour): 11:30 - 12:55

WELCOME TO WORKSHOP!

Welcome to eighth grade language arts -- workshop style! The focus of this course is on the four "strands" of language arts: reading, writing, speaking, and listening. That's exactly what you can expect to find in our Reading-Writing Workshop. Students will be reading and writing, as well as sharing, collaborating, and conferring with others in the classroom on a daily basis. We will explore different types of literature and writing, emphasizing mechanics and content in both areas. Mainly, we will be learning what good readers and writers do, and practicing skills for literacy.

What is workshop?

Reading-Writing workshop means:

*Time is given in class for reading and writing.

*Students are expected to also continue in-class reading and writing at home.

*Students are encouraged to explore their own interests for reading and writing.

*Whole class lessons focus on improving reading and writing skills.

*Students are expected to reflect on their own literacy learning.

What about class work and homework?

*Students are required to read 30 minutes a day, M-F, outside of school time. (This is in addition to any class time given in language arts or in C.U.T. time classes.)

*Students are required to write a minimum of 3-5 pages of rough draft writing each week and to keep drafts in their writing folders.

*Students are required to maintain a Writing Folder of work-in-progress and skills lists.

*A lot of class time will be devoted to writing and revising, however additional homework time will be necessary to complete requirements.

And grading?

*Each week Writing Folders will be evaluated for completion of rough draft writing and for keeping writing and reading lists up-to-date.

*Each week Reader's Response Journals will be evaluated for completion of three full-page responses to student's individual reading.

*Completion of daily lessons and class participation will be noted and evaluated.

*Each card marking, students will develop and turn in a portfolio or work with reflection of their own learning in the course.

*The progress report grade will be based on the completeness of required assignments.

*The marking period grade will be based on the complete portfolio - a product of all of the above.

How will you know how your child is doing in language arts?
   *You should see a lot of reading and writing happening at home! If not, please call me!
   *Students will periodically be sharing work with you at home.
   *Mid-mark evaluations will be sent home at the five week point of each marking period.
   *If you ever have questions call me!

What materials do students need?
The school will provide:
   *A manila folder which can be used as a student portfolio.
   *Classroom and library books.

In addition, students will need:
   *Pens and pencils for writing every day!
   *A **three ring binder with dividers** to serve as a Writing Folder
   *An 8 1/2 x 11 **composition notebook** (to serve as a Reader's Response Journal).
    *Books, books, and more books!

   While there will be some whole class and small group reading, students will be
expected to pursue independent reading throughout the course. There is a wide variety of
literature available at Holmes for students to choose from. I do encourage you, however, to
take your child outside our school building to discover books of interest in other places.
This can include public libraries, local bookstores, used bookstores, or even borrowing
from friends.

An invitation....
   *Questions? Call me at 953-3932. I am available from 8:15 - 9:15 and after 3:00 p.m.
   *Interested in visiting our classroom? Please let me know when you'd like to come in!
   *Would you like to volunteer in the classroom to:
    -work with small groups of students to listen to and respond to their writing?
    -help students with publishing their writing?
    -share with us your personal or professional reading and writing experiences?
    -any other ideas? If so, give me a call as soon as possible so we can make arrangements.

A request....
*The more I know about each student, the better able I am to meet each student's needs.
**Please take a moment to write to me about your child. What should I know as his or
her language arts teacher?** *Responses can be delivered to me through your child or can be
sent directly to the main office to my attention. I appreciate your time!

THE STUDENT TIMES

A PUBLICATION OF MS. KING'S THIRD HOUR LANGUAGE ARTS 8 CLASS, HOLMES MIDDLE SCHOOL

EDITORS:Dan Cox, Stephanie Rothenberg, Adam Vincentini, and Kim White
ISSUE #1   FALL, 1995

THINGS WE USE FOR EVERYDAY LIFE

We have many things available to us in writing workshop. We use computers to write pieces and to save data, and printers to print the data. A pencil is also used, or a pen can be used when desired. These materials are used for everyday life. We use other things such as date stampers, markers, printers, white out, books, paper, stapler, and paper clips. Hole punchers are used for papers that go in our black binders. We are provided with all the tools to have a successful Language Arts class.

By: Erich Shrewsbury, Misty Evenson, Joe Katrich, Jamil Azar, Aaron McCabe, and John McLean

Writing made Right

There are many different types of writing. There are also a variety at things to write about,like short stories, poems, letters, and many more. Some people write about sports, memories, letters to parents and friends. A good writer tries writing a different way, most of the time. Writing is worked on from Monday to Wednesday. Step of writing include first, brainstorming ideas, then draft (1-3) with conference sheets, conferencing, then self edit. After that you turn in all those sheets for a final edit and be looked over by Ms. King.

By: Jamil Azar, Cindy Galka, Joe Katrich, Dustin Mojak, Aaron McCabe, and Dan Cox

Brain Storming

Brain storming is great way for writing ideas. It helps for ideas on your drafts. Like webs, jots , and other things using them for ideas is good to. Also just putting ideas on paper helps. Before every first draft Ms. King tells us to brain storm.

by: Nick Soper , Steve Holden, Brad Langohr , and John McLean

Conferences "R" Us

Conferencing is when you talk with a group of people about a piece of writing and see what they think about it. They give you two pluses and a wish. Two pluses are when a person gives you two good things to say about your piece of writing. A wish is something they want to change about it. Two people can conference at a time. Conference records are pieces of paper that you write your two pluses and a wish on. It also has a post conference plan that is where you write what you are going to do next to your piece. Conferences help people become better writers. Many say it's fun.

By: Dan Cox, Megan Meldrum, Kelly Bruce, Cindy Galka, Misty Evenson, and Kim White

By: Kim White, Josh Swim, Mike Shkreli, Mike Harris, Mike Cervi, and Joey Kosky

FINAL EDITING

Editing involves a lot of independent work. After going through the conferencing stage, editing is necessary. Self editing is where you go through your piece of work, correcting all punctuation, spelling, and sentence structure. Editing could be considered a form of self-correction.

After the self-editing is completed, the piece of work is turned in for teacher editing. In this stage Ms. King goes over the piece for final corrections. She confronts us at this time in what we call an editing conference. In this conference we discuss the changes the she recommends. This is the final stage before the piece is finalized.

Come Sit in the Author's Chair

The author's chair is shiny red and people from the class come and sit in the chair and share their pieces of writing to the class. After there done the whole class gives them two pluses and a wish which means two good points in your piece they liked and one thing they wished you could have added to your piece. But some people get nervous. But after you read your piece you get a lot of good ideas.

By: Craig Sharpe, Angelica Placinta, Adam Vincentini, Steph Rothenberg, and Megan Meldrum

Mini Lessons

Every couple days we start the class with a mini lesson. A mini lesson helps understand different ways to write. We have done mini lessons on the way we do things in class like, discussing evaluation points, conference record; turn in check list, words that show not tell and noun plurals. We have also had mini on reading workshop how we should write in our lit logs. How we should not write plot summaries. We should critical think. In our lit log we have also

learned how to make a plot triangle about our books.So mini lessons are good because they help us become better writers.

By: Mike Soho, Joe Kosky, Jennifer Schmid, Mike Skrehli, Joey DeCarlo, and Craig Sharpe

About Working Together

Group work is exciting because there's more than one brain thinking. It is an excellent way to get to know other people better. It allows us to work with other people and still learn.

When we are in a group, we share our ideas with other people in the group. These groups can be fun, though in other ways they can't because we could get stuck with people who don't want to work. Sometimes we get a lively group and everything works out.

By: Stephanie Rothenberg, Joey DeCarlo, Amanda Paglione, Josh Swim, Mike Soho, and Brad Langohr

Social Kids
Get Down to Reading

Silent reading is a time to read and to do it silently. No talking is allowed, but we can write in our literary log to who we want to. Sometimes we read two times a week for the full hour in Reading Workshop. A lot of the time we spread all around the room, but some people stay in their seats. Some people read long, long, long books, and some read shorter books.

by Nick Soper, Mike Cervi, Dustin Mojak,Katie Jahnevich, Kelly Bruce, and Eric Shrewsbury

Writing in Literary Logs

You can write to a person about the book you are reading. You can also write to Ms. King. You have to write at least once every two weeks and turn it in to Ms. King. You tell how your book is coming along. You also tell if its good or interesting or if its bad or boring. Some people say it's just like writing a note to your friend.

By: Angelica Placinta, Amanda Paglione, Jennifer Schmid, Adam Vincentini, Mike Harris. and Katie Janhevich

THE STUDENT TIMES
ISSUE #1 FALL. 1995

> **Seeing Common Ground:**
> **A Parent's Guide to Process Writing**
> **Instruction and Assessment**

Dear Parents,

Too often the "new terms" in education create a gap between teachers and parents. As new movements and practices in the teaching and learning of language arts come along, it is often confusing to understand a teacher's classroom expectations and requirements. As we learn more and more about how students acquire language skills, language arts instruction continues to change from what we remember from our own schooling.

This handbook is intended to be a guide to understanding how a process approach to teaching and assessment work in my middle school classroom, and in many other classrooms where this approach to teaching and learning are used.

In the three sections of this handbook: Process Writing, Portfolios, and Authentic Assessment, I have defined each term so you can better understand each and how it works in the classroom. In addition, with the cooperation of many of my seventh and eighth grade students, I have included stories about how these practices work in the classroom as well as samples of what students have said and written throughout.

It is my hope that this guide will help you understand our classroom and your child's work in language arts this year. I also hope it serves to give you ideas as to how you can work with your child at home to become a lifelong learner of language and literacy.

Sincerely,

Julie King

Julie King

(PROCESS WRITING)

What does it mean?

Process writing is an approach to teaching writing which recognizes that most writers take a piece of writing through several stages before the "final" version is completed. In the past, writing instruction has often involved assigning, collecting, correcting, and returning papers to students with the hope that they learn from their "mistakes" and avoid these mistakes on the next assignment.

TRADITIONAL APPROACH:

I can remember my tenth grade composition class; the class where we "learned to write." Each week we were given a five hundred word writing assignment, usually focusing on a different kind of writing. We wrote a variety of papers: narrative, description , comparison/contrast, categorization, and persuasive essays, to name a few. We would receive the assignment on Monday, with little discussion about the expectations of us as writers. Sometimes we were given a few minutes in class on Monday to begin our papers, then we spent the rest of the week hearing about different types of sentences and paragraph unity.

We never really applied those ideas to our papers in class; however the teacher assumed we would use these skills correctly in our work. We did learn the "formula" for exposition: a three part thesis with an introduction, three body paragraphs, and a conclusion. Sometimes we were required to show our thesis sentence to the teacher for approval.

On Fridays, we handed our papers over to the teacher, with a final draft, a rough draft and an outline. On Monday, she returned them to us with red marks and a grade on the last page. If we had over a certain number of red marks, we were required to recopy the incorrect sentences or misspelled words ten times and hand in our "revisions" by the next Friday. I can't remember whether or not this could improve the grade on the paper.

This approach to "teaching writing" has been used traditionally for many years, and has been successful in teaching students that writing has a formula and the writer must meet the expectation of the teacher-audience when using that formula. This approach does not offer the kind of coaching and teaching that a process approach allows. The *traditional* "instruction" occurs before students begin writing with lessons and lectures about the rules of writing and not again until after they complete a piece.

1.

In the past, little attention has been paid to working with students a
they engage in the *actual writing*. Over the past 15 years, however,
educators have learned from professional writers that there are many
identifiable stages that a piece of writing goes through before it reaches it
final version. Further, students can and should be taught about writing at
each stage of the process, to allow them to develop more fully as writers.

A PROCESS APPROACH:

Lauren was one of my seventh grade language arts students. Over
the summer, she had an incredible experience with her family in the birth
of her cousin, Haley Rose. During the fall semester, students in my
language arts class began developing ideas and exploring many different
kinds of writing of their choice. One week, students created "positive /
negative charts. " They listed a number of important events in their lives,
and ranked them according to which were the most positive and the most
negative. When they had completed their "positive / negative" charts,
students talked with each other about some of their experiences and chose
topics for writing.

When Lauren ranked the significant events in her life, one of the most
positive was the birth of her cousin. She immediately knew that this was
something she really wanted to write about. She relates,

> ...for some reason I had just kept on thinking about the
> past, what happened...all the things with decorating and
> the baby shower. And it made me think of a story.... When
> we did our plus and minus charts, for "our good things" I
> wrote "my best thing that ever happened to me was
> when my cousin Haley was born" and then I kept on
> writing about it. I wrote a good two pages about it and I
> got a story in my head so I just started writing in my
> journal. And I got maybe two pages down.

Lauren's excitement about this topic was obvious. The assignment was to
explore a variety of topics she cared about, then to choose one and create
piece of writing about it. She was enthusiastic, which showed in her
writing because she was not trying to fit her ideas into a formula, but
rather was concerned with telling her story so others could understand
how she felt. She spent a great deal of time working on this piece, called
"The Big Surprise," taking it through her own process, which is what real
writers do.

2.

(PROCESS WRITING: STAGES)

Process writing involves stages such as *prewriting, drafting, revising, editing, proofreading, polishing, sharing and publishing*. General definitions of these stages are provided below; however they are often overlapping and different teachers may use the terms differently.

What is most important to understand is that process writing instruction fosters the development of student writing through many stages, recognizing that individual writers have different approaches and different needs. While Lauren's process for her writing will differ from that of others, the process she went through can be identified to show how each of the stages work together.

*prewriting: writing before you write

*drafting: getting it all down

*revising: reseeing and changing

*editing: changing content / changing mechanics

*proofreading/polishing: getting it ready for publishing

*sharing/publishing: taking it to a larger audience

3.

(PREWRITING: WRITING BEFORE YOU WRITE)

Prewriting is any activity which helps the writer come up with ideas about what might later go into a piece of writing. It is not about right or wrong; but rather about freely releasing possibilities for writing. There are many methods of prewriting which can help a writer get started. Some students may *free write* or *brainstorm* - both are methods of writing down anything that comes to mind, quickly, to help release ideas. Other students may need to talk, or share ideas with other students before they begin writing. Other types of prewriting are more visual, as students may draw pictures or symbols which represent the ideas they might later write about.

Once students get an initial idea about what to write, they often can continue in the prewriting stage to gather more information about the subject, or come up with details to include in the piece. Often students can begin organizing information at a prewriting stage. They can do this by creating a *web* or *cluster* (charts to organize information) or by actually creating an outline. **During prewriting stages, correctness of mechanics such as spelling or punctuation is not emphasized.** What is most important is giving the writer an opportunity to gather ideas and information to work with later.

PREWRITING IN ACTION:

Lauren's prewriting began when she first decided to include the birth of her cousin on her positive negative chart. She relates,

> When I started writing about Haley all kinds of ideas kept popping into my head and the sequence of when she was born... when my aunt told us and everything and I got a story in my head. I just first started jotting down ideas... , just regular plain ideas and then it wasn't going very far...because I was kind of having some trouble remembering things. So that day I went home and called my grandma (to ask) her exactly what she remembered. I started remembering things like the day she was born and the time.

The "positive / negative" chart was a place where Lauren could start to gather ideas for writing. Once she had a story in her head, she wrote down everything she could remember. Later, she gathered more information by talking with her grandmother. All of these strategies Lauren used to begin her piece can be considered part of her prewriting.

4.

WHAT YOU CAN DO AT HOME:

Many writers experience what is known as "writer's block." Students often tell me, "I don't have anything to write about!" That is natural, and happens to all of us. If your child is frustrated, or having difficulty thinking of things to write about, there are several things you can do at home to help:

-Talk about interests, hobbies, memories, and important experiences.
-Select an interesting topic help your child list everything he or she
    knows about the topic. (This is called brain storming.)
-Encourage your child to draw pictures or images that might help get ideas
    flowing.
-Look at things you or your child have read and found interesting for
    examples of possible topics.
-Choose a topic and write together for 2-3 minutes without stopping,
    putting down any ideas that come to mind. (This is called free
    writing.)

5.

A FINAL NOTE:

Writing instruction as a process has been in use in classrooms for many years. It is an approach to teaching writing that values the individual interests and levels of the students, and our understandings of how this works in the classroom increases as we learn new ways of teaching students strategies through each stage of their writing.

Many teachers also use the terminology, "The Writing Process," to describe the stages of writing that students in their classroom use. In some ways, this implies that every writer moves through each stage, lock-step, in completing a piece of writing. As writers mature, however, they become more independent in how they approach a writing task, and need the flexibility to move back and forth between the stages. **It is important to recognize that each writer will develop his or her own process in developing pieces of writing that are meaningful to them.**

14.

Appendix B

This appendix contains the following materials developed by Kathleen Hayes-Parvin:

- Poetry teaching letter
- Memoir letter
- Invitation to write for Class Heritage Book
- Student-led parent conference invitation

October, 1995

Dear Parents,

We hope you enjoy our first publication. We began the year with poetry so we could focus in on the structure of language. You might notice some of the writer's tricks we've incorporated into our poems.

Look for detail, alliteration, line breaks, the use of three's, and using old words in new ways. Our writing has greater impact in part because we're learning to use vivid verbs and pare down unnecessary words. Watch for the use of the five senses in our poems. And just as published authors do, we're writing about things that really matter to us.

Included in our anthology is a comments sheet. Please take a minute to respond to us. What did you notice, wonder, feel, what surprised you or connected to your own experience, what reminded you of another author or poem. Any way you choose to respond will be valuable to us.

Thank you for making the time to read our poetry. We're proud of our strong beginning.

Sincerely,
Language Arts Class, 1995-96

November 15, 1995

Dear Parents,

Memoir is a literary genre that helps us find meaning in the events of our lives. Unlike autobiography, memoir does not attempt a complete timeline of life experiences. Instead, it focuses on a few select moments in our past that together, reflect larger truths about our existence.

Memoir is an opportunity to reflect on who and what we are as we create meaning out of our lives experiences. Memoir can be crafted into picture books, poems, essays, letters, short stories, young adult and adult novels. A trip to the library or bookstore will yield countless examples of memoir as it's particularly popular today.

Over the next six to eight weeks, we will pursue an in-depth study of memoir that will culminate in a class book. We invite you to write a personal memoir that we will publish in our book next to your child's.

I, too, plan to write for our book. I intend to explore several childhood events to begin to understand why I am the teacher I've become. This is my first experience writing for a class book and the first time I've issued this invitation to parents. Let's take the plunge together and model literacy for our youngsters.

OUR DEADLINE FOR ACCEPTING PIECES IS FRIDAY, JANUARY 12, 1996. The extended deadline takes into account the holiday season that is almost upon us. However, we welcome your writing any time before then.

I will be available to assist you in any way possible and will act as editor for your pieces. If you have any questions I can be reached at school. My preps are 10 a.m. and 1 p.m..

Sincerely,

_____ YES, I PLAN TO SUBMIT A PIECE.

PARENT SIGNATURE

YES, I RECEIVED THE INVITATION TO
WRITE FOR THE CLASS HERITAGE BOOK.

PARENT SIGNATURE:

CHILD NAME:

YES, I PLAN TO WRITE FOR THE
PUBLICATION.

PARENT SIGNATURE:

PLEASE PHONE ME. I HAVE SOME
QUESTIONS ABOUT MY WRITING.

NAME:

NUMBER DURING DAY: EVENING:

I WOULD BE WILLING TO VISIT THE CLASS
TO READ MY PIECE.

NAME:

NUMBER DURING DAY: EVENING:

May 20, 1996

Dear Parents:

Please join your child and me for a unique conference experience. We invite you to visit room F-110, Tuesday, May 28, to view and discuss you child's work and progress in Language Arts.

Approximately five parent-child conferences will take place simultaneously. I will oversee each conference and be available to answer questions. However, your child will be the one to sit with you and explain his/her portfolio.

Language Arts involves reading, writing, speaking, and listening. Your participation provides a meaningful opportunity for your child to integrate all of those skills. In addition, by attending, you send the message that education is important to you and you want your child to do well in school.

This conference provides your child with an opportunity for self-assessment and a chance to build self-confidence. It is a stepping stone on the road to future college and/or job interviews. I am sure you will find it worthwhile.

If you are unable to attend at your assigned time, please note a better time below. I will call you and confirm the change. Thank you for all of your support this year. You have made a difference for your child and I am most grateful.

Sincerely,

Kathleen Hayes-Parvin

I plan to attend my conference at　＿＿＿＿＿＿＿＿＿＿＿

No, I am unable to attend. I would prefer to come:
＿＿＿＿＿＿＿＿＿＿＿＿＿＿＿＿＿＿＿＿＿＿＿＿＿

I can be reached at home:＿＿＿＿＿＿＿＿＿work:＿＿＿＿＿＿

Parent name:＿＿＿＿＿＿＿＿＿＿Child name:＿＿＿＿＿＿＿＿

Appendix C

This appendix contains the following materials developed by Carolyn Berge:

- Parent Involvement at Home handout
- Walking Journal letter
- Parent volunteer form
- Parent workshop topic survey

PARENT INVOLVEMENT AT HOME
No sign-up needed for these
most important contributions:

Often, parents are too busy to offer time in the classroom. I, for one, am a parent who seldom has the opportunity to volunteer in my own daughter's school. But we can still help out by doing some of the following valuable activities with our children at home.

1. Read with your child--anything and anywhere. Share the newspaper, the cereal box, road signs, products at the supermarket, and, of course, books! Our Multiagers should be reading every night for at least 10 minutes, preferably before they get too sleepy. Don't make them read that cozy bedtime story. Save that delightful duty for yourself! Remember, you are the most important model of literacy in your child's life.

2. Write to and with your child. A thank you letter for cleaning a messy bedroom (don't we all wish!), a friendly note in the lunch box, or a "TO DO" list. Together, you can compose a letter to a friend or relative, jot down a shopping list, or label a photo album. Children who see writing as a necessary and meaningful part of every day life are usually eager to gain independence as writers themselves.

3. Reinforce the real life math that you automatically do at home: count out the silverware when setting the table, estimate how long it will take to finish raking the yard, think about numbers used in baking, traveling, and sewing, or the shapes used in building or drawing. Make your child aware of the importance of numbers and problem solving every day.

4. Talk with your child. Read over the class newsletters and ask questions about school. Show lots of interest and respect for the ideas and thoughts your child expresses, as well as the work he/she brings home. Your praise insures rapid growth.

5. The basics are always essential--enough sleep, a good breakfast, and a warm hug!

WALKING JOURNAL

1997-1998

Dear Families,

Your child has just brought home a very fun and important binder. It is our WALKING JOURNAL. We call it that because every day, a different student will walk home with it, share it with his or her family members, and write a little something on one of the empty pages. The fun thing is that there are absolutely NO directions! Whoever wants to write is welcome to do so--children, parents, grandparents, even pets (with some human translation, please). There are no assigned topics. We, as writers, may tell about memorable events or everyday happenings. We may want to share favorite poems, stories, games, or songs. Adding photos, drawings, or cartoon might be fun. We may want to ask questions or pose problems or respond to the thoughts of other writers. It is all entirely up to us!

The only thing to remember is that your writing will be read by all of the families in the classroom. What a wonderful audience! From an educational standpoint, the purpose of the Walking Journal is simply to model and encourage written communication. But mostly, it is fun for all of us to learn more about our extended family of learners.

Please take time to read and write in the Walking Journal. If you can't get it done overnight, feel free to take a day or two. Hopefully the binder will circulate a number of times before the end of the school year. Thank you!

Sincerely,

Carolyn Berge

PARENT VOLUNTEER FORM

Here are some ways you can help in our Multiage Classroom. If your schedule allows, check the tasks that interest you and return the form to school. We will work out times and details later. THANKS!

_____ Compiling Scholastic Book Orders

_____ Assisting with Computer

_____ Sharing travels, occupations, hobbies, etc.

_____ Serving as an Art Angel

_____ Serving as a Science Angel

_____ Working with individual children on reading, writing, or math

_____ Coordinating our Classroom Newsletter

_____ Going on field trips

_____ Helping with class plays

_____ Working on special Theme Projects

_____ Supervising Reading, Writing, or Math Clubs

_____ Shopping at the Scrap Box, picking up supplies, etc.

_____ Typing children's stories for publication--at home or school

_____ Donating supplies: Old stationary, fabric, etc. as needed

_____ Working on a project at home

_____ Other--Please feel free to write down your ideas!

NAME _____

PARENT WORKSHOPS

Curriculum Night is a meant to be an overview of the subjects taught
in our Multiage Classroom, and I realize that many parents will still
have lingering questions about "why" and "how" certain things are
taught. This year, I would like to offer families the option of attending
some workshops around some of the major issues. From the list below,
please check the topics that seem most relevant to you. Please
prioritize if you have more than two favorites. Thank you!

Carolyn

XXXXXXXXXXXXXXXXXXXXXXXXXXXXXXXXXXXXXXXXXXXXXXXXXXXXXXXXXXXXXX

_____ Multiage: How It Works and Why Do It?

_____ Literacy: Reading and Writing, Speaking and Listening
For those interested in phonics, invented spelling, and how to
respond to a child's writing when you can't read a word of it but
know it must be wonderful!

_____ Math: It may be "Everyday" but not in my day!
How to understand the stuff your child brings home and why we
don't just teach "how to carry and borrow" anymore!

_____ Multiple Intelligences: Why it is so important to work with a
child's natural learning style and how we can recognize a child's
strong areas and use them to enhance learning at home and
school.

_____ TIGERSKS: How and why we encourage students to develop skills
that make them lifelong learners. Thoughtful, Industrious,
Generative, Empathetic, Strategic--Knowledge, and Self-esteem.
Your kids know all about these, do you?

_____ Learning through Inquiry: How we develop curriculum with,
instead of for, children.

Appendix D

This appendix contains the following materials developed by Ronda Meier and Amy Pace:

- Defining a Parent Study Group handout
- Suggested parent study group articles

Defining a Parent Study Group

What is a Parent Study Group? It is a group of people who gather together to read, share, and discuss topics and issues in raising literate children. These issues may be related to education such as multiple intelligences, reading, spelling, self-esteem, or other issues related to parenting.

Our parent study group is starting small. But if you know of another parent that is interested, please invite them. Everyone is welcome. Our first meeting date is Tuesday, October 8 from 7:00-8:30 pm. We will meet in our classroom. A Monor sixth grade student will be available to baby-sit here during the meeting if you need someone to watch your child.

At the meeting we will be discussing the article we sent home earlier in the year, "Your Child's Brain." If you still have it, please bring it. Extra copies will be available at the meeting. Time will be provided for us to read a short article entitled, "What Motivates Children to Read." We would also like to brainstorm and select topics our group would like to discuss at future meetings. We will set another meeting date, so please bring your calendars.

Suggested Parent Study Group Articles

Begley, Sharon. "Your Child's Brain." *Newsweek*, 19 February 1996: 54+.

Curtis, Wendy. "Spelling Bees for Children: Why?" *Language Arts Journal of Michigan* 12 (1996): 50–51.

Gambrell, Lisa. "What Motivates Children to Read?" *Scholastic Literacy Place: Teacher's Desk Reference.* New York: Scholastic, 1996.

Neill, Monty. "Principles for Assessment," *Talking Points* 8.3 (1997): 26–27.

Routman, Regie and Donna Maxim. "Invented Spelling: What It Is and What It Isn't." *School Talk* 1.4 (April 1996).

Weaver, Constance. "On the Teaching of Spelling." *Michigan Literacy Consortium Journal* 28 (Spring 1995): 24–25.

Whitin, David J., and Phyllis E. Whitin. "Inquiry at the Window: The Year of the Birds." *Language Arts* 73 (1996): 82–87.

3 An Introduction to Community Organizing

Last fall, as I was beginning to interview community organizers for this book, the parks department in the city in which I live initiated a ballot proposal to build a $2.4 million, 12,000-square-foot "Environmental Education Center" in the city-owned park across the street from my house. This park is a treasure in our neighborhood and in the city: acres of open space where kids play, a wildflower meadow which changes through the seasons and boasts six-foot flowers in July and August, acres of wooded trails leading to a pond filled with salamanders and frogs, a very low-tech environmental program featuring a "critter room," children's gardens, a compost demonstration center, and some hands-on outdoor classes designed for school-aged children in the area. This proposal had gone through the usual approval process: Various governmental committees had given their OK, including the unanimous support of the City Council. The first we neighbors heard of this ballot measure, however, was in a flyer put in our mailbox, inviting us across the street for a meeting at "the homestead," the old home that sits atop the hill that was the former residence for the couple who willed their fifty acres to the city to establish a children's park. People came away from the meeting a little confused about this proposal, wondering why on earth this low-tech, down and dirty, environmental program housed in the midst of a residential neighborhood wanted to expand so drastically. One neighbor—someone we only knew in passing—asked if we wanted to meet with some other neighbors on Sunday night to talk about our impressions of the proposal.

From that confused response to the parks department proposal came my first hands-on introduction to community organizing. The first meeting led to more meetings, and to conversations with city council members, with the parks department officials, and with the staff of the park's education program as we tried to discover the motivations behind the construction of this center. Meetings multiplied as we began to talk within our neighborhood group to figure out, first, our own individual stances toward the building and, then, to come up with a consensus group stance as we decided to publicly oppose its construction. Our group grew as we talked with our friends and colleagues about why we opposed the building, from about twenty interested neighbors to more than two hundred people around the city, who signed our petition and our signature ad for the newspaper and who contributed money for us to publicize our campaign. An unlikely coalition of characters began to emerge: a real estate agent who was also an environmental activist, a concert pianist, a therapist, a social worker, a nuclear engineer, a sculptor, a homemaker, a public interest attorney and community organizer, and an English professor who, ironically, was on sabbatical to write a book about community organizing! Our members ranged from a seventeen-year-old who was adamantly opposed to changing the nature of the park which provided so much joy to him growing up, to older neighbors who knew the original owners of the land and protested this change as antithetical to the spirit and intention of their endowment. Our supporters around the city included Republicans and Democrats, conservatives and liberals, retired folks nervous about the tax increase this proposal would entail, and environmental educators worried about the overuse of land that such an expansion would cause. Our message was honed by a few core group members and supported by the larger group; our campaign against the proposal was waged by a large number of us who called our friends and colleagues to tell them why we were opposed, testified at city council meetings, wrote letters to the editor, called in to a local talk radio show, had lunch with various members of the city council, and handed out leaflets in neighborhoods and at gathering places in town.

I found myself doing things that I, in my basic nonconfrontational demeanor, had never before imagined myself doing: approaching strangers and telling them about our reasons for opposition, walking door-to-door in the pouring rain to distribute flyers to yet one more neighborhood, writing my first-ever letter to the editor, and cold-calling people to urge them to get out and vote on the day of the election. I found myself quickly acquiring knowledge about environmental education that I had never possessed before: learning to talk about things like "carrying capacity" and "environmental assessments," reading Aldo Leopold's treatises on caring for and using the land. I found myself getting a crash course in organizing strategies: discovering how to get the attention of the press, how to sculpt and shape a message, how to speak in sound bites, and how to organize a campaign. I became amazed at the power and vehemence of this seemingly small fight of a neighborhood opposed to a building in its park. People on both sides became incensed about each other's stances and information distribution. Accusations of being "antienvironmentalists" were hurled at our side because we opposed this Environmental Education Center, a charge that has caused environmentalists all over the city to talk about the best means for environmental education (an environmentally sustainable building or open spaces?) and the best use of funds to support such efforts (busing more kids to a single nature site or educating children in the open spaces adjacent to their own schools?). The letters to the editor poured in fast and furiously; the local newspaper editorialized against the building; yard signs for both sides went up all over town. At times I just sat back and shook my head in wonder at the number of people our small campaign was reaching.

The night of the election, more than fifty people gathered at our house to watch the returns come in. The ballot measure was defeated by a three-to-one margin, making it the first parks proposal ever to be defeated in the history of this city, a very pro-environmental and generous city when it comes to supporting its extensive park system (proven, interestingly enough, by the passage that same day of a second ballot proposal for increased funding to maintain the many parks). Among those present for the celebration: a city council member, a reporter from the local paper, and a radio reporter from the local NPR station. And since the election, the issues raised by our campaign continue to occupy the hearts and minds of many around the city. Several months later, I served on a committee to nominate nine people to a task force charged with looking at the future of the space at this particular park and its place in the environmental education program of the city—the outgrowth of a public meeting on the park's future held four months after the election and packed with citizens (including the mayor and four city council members). Our campaign moved from a few neighbors' concerns about the construction of a large building in a park to a citywide discussion of the very idea of environmental education. Sometimes I still ask myself, How did this happen?

Of course, the irony of my participation in this experience was not lost on me. Here I was—a neophyte when it came to community organizing, immersed in the academic's approach to a new topic (reading, writing, interviewing others) for the research I was undertaking—suddenly thrust into a hands-on experience. Even at my most passionate moments of the campaign, when I was publicly disagreeing with someone from the opposition when he gave out what I perceived was less than truthful information or when I worked with my eight-year-old son as he wrote a from-the-heart letter to the editor about saving *his* park, I was constantly aware of the process I was going through and the strategies I was learning. I kept comparing my experiences with the experiences I had been reading about, with the words of the community organizers I was interviewing, and with those teachers who were doing parent outreach in their classrooms—as I began to understand what community organizing was truly all about.

Community organizing, I came to realize, is really a general term for a lot of different approaches, techniques, strategies, and mindsets which are held together by a very basic commonalty: people coming together to create change—whether it's getting a stop sign for the bad intersection at the end of your street or trying to raise people's awareness about the hazards of the medical waste incinerator in your local hospital or trying to change people's minds about the usefulness of an expensive building to teach environmental education. At its simplest level, community organizing arises from that moment of frustration, when something affects us personally, just as it did for members of our neighborhood group—when we were informed about the ballot proposal as a fait accompli, when our input, as neighbors, as users, and lovers of this park, was not sought or even considered. Thus, organizing begins, according to Lois Gibbs and Will Collette, "when one or two people become convinced something is wrong" (1). Ordinary people, and not always experienced or professional organizers, frustrated by an event or an action, begin to realize that in order to make change happen, they have to do something; and that something usually involves talking with other people, trying to help them understand the problem and the frustration, hoping to light a similar fire of outrage in them, and together trying to effect a change—whether that's a change in mindset or a change in policy. Gibbs and Collette reduce all the complexity surrounding community organizing to its simplest level: "Organizing is real complicated," they tell us. "First you talk to one person, then you talk to another person, then you talk to another person . . ." (59).

But at another level, community organizing *is* a very complicated process, involving much more than a group of people getting together to try to create an isolated change. For a number of practitioners, community organizing at its core is also about social justice issues, about the empowerment of people who traditionally are not empowered by existing systems of government and economics. According to Dan Cantor, a longtime community organizer for a number of groups, one of the core beliefs behind a community organizing approach is "that people should be involved in their own self-governance." For most of those who practice community organizing over time and who theorize about its value, its real impact is less the single-issue win, but more the effect that such a win can have. In other words, while a community organizing campaign might begin as a community drive to effect change about a single issue, the feeling of empowerment that accompanies that win begins to permeate the community and expands onward. People who join a community organizing campaign to achieve a specific goal often feel the rush of discovering they can make a difference through their hard work and passion, and this feeling often begins to inform their experience in other arenas: People discover they actually can help inspire change and are then more able and more committed to continue their role as change agents, often with related issues, but sometimes with new ones. A number of us, for example, took on another city department a month after the election when it decided not to open our neighborhood outdoor skating rink because of "low use" by the area residents. A campaign of phone calls, e-mails, and a petition took about one week—and resulted in their changing their minds. One member of our group has since been elected to city council; two others have been asked to run the next campaign for another city council member. For many experienced and successful organizers, this goal of empowerment is the ultimate goal of any effort: The winnable issue is important, but people's changed perceptions of their role in their community is paramount. Once people feel differently about their role, once they begin to feel that they are able to contribute to change, a different kind of relation to governance can follow. A perfect example of this can be seen in the title of one of Lois Gibbs's books: *Dying from Dioxin: A Citizen's Guide to Reclaiming our Health and Rebuilding Democracy*—a book which on one level offers some specific advice on how to organize a campaign to reduce toxics in our environment but also is quite clearly about how such an approach can help us regain the kind of democracy in which all citizens have a voice.

Thus, much of what we read and hear about community organizing focuses on those who traditionally have not been empowered by the system. Historically, community organizing arose from this notion, starting with the settlement house movement of the nineteenth century in which organizers worked to create social reform for poor people. Saul Alinsky, perhaps the name most connected to the community organizing movement in the United States, continued this work in the 1930s, '40s, and '50s through his creation of the Industrial Areas Foundation (a group which continues to be active today, although much modified from Alinsky's original approach). According to Gary Delgado, Alinsky's movement could be called "urban neighborhood organizing . . . organizing that extended beyond the mere leveraging of additional goods and services: building organizations of poor people that could challenge the existing balance of power" (*Beyond* 9). Alinsky, who became an extremely controversial figure, due in part to the abrasive nature of the tactics his groups used against public officials, has also become in many ways the central figure in the community organizing movement, the person whom campaigns are named as being like or unlike. Despite the strong feelings his name evokes for people, many of the key notions he developed have become standard practice in organizing campaigns: recognizing that numbers count and that, to be effective, a campaign must enlist a good-sized group; always starting with "where the people are," that is, creating a campaign that meets the needs and desires of the community; introducing a professional organizer whose role is partly to develop "indigenous leadership," local people from the community who begin to take on leadership roles; and starting with small "winnable" campaigns as a way of building power for the organization (Delgado 10–11).[1]

What is named as community organizing at present in the United States has branched out greatly from the work of the settlement houses and Alinsky to include a wide range of experiences and movements, ranging from the kinds of campaigns launched by Lois Gibbs and Candy Lightner mentioned in Chapter 1 to the work my group launched against the ballot proposal; from the advocacy work of groups like the Sierra Club to the adversarial tactics of groups like Greenpeace; from the education and consciousness-raising work of Paulo Freire and his followers to the community development work of social workers. Somehow all these diverse groups are held together by some commonly shared beliefs, despite differences in tactics and in key issues, differences which are known in some circles as the "signature styles" of various groups. Looking at these common elements can help in identifying just what it is about community organizing that makes it community organizing, what it is that ties Freire to Alinsky, ACORN to MADD.

First, I've noticed that all community organizing groups depend on a particular view of community—that *community*, rather than *individuals*, serves as the basic "unit of practice" in their work. Barbara Israel, a public health professor committed to a community organizing approach to her field, explains it in this way:

> There are levels of thinking about identity and practice . . . , and much of health education and public health is focused on the individual level: trying to understand why individuals behave the way they do and to change their individual behaviors. It's not the priority in the work that I do. Rather [I] think about commu-

> nity as a unit of practice, . . . the organizational and social net-
> works and interactions and relationships that exist within a com-
> munity . . . [the] strengths and resources as well as community
> for collective action, and then that becomes your unit of practice.
> Now within that there still could be a community to get involved
> in efforts to change individual behavior, community to get in-
> volved in efforts to change policy, but it's this notion of collec-
> tively bringing people together to bring about change.

Community, for these practitioners, becomes an identifiable entity
(albeit embedded within larger systems), providing resources, networks, interactions, and various relationships, and, as such, serves as a
source for collective action in ways that an individual consumer or
recipient of services does not and, indeed, cannot. Considering community rather than individual as the unit of practice has important
implications. In the world of public health, for example, a campaign to
stop teen smoking focuses not on how to get individuals to quit, but
rather on how to get a particular group to change its behavior toward
smoking. Community as a unit of practice within the world of social
justice leads organizers to be less concerned about finding a way to
acquire clothing for an individual family in need and more concerned
with how to provide clothing for an entire community, perhaps by
changing the circumstances of their poverty. Community, as we'll see
shortly, can be defined differently depending on the situation—in terms
of neighborhood, in terms of socioeconomic connections, in terms of
compelling interest, in terms of age or even gender—but for community
organizers, that it is the unit that becomes the source of strength to
create change.

Second, all community organizing recognizes that communities
are made up of a variety of individuals, each with different needs,
interests, and abilities, and that within the community organizing
structure these individual members take on different types of roles.
Most commonly, the roles tend to break down into organizers, leaders,
core group members, and other members. *Organizers* usually are those
who spark the initial interest and help keep people going—and often,
but not always, they come from outside the community. Organizers,
according to Tracey Easthope, a longtime organizer with an environmental group known as the Ecology Center, have the charge of helping
change people "who are concerned about something very particular to
their family to people who are concerned about more"—in other words,
to help people transform their personal fights into a focus on becoming
"proactive at the community level." Organizers, she continues, have the
responsibility of helping people see that they have "enormous power,

just enormous power." *Leaders*, or as some groups call them, "indigenous leaders," are usually seen as people from within the community who take on the roles necessary to keep a group going, serving alternately as researchers, cheerleaders, spokespeople, meeting chairs, and so on. The long-term effectiveness of a community group comes down to these leaders, especially since, for many practitioners of a community organizing approach, the organizer's role is "to try and get [the leaders] to take it over" (Easthope); ultimately, the organizers leave and the leaders in the community are the ones responsible for keeping the group going. Usually, the leaders of a group form the *core*—those charged with some decision-making power, who bring their suggestions and conclusions to the group at large for approval or disapproval. The *membership* role, in most groups, is the role reserved for the large number of participants who do much of the work of mounting a campaign, and by so doing, maintain certain rights of representation, making sure that their interests are properly expressed by the leaders, organizers, and core group.

What varies across many of these groups is how these roles actually play out. Whether the organizer comes from within or outside the group makes a huge difference in the overall approach; likewise, whether the members are seen as active participants in the process, as silent participants who desire representation, or as clients seeking help, makes a difference. Some people are beginning to see the definition of roles within a community organization in feminist terms, moving beyond the traditional definition of leaders as those who are most vocal and articulate to a consideration of other issues, such as shared leadership and a recognition of a variety of roles for different abilities and interests. Tracey Easthope has seen what she calls a feminist model of leadership in action, one which allows more people into a variety of leadership roles, some of them perhaps untraditional, one which looks more toward the long term. Speaking of a long term fight waged by a local group against the building of a hazardous waste facility, Tracey explains their leadership style:

> The leadership of their organization changes every year and they have leaders with different abilities. . . . They have more leaders than any fight I've ever seen. They have only a few high-profile leaders. It's totally inspirational, and I think it's because they had shared leadership. This is a totally different model from what I consider the male-dominated model of leadership, in which you say there's certain people with leadership skill and I am going to take them and mold them. . . . It might be good [to have] people who are well spoken, people who are eloquent . . . people who

know how to move political agendas or who might be good as leaders of large political movements. But I'm not sure it's the best model. [A shared leadership model] insures that you're not going to suffer if one person or many people leave, which is a huge problem [in many campaigns].[2]

The third component of community organizing that I've noticed is that all community organizers recognize change as the ultimate goal of their work. Change can take many forms, as mentioned earlier, from the immediate goal of getting a stop sign put in at the end of the street to creating a more empowered group which feels able to become a consistent, active voice in their own governance. What constitutes change and what tactics might be used to create change are defining qualities of the signature styles of various groups. For some community organizers, the concept of change is focused on the design of "winnable issues," that is, issues that are within the realm of a particular group's grasp and which will help the group experience the kind of success they need in order to go on. For some, it has to do with balancing the concepts of individual change, policy change, and social change. Candy Lightner's creation of MADD serves as a good example here of the various kinds of change a community organizing campaign can bring about: Her group effected individual change when people elected to swear off drinking and driving; they created policy change when legislation resulted which raised the penalties for drinking and driving; and they also pushed for social change as they helped remake a cultural mindset which had previously considered drinking and driving a regular way of life.

Although change is generally seen as the ideal end of most community organizing, it's important to note that many groups emphasize an integral connection between change and empowerment. According to Nina Wallerstein, empowerment itself is "a social action process that promotes participation of people, organizations and communities toward the goals of increased individual and community control, political efficacy, improved quality of life, and social justice" (qtd. in Minkler 9). Again, while the word *empowerment* seems to enter into almost all attempts at community organizing, the extent to which it takes precedence in a campaign varies. As mentioned earlier, for some organizers empowerment is the goal, with any victories along the way tending to serve mostly as additional fuel. For other groups, winning the immediate goal is of primary importance, but the empowering feeling that accompanies that win helps people to feel motivated to go on with their activism.

How a group perceives itself in terms of inherent power structures sets the stage for the kinds of responses and tactics it mounts. Briefly, those groups who see themselves as oppositional to an intact power structure tend to see their mission in confrontational terms and to see the power structure as a target of its campaign, an enemy who must be stopped, who must be, according to Gary Delgado, identified, isolated, and iced (Delgado, *Organizing* 123). For groups who don't see themselves as so separated from the power structures, tactics tend to be more collaborative; these groups operate under a belief that there are common interests which may be reconcilable (Rothman, "Approaches" 44–5).

While these characteristics became increasingly clear to me as I uncovered numerous examples of community organizing, I also found that the ways in which various community organizers approach these characteristics vary. In part, this variation results from the very broad nature of the term and the many disciplines of study that lay claim to it: from social work to public health to natural resources to political science. As I began to read into these various disciplines, each with its own language and terminology, and interview a number of practitioners, I was struck by both the connections and the distinct approaches they employ. One of the seminal works in the field of social work, authored by Jack Rothman in 1968, talks about those connections and disconnections, suggesting three different "models of community organizing practice": locality development, social planning, and social action. Rothman created a chart in which he analyzed these three approaches in terms of a number of concerns: their assumptions about community structure; their basic change strategies and tactics; their orientation toward the power structure; and their conception of the client population and role. In his recently revised version of that piece, though, Rothman admits that rarely does any community work fall into the kind of distinct categories he originally suggested ("Approaches"). Rather, he now argues, most community workers "mix and phase," within and among those categories as they go about their work, mixing the strategies and techniques from the various approaches depending on the needs of the community and the demands of a particular project, and phasing in and out of a particular model depending on the part of the process they find themselves in on a given day.

Various community organizers I've spoken with agree. Barbara Israel explains, "Because there are so many different types and ways of thinking about community organizing, I just find it more useful to use that term as a generic umbrella term. . . . When I teach, I talk about . . .

different models, . . . [but] rarely are they totally distinct." What is similar among the models and what is most important, she believes, is "this notion of collectively bringing people together to bring about change . . . and that's true regardless of which of these models you're using."

If this is true, why even bother looking at various approaches or models? For me, a newcomer to the world of community organizing, defining some way to make sense of the various approaches was essential. Even as I recognized that most community organizers mix and phase, my initial look at the great variance of approaches and distinct language employed by practitioners and theorists in different fields, all claiming to be community organizers, was overwhelming at first. As I was striving to make sense of this huge umbrella term, always with an eye toward thinking about what might be of use to teachers, it helped me to break down the multitude of approaches into what I see as five orientations toward community organizing, adapted from Rothman and informed by the teaching of Barbara Israel: education, planning/development, mobilization, social action, and advocacy. These orientations are, of course, not distinct, but, rather, might be seen as a set of circles, with each orientation overlapping each of the others, as shown in Figure 1.

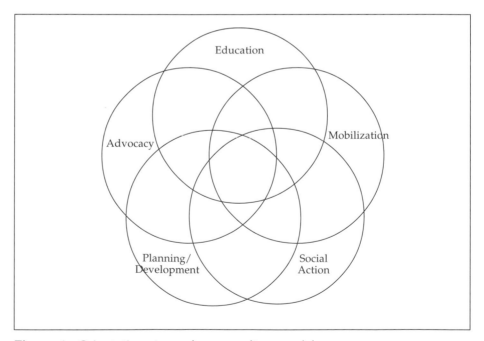

Figure 1: Orientations toward community organizing.

To try to make sense of these orientations, I will, in the rest of this chapter, explain them, first by giving an illustration of what I mean by the orientation, and then by discussing them in terms of the three characteristics mentioned above: how each orientation defines community and the role of community members; how each sees the role of organizer and leaders within the community; and how each deals with the concept of change and empowerment. As teacher educators and teachers read these sections, my hope is this: that you will look at the examples and characteristics which define each orientation always with an eye and an ear toward how these might apply to the work of classroom teachers. Are there elements of any specific orientations that would seem to transfer to teachers' attempts at outreach to parents? Are there ways teachers and teacher educators can see mixing and phasing among these orientations in order to create a model of community organizing specific to our needs? Clearly, the examples I have chosen to illustrate each orientation take us out of education and into other disciplines—but, in fact, that's the point: What is it we can learn from these other worlds?

Education Orientation

In their article "Freirean Praxis in Health Education and Community Organizing," Nina Wallerstein, Victoria Sanchez-Merki, and Lily Dow describe a program in which they have been involved for over a decade, a program that in essence defines the education orientation of community organizing. Entitled ASAP (Adolescent Social Action Program), this program targets teens in New Mexico who are mostly American Indian, Hispanic/Latino/Latina, and low-income Anglo-American "to reduce morbidity and mortality among adolescents who live in high-risk environments, to encourage them to make healthier choices in their own lives, and to facilitate, via empowerment education, their active engagement in political and social action in their communities" (196). For seven weeks, small groups of teens travel to a local hospital and the county detention center to meet, interview, and come to know some of the patients and jail residents whose problems include substance abuse, violence, HIV infection, and other "risky behaviors." The youths who participate in this program are supervised by trained university graduate students who help facilitate a way of learning with and from the patients and jail residents: The adolescents learn how to listen and how to conduct interviews with others; they then spend time afterwards dialoguing with their peers about what they learned and how their own experiences relate, analyzing their learning in terms of the personal, "social, medical and legal consequences of risky behaviors" (196). As a next step, the participating teens are offered two options. They can join in some kind of peer education project to model for elementary-age students the ways of listening and analyzing that they have learned, or they can work on a social action project that turns into a kind of community organizing. Over the years, ASAP students have done community-based research, resulting in community murals and organizing campaigns in their communities; they have written pieces and produced videotapes used in educating others; they planned exhibits for the New Mexico State Fair ("A Day Without Alcohol is Fair") and worked with Street Reach, a gang prevention project; and they have been active in the New Mexico Peer Leadership Conference, as well as many more activities.

What Wallerstein and her colleagues have accomplished and what I am naming an education orientation to community organizing has been named by others as consciousness-raising or popular education. For many of its practitioners and theorists, the primary source of this movement is the work of Paulo Freire, a name familiar to English educators and teachers. For Freire, the teaching of literacy became, in essence, a community organizing activity. Working primarily with working-class Brazilian peasants, Freire instituted a way of teaching reading which involved community members' connecting words and pictures (specifically selected because of their potential to support critical thinking) to their direct experiences. By using prompts which linked to the lives of the people, Freire encouraged his students to participate in a dialogue about their own worlds, sharing their own understandings and listening to the experiences of others. For these "student-teachers," as Freire called them, learning to read became both a dialogue in which they were sometimes teachers and sometimes learners in a kind of critical reflection about their own existence and the existence of the others in their community. Integrally tied to this new knowledge, an essential component of literacy for Freire, was an action component. This kind of critical reflection, he believed, should lead people to feel empowered to act upon their lives.

In similar fashion, the education orientation of community organizing relies upon listening to others, reflecting upon what they have said, participating in a dialogue with others as a way to learn more, and taking action as a result of that new learning. Vital to this orientation is the notion of community members reflecting on their lives, identifying for themselves the issues of concern, and being responsible for creating change. In the ASAP program, for example, teens conduct a dialogue with others about issues of health and safety and are then able to reflect in a critical way with others in their own community about what they have learned, mixing their own knowledge and experiences into that discussion. Students follow a problem-posing format, asking themselves and their peers questions about how and why these risky behaviors become a part of the lives of the jail residents and hospital patients, and are then able to think with others about how those behaviors have been or might become a part of the lives of people in their own communities. Students then formulate an action plan, working with others to enact some sort of outreach to raise the awareness of others in their communities, to help change behaviors.

An education orientation to community organizing can range from more formally structured enterprises like ASAP and DELTA (Development Education and Leadership Teams in Action, a training program for community organizers, mostly in Africa, which uses Freirean concepts as the basis for their work[3]) to less formal consciousness-raising (CR) groups. CR groups, as some might recall from the '60s, served historically as a place for usually small groups of people interested in a similar topic to talk with others about their experiences, to share knowledge gleaned from reading, and to try to make some transformations in lives, encouraged by the support and energy of the group. CR groups continue to form today (although often with other, less-charged monikers) around a number of issues, from a group of college students coming together to learn more about ecology and recycling to a group of mothers joining forces to learn about their daughters' upcoming journey into adolescence.

How does the education orientation define itself in terms of the elements identified above? First, community is most often identified by interest area; that is, people come together because of a specific interest in the issue under discussion: the environment, the emerging adolescence of daughters, the risky behaviors of a certain population. Beyond that common interest, though, groups that come together for this kind of education slant generally share other characteristics as well—sometimes gender, sometimes age, sometimes race, sometimes class. Oftentimes, not all of the members of the group will know each other before the group gets together, with members responding to an advertisement or flyer or tagging along to a group meeting with a friend. As a result, the group (brought together, for example, because of the need for that stop sign) doesn't always have an immediate reason to cohere, and the community may take time to develop. Other times, this kind of group is an outgrowth of a group of friends who have casually talked about similar interests over time; the group then becomes a way to formalize their learning on a specific subject.

The roles of community members in this orientation don't always have clear lines of demarcation, something that makes sense given that the intentional engagement in dialogue and shared learning is the basis of its makeup. Thus, much like Freire's notion of teacher-students and student-teachers, membership in an education-oriented community organization implies times of facilitating and times of listening to others. Often, the role of leader is renamed as either animator, whose job is "stimulating people to think critically and to identify problems and new solutions," or facilitator, whose job is "providing a process through which the group can discuss its own content in the most productive possible way" (Minkler and Wallerstein 42). Although organizers can come from the outside, oftentimes they are members of the community.

As with all types of community organizing, change is an important element of this orientation. Change here may simply be personal—the changing of minds based on the new kinds of learning that have taken place, individual change as the result of one's consciousness being raised within the group process. Often, though, the change in personal understandings has an impact that expands outward; that is, once the consciousness of the members of the group has been raised, action often develops. In some cases the outward action may be what Berkowitz calls *incidental (Community Impact)*: simply by informing others about your new learning in casual conversations, you are taking action and helping to change their way of thinking. Other times, it may be what he calls *prearranged*: a specific occasion planned to help others learn what you have learned. Renee Bayer, one of the organizers whom I interviewed, recounts a specific incident which might help clarify the kind of change to which I am referring, an occasion she calls her first formative experience in community organizing:

> When I was a freshman in college . . . , [some of us] elected an independent study to look at ecology. . . . We ended up doing it in the dorm and we ended up organizing the first recycling center in a dorm and we organized nutritional sessions in the cafeteria and got them to change over to offer vegetarian entrées every night! They had never even considered doing something like that. We brought in speakers, we wrote newsletters that we posted in the bathroom stalls so people would have something to read about ecotactics! We rotated facilitation of meetings so we'd learn how to facilitate, how to develop an agenda. . . . We would go to the literature, figure things out and talk to different people. Some of

> them were older, like seniors . . . , so they were teaching literature
> [on the environment] they'd been reading over the years.

A classic example of the education orientation, this experience demonstrates the several kinds of change to which I referred: individual change as the participants began to learn more about the environment, outward change that was incidental as they talked to different people about their learning, and outward change that was prearranged as they posted letters in the bathroom stalls and approached the food service staff to ask for a change in menu.

What this anecdote also represents is the connection in this orientation between change and empowerment. While empowerment certainly can occur as people become more knowledgeable and more confident about their ability to act, there is rarely a specific, identified opposition against whom a campaign is directed. Rather, the group operates first and foremost for its own self-knowledge, knowledge gained only through its community dialogue.

This is not to say that an education orientation is without serious risk. Certainly the kind of popular education practiced by Freire and others can be extremely threatening and has resulted in some terrible consequences for both the organizers and the community members who participate—because of its emphasis on people discovering the root causes and underlying structural factors of social problems. Many of the versions of popular education which exist in Latin American and developing countries, then, are fraught with danger because of political opposition to the empowerment that often results for the participants. Outside organizers have to really think about "the potential implications" of their work, "because, if you're an organizer, you can leave. Usually others cannot" (Israel). And in many situations, a group gaining knowledge and feeling newly empowered can be a real threat to the status quo, to those already in power.

Planning/Development Orientation

In most cases, a planning/development approach to community organizing is situated in the world of social work or community health.[4] For some organizers, this approach is met with some disdain. As one organizer told me, "One of the pejoratives that all community organizers use, if you really want to put something down, is . . . 'That's just social work,' which suggests it is oriented toward a single individual or tiny little group but that it does not attempt to alter their relations of power in society." And certainly, as I read through volumes of materials on this approach and talked to some practitioners, this label has some element of truth. At one extreme, this type of approach seems much more concerned with a problem-solving approach to a specific community concern than with some of the other issues identified as key to a community organizing way of thinking. In Rothman's words, the planning/development mode, in its most traditional sense, "emphasizes a technical process of problem solving regarding substantive social problems, such as delinquency, housing and mental health." It is "data-driven and conceives of carefully calibrated change being rooted in social science thinking and empirical objectivity. The style is technocratic, and rationality is a dominant ideal" (Rothman, "Three Models" 30). Again, at this traditional extreme, people considered expert in an issue (people from a university or social agency) receive a grant to work in a particular kind of community. They enter the community and, using quantitative data and often sophisticated statistical tools, administer a needs assessment, formalize some kind of decision analysis, and conduct evaluation research. As Rothman captured in his original chart of models of community organizing, what he calls a social planning approach sees the community members as clients, as consumers or recipients of the services offered by the expert planners. According to Barbara Israel,

> The social planning approach is the one that in some ways is . . . the least grassroots. It's the least likely to address issues of empowerment, control, shared control, but it's also the one that health professionals are most likely to [use]. . . . But . . . there's a lot of potential [because] that might be the only place that public health practitioners will interface with community members at all.

The examples of this planning/development approach that I gleaned from those with whom I spoke certainly push this traditional definition past its organizationally driven mentality with limited commitment to community members. These community organizers, firmly situated in the worlds of social work and public health, may have outside grants as one impetus, but their focus shifts from planning *for* a community to planning *with* a community. One example comes from the public health work of Renee Bayer, who has spent most of the last decade working in various communities in Detroit. In one particular project, she received a community development grant to work on issues of maternal/child health education in an urban setting. Convinced that she wanted both to involve and to learn from the community as she conducted this work, she began by bringing together some people from different organizations in the city who were already working on maternal/child health issues in order to form a kind of advisory board: a woman from a church group, some representatives from a large community-based organization, someone from the police mini-stations, and someone who lived in public housing and had been active in other projects she had done. As Renee explains, "We got together and started talking through a bunch of strategies and . . . one thing we came to conclude was the public housing site in the community really was in need of some kind of organizing structure to look at maternal/child health and . . . more education in the neighborhood." Over time, this group began to think about what might actually be done in this neighborhood community, but always under the auspices of Renee's grant. "I had to tell them my limits," she explains. "That's a really important community organizing point, to make sure people know exactly what they can expect of you. And they were really savvy. They wanted to know: 'What are we? What do you do with our information? Do you take that to your professors you work for? Does it change anything we do? Do we have a budget? On what level are we operating?'" For Renee the answers became the kind of balancing act common to a social planning orientation: "I had to tell them, you're basically operating as advice to me. . . . No, you don't have any control or power, but you can expect what you and I decide we'll do, we'll do. As long as it's within the parameters I told you about."

The group over time chose to organize a community group, beginning with a single meeting to which one of the advisory board members brought a lot of her friends from the community. Renee showed a movie about birth that day and then began to talk with the women about what they might want to do. She asked them if they wanted to keep meeting, what they wanted to learn, how often they wanted to meet, how they wanted to organize their time. The women began to talk about what their vision was for a healthy community, where they were at that point in working toward that vision, what things might be standing in the way of achieving that vision, and so on. Eventually about twenty women came regularly to a series of meetings over the next year, comparing notes and learning about issues of nutrition, prenatal care, parenting techniques, and more, as they talked about their own kids, the kids of their friends, and the kids in the community. Their eventual goal was to have these women then go out and organize their own parenting classes with others in the community. Renee's role, as she saw it, was to help provide them with some initial content, to learn from them about their own parenting issues, and to help them learn some of the skills of organizing a group, so that this "parenting class" could continue to expand outward. This group turned into a grassroots advocacy group, which has now been going for seven years.

In a planning/development orientation, the community is usually defined by the geographic area but is identified as well because of some specific perceived need or problem within that community, such as a drug problem, a lack of prenatal care, illiteracy, or a lack of recreational activities for youth. What's significant, I think, is that the initial identification of the community and its needs is done by outsiders. This is not, for instance, the self-selected group that you find in the education orientation, although, once the initial identification has been made of a community or area, oftentimes the actual participants do volunteer.

The roles taken on by various members of the group vary, but inevitably the organizer is an outsider: someone who comes into the community from outside its boundaries, often a professor or a graduate student or a representative from a social services agency. This organizer, despite the care and commitment that she/he brings to the situation, does enter with an outside agenda, such as a grant or a research project, which helps form the parameters of the organizing that can be done. Cheryl Walter perfectly captures the dilemma this can cause for a conscientious organizer:

> Although the imperative "Start where the people are" is familiar to most health educators and other social change practitioners, more often than not we start where we are funded to start, which has powerful ramifications for how we interact with community, the strategies we employ, and what priorities or needs of the community will be elicited, supported, and sustained. (70)

This kind of double commitment—to both the community members and to the funded research—can be an intricate balancing act for all organizers. Barbara Israel sees several challenges in this: "One is the challenge . . . between research and action, trying to create a balance so that we all agree what the importance of the research is and how that information can benefit the community—and at the same time, how to do that in a way that doesn't slow up the action, what may seem more beneficial to the community than what the data's going to show." She adds, "And even though we think this is participatory and democratic [and] you're just facilitating, you can be imposing a process." There is also the issue of trust. "You can establish trust, but it's never a trusting relationship forever. Just like your other relationships, there are always potentials for violating trust and making mistakes." Renee, who also trains graduate students to work in public health settings as community organizers, talks about how important it is for outside organizers to think hard about who they are, where they come from, and what tensions might exist when they walk into a situation with people from other backgrounds and cultures: "The students I send in, they can't change that they're college-educated, that they're coming from University of Michigan, which is baggage. When you go into a room and say, 'I'm from U of M,' you bring that with you. And there's no getting around it. You just have to think about that and what that means and acknowledge it."

Creating trust with others is key to this orientation, especially as leaders emerge within the community. The role of community leaders certainly varies in this orientation, depending on how close the model is to the more traditional rendition. In its very rigid rendition, leaders and the rest of the community are valued because of their ability to provide the organizer with information through surveys or interviews—valued, that is, as a kind of informant for a final analysis and report. In a model more like Renee's maternal/child health group, community leaders are very important for their potential to transform their community, to learn how to create and lead their own groups and continue meeting after the grant runs out and the organizer leaves.

In almost parallel fashion, the conception of change and empowerment in a planning/development model varies depending on how traditional an approach is taken. In its most traditional form, the organizers are often part of the power structure; they are employees of organizations charged with fact finding who may then return to the granting agency, submit their data, and eventually institute some change far down the road. For others, change is an inherent part of the work they undertake. As Barbara Israel mentioned above, the tension becomes one of collecting the information within a community that has probably come together because they want to create some change, and also actually helping to put a plan into action. If the experience is to be successful for the community members, change must happen in a timely fashion—and not be put on hold, waiting for all the data to be collected and analyzed, a process that tends to take place away from the community.

Mobilizing Orientation

The sometimes romantic image of community organizing that most people seem to carry in their minds arises from the mobilizing orientation. The outraged group of neighbors—distressed because of recurring accidents on their street or by a potential hazardous waste site in their neighborhood or by the proposal for a new housing development to be built on farm land—band together to fight city hall. Their impassioned speeches to bad guy city officials lead the officials to see the light; the neighbors emerge victorious with a new stop sign installed, a ban on the waste site, or the knowledge that there will be no development on the farm land. In the city in which I live, examples of this mobilizing orientation arise almost daily. Just in this week's newspapers, I read about the battle to save a historic art deco building which currently serves as a bus station, the fight to prevent the construction of a new highway exit through a residential neighborhood, the campaign to preserve certain open spaces from the spreading developments that are springing up everywhere, the protest against a particular design for rebuilding a small but central bridge which would result in permanently closing certain streets and changing some long-standing traffic patterns, and the new fight by a group of dog owners to establish a "dog park" for their pets to run off-leash.

The lengthy example with which I began this chapter crystallizes a mobilizing orientation. My neighborhood became unhappy with a particular ballot proposal which we felt would change the character of the neighborhood. Further research into it convinced us that it also would not be the best way to further the center's goals of environmental education for children. After thinking hard about the issue, first at a personal level and then at a small group level, we began to take our message outward: to the larger neighborhood, to the environmental educators and activists in the city, to city officials and to the public at large. Our goal was immediate and clear: to defeat the ballot proposal which would support the construction of the new building. Our tactics were fairly simple: to reach out in a convincing way to as many people as possible through personal contact and the media. And the pattern we followed is one familiar to the mobilizing orientation: People immediately affected by an issue get upset, they band together to ask, "Why don't we do something about it?" and then they forge a campaign to move forward and try to do something. These people unite over a specific, usually narrowly defined, issue—something that affects the small group in immediate and powerful ways—and come together for a short time to try to effect change.

Characteristic of the mobilizing orientation first and foremost, then, is this notion that the campaign is short-term. Generally, people come to the fight because they are outraged and they are committed to devoting high energy and lots of work for a limited period—until the school board or city council will meet and make a final decision, for example, or until the election is over. Of course, in reality the idea of limited time invested may not be accurate: perhaps the school board tables the discussion for six months, or, though the election sends a definitive message, the members of the organization realize that is just the start of their work. Oftentimes people who get involved in a specific fight for a particular issue find themselves drawn into the larger issues which surround the fight, as in the case of Lois Gibbs and the Love Canal story. Andy Buchsbaum, an attorney and environmental activist and organizer, shared the story of one group, the Milan Citizens Against Toxics (MCAT), whose struggle to prevent a hazardous waste disposal company from putting an incinerator into their community turned into an eleven-year battle, one that just ended this year. "They began on that issue [preventing the incinerator]," he explains, "but they decided to become involved in many different environmental issues that affected their community. They testified, contacted legislators, made presentations to city councils. As a result, they developed allies throughout the state who actively supported them in their fight against the incinerator. After 11 years, the company finally gave up." Tracey Easthope, too, speaks of how the short-term fights often become longer: "I have lots of memories of people saying, 'When I got into this, if I knew I'd be doing it two years later, five years later, eleven years later, there's no way I would have done it.' I think that's a real important thing to recognize about fights, that they don't end. . . . What's that quote? 'The curse of democracy is you have to be ever-vigilant.' . . . There is a vigilance that is required."

A second characteristic of the mobilizing orientation is that the campaign usually begins in outrage—outrage because something very personal has happened or has the potential to happen to an individual. Tracey Easthope shared some of the stories she hears on a daily basis, many of which she characterizes as

> extremely grim . . . I got two mercury contaminant calls recently . . . [people who are] contaminated with mercury . . . because [they] have so many dental amalgams in [their] mouths . . . , [a woman] who's trying to get her workplace to stop spraying pesticides . . . , a woman whose kid is contaminated and she thinks that the water at the day care [is bad]. It's well water and they're surrounded by landfills.

What makes the personal response turn into community organizing is when that angry or concerned individual contacts others to help effect some change—either people who might be affected in the same way or people who sympathize with the problem and think they can help. Tracey explains that for most of the people with whom she works, "in order for them to heal or to change the power, they have to become organizers." Thus, the core community that emerges from a mobilizing orientation can vary: It might be neighborhood based (others in the same geographic area affected by the hazardous waste incinerator); it might be issue based (people across the state or country affected by mercury amalgams); it might be race, gender, or class based (African Americans incensed by the high number of toxic waste cites located in black, urban areas).

The leadership that emerges in a mobilizing approach varies as well, but most times the lead organizer is either the person first affected or outraged or some other person brought into the fight early on—in other words, an ordinary person not necessarily trained in community organizing or even familiar with the political process necessary to achieve some changes. Bill Berkowitz's book *Local Heroes* is filled with examples of these "ordinary people" who work to create change in their communities through community organizing. According to Ellen Cassedy, one of those he interviewed for the book and the founder of the group 9 to 5, "The truth is you can be a regular person and lead a pretty normal life, and be active in social change" (310). Lois Gibbs cites her own experience and stresses how everyday people can become the leaders of organized movements. She says to those who say they can't do it, "You can't say that. I mean I was where you are. I was worse than what you are, because at least you know where city hall is!" (qtd. in Berkowitz, *Local Heroes* 115). She further explains how she helps others overcome their fears of organizing:

> In teaching people . . . I make them talk to me: "What do you feel most insecure about? What is hardest for you to do?" And we'll go on and say, "well, how do you think we can overcome that? Let's talk about it. You think somebody's going to slam the door in your face. Okay, let's go over there and we'll practice. You knock on the door, and I'll slam it in your face. And then we'll see what happens." And you know, it would be a silly thing and we'd all be giddy and laughing which would take the tension out of it. "We're going to slam the door in your face, let's go!" And they would do it and I'd slam the door in their face, and I'd open up the door and I'd say, "Did you lose your nose? Did you lose an arm? Did your pants fall down? And what happened?"
>
> And then help them think that nothing happened; the door got slammed in my face. "So now what are you going to do?" "I'm going to go to the next door." (116)

Within the community, then, ordinary people generally take the lead roles as organizers and other kinds of leaders, often in shared ways. And as might be expected with a community-run effort, people tend to take on different roles which are comfortable for them. In our campaign to stop the construction in the park, this was certainly true: Someone who was fairly articulate took on the role of spokesperson, others who could write well composed letters to the editor, another person skilled in graphic arts produced that literature, and someone with strong ties to the community took the lead in fund-raising. Within this structure there was still plenty of work for people who did not choose to be leaders but wanted to be involved, such as handing out literature, making phone calls, and copying materials.

In some cases, those involved in a mobilizing approach turn to outside, experienced organizers to help them through the battle, a role that is a typical one for Tracey Easthope to play. Her job as she sees it is to help people define their problem and to help them figure out what to do next.

> It's not like people come to you with a ready-made problem. . . . They'll come in the way that it has become meaningful to them and then you take the problem in [that] way . . . and work on it that way. And then, what I hope, is that people will be transformed in some way. What I try to work on is changing people from people who are concerned about something very particular to their family to people who are concerned about more and willing to organize. . . . The first question always is, "Who's your audience" and "Can you win? . . ." The second rule . . . is, "Everything is local." Every fight you win is a different combination of things. . . . But what I often do in my work is . . . talk [people] through the process of mounting a campaign.

At times, then, a group that is mobilizing for a short-term campaign will work from their own expertise; at other times, they might bring in an outside organizer for advice.

A third characteristic of the mobilizing approach directly affects its stance toward change and empowerment. Clearly, the goal of those involved in these kinds of campaigns is a specific change: to stop something, to add something, to force a new policy or a new action. Generally, the group focuses on the immediate and specified change; it's the movement toward that change that ties the group together. But what often affects the success of these groups is the presence, at times, of an identified opposition to the position the group has staked out: the company that wants to put in a hazardous waste facility; the state department of transportation, which has a vested interest in putting the highway exit through a particular neighborhood; the dentists who have used mercury amalgams in fillings for years and don't want to admit the danger for fear of lawsuits; or, in the case of my own battle, the parks department that placed the measure on the ballot and desperately wanted to put a new building in the park. The range of what I am calling opposition here is clear, I think: not always is the opposition the classic "enemy," the bad guys who are trying to pollute the land or ruin a neighborhood; rather, the opposition is oftentimes merely a group whose interests are very different from yours. Also significant is the notion that in most cases the stance of the opposition has been staked out before your group has come together; in fact, it is often that oppositional position which inspires the formation of a mobilizing group in the first place.

The absence or presence of an oppositional group in many ways defines the kind of campaign that a community organization has to run. As I mentioned in Chapter 1, the presence of an opposition often forces the organization to see itself as reactive rather than proactive. When a group is proactive, it is able to organize and educate a public before a specific problem arises; when a group is reactive, it is responding to a problem or against an opposition that has generally already reached into the public's consciousness, and this opposition's presence forces the group to wage a campaign *in response to* rather than merely *informing about*. And when a group is waging a reactive battle, the kinds of approaches and strategies they can use are of a specific kind. Although some organizers talk about the three I's of organizing against an "enemy" ("identify him, isolate him and ice him" [Delgado, *Organizing* 123]), for many experienced organizers, the issue becomes one of "strategic thinking." Andy Buchsbaum, former program director for PIRGIM (the Public Interest Research Group in Michigan, a state affiliate of the larger national Public Interest Research Group) defines strategic thinking in this way:

> Of course you have to do all the things you would normally do to make your own group work well, the proactive things that keep it going. But then you have to add what I call strategic thinking .... Strategic thinking is something everybody has to do or should do in various aspects of daily life. Strategic thinking involves trying to convince somebody of something and anticipating their reaction to what you're doing or what you're saying—which forces you to circle back and change what you were going to do or say in anticipation of that reaction. So, in a political context, it's "this is what we want to happen and this is how we want to get there, but we know the other side is going to oppose us, and

therefore we have to anticipate their response and change our plans accordingly." In everyday life, it might be "I've been over-charged for something I've ordered in the mail and I'm going to call the company and so I've got to think: who do I want to talk to, what are they going to say, do I have all my receipts or initial order form before I call them?" I want to make sure I can antici-pate their response. That would be an example of strategic think-ing.

Strategic thinking helps staff members map out their approaches in a number of areas: determining how best to access the media in order to get the most coverage, how best to frame an argument that would carry weight with a particular legislator given her history and stances on similar topics, how and when to compromise and negotiate, and how to reach the largest number of people.

As an experienced organizer, Andy Buchsbaum has developed a repertoire of questions he asks himself as a campaign gets under way, a kind of guide to strategic thinking:

1. Who are the decision makers who can give you what you want?

2. How do you convince those decision makers? On the merits of the proposal or through pressure?

3. What are your resources and who are your allies? Can you in-crease either by changing your goal or message?

4. Who are your opponents and their allies, and what resources do they have? Can you neutralize their allies or decrease their resources by changing your message, your allies, or your goals?

5. Where is your issue on the public's radar screen?

6. What is your message? It isn't the same as your purpose; rather, it should be the communication of that purpose.

7. What is your schedule for decision makers and other goals?

8. What tactics should you use and when: petitions, public meet-ings, door-to-door meetings, mailings, telephone calls, talk ra-dio shows?

While, as this list clearly indicates, most strategic thinking depends heavily on the situation, certain tactics are commonly used by many organizers. One has to do with numbers: ascertaining how many people you need to talk to in order to reach as many people as you can. Andy refers to this as "the gossip factor." He explains:

Simply talking to enough people and getting them talking about something can start a sea change, a paradigm shift in the way a governing structure looks at an issue. Now it's issue specific, ob-viously. . . . [But] the theory is if you talk to one-third of the people in a closed community about an issue, the other two-thirds of the

> people will know what you said, because of the gossip. . . . There are different ratios, depending on how large your community is and what kinds of input they're getting. . . . [When PIRGs did campus organizing] PIRG organizers would plan their entire organizing strategy based on the gossip factor. . . . If there are 30,000 people on campus, our target number was always 10,000, 'cause we figured if we talked to 10,000 people the other 20,000 would know.

Most community organizers familiar with the mobilizing orientation add that there are two necessities for a successful campaign: content knowledge about the issue you're addressing, and process knowledge about how to be an effective advocate. Knowing the content information is vital; if someone involved in a community organizing campaign makes a mistake on content, they can easily get undermined by the opposition who will use that mistake to their advantage, sometimes claiming that the one factual error might be indicative of a whole campaign. According to Marc Caplan, author of *Ralph Nader Presents a Citizens' Guide to Lobbying*, "Do not climb out on unsupported limbs (the counter forces have a raft of saws)" (30). Lois Gibbs and Will Collette talk about the importance of gathering information for your campaign. They explain that while some people might see this information-gathering stage as a waste of time when action is required, they feel it is imperative. Using the example of their experience at Love Canal, they say,

> Since the dump there looked like a harmless open field, most people were unaware that a hazardous dump site was in their neighborhood. After contacting local and state government offices, residents discovered that Hooker Chemical Corporation at one time owned the property and had dumped about *20,000 tons* of chemical wastes. . . . These facts settled suspicions local families had about why their kids were so sick, neutralized the doubters and gave the residents the ammunition they needed to start their organization and win. (8)

In addition to this kind of informational knowledge, organizers need to be knowledgeable about the process of mounting a campaign. Numerous handbooks and how-to manuals exist, most of which lay out step-by-step instructions for how to proceed.[5] Generally, these manuals agree on a few important steps: gathering information, organizing people to gain sufficient numbers to be heard, and going public with the message. (For more on the specifics of these steps, see Chapter 4.)

As mentioned earlier, for those whose work falls under this mobilizing orientation, the short-term action and not the long-term change is the main goal. Still, long-term change is often a side effect of the work. People generally become inspired by the heady feeling of being able to effect change and may go on to work on other things, understanding now that it is possible for everyday people to become empowered and change the status quo. Others discover that what they believed was a short-term battle is in fact a lifelong struggle: to protect the environment or to keep a neighborhood safe. But this kind of relationship to empowerment is really a side effect of the work, and not the motivating force of this orientation—a contrast, you'll see, to the next orientation, that of social action.

Social Action Orientation

Long-term change in the power relations among various groups is the identifying characteristic for those who follow the social action orientation to community organizing. For these people, organizing communities on a specific issue is really a means to an end: It's good to achieve the short-term goals of change that motivate the mobilizing folks, but that specific action or change can only be seen in light of the big picture—empowerment of people who have traditionally been disempowered by the status quo.

One group whose work might serve as an exemplar of the social action approach is ACORN (the Association of Community Organizations for Reform Now). Although no single group captures all the nuances of this orientation, much of ACORN's story is indicative of the key elements and values of such an approach.

Beginning in the early 1970s, ACORN started to organize mostly in southern cities across the United States around what it considered social justice issues, particularly among working-class and poor people. They developed an operating method of waging a campaign about a specific issue that might be significant to a particular neighborhood and might also serve the purpose of opening people's eyes to larger issues of power and empowerment. Their first campaign, for example, was a furniture campaign, in which organizers tried to initiate contributions of furniture for low-income people; other popular issues have included neighborhood safety, welfare rights, zoning, and urban renewal. According to Delgado, there is an ACORN truism: "Rather than organizing around racism, we involve our members in campaigns that affect all low- and moderate-income people, building solidarity" (*Organizing* 193).

The core of their work, which has been replicated in numerous cities around the United States and in each campaign they wage, relies on their organizing drive model, a seven-stage model which takes six to eight weeks. First, professional organizers gather information about the community, talking to neighborhood leaders, for example, to find out what the "hot" issues are for that neighborhood. This step allows the organizer to make connections with neighbors, come to know them on an individual basis, and neutralize some opposition that may be present. Next comes "contact work," in which the organizer knocks on doors in the community, trying to achieve at least these three things: to learn more about the neighborhood issues, to recruit a number of people who might participate in a new organization, and to try to find ten to fifteen folks who seem to have leadership potential and who might serve on a neighborhood organizing committee. Third, the organizing committee works together to specify an issue and to legitimate the drive by developing an organizing letter, signed by all members and mailed to all neighbors. The next step is to prepare for the neighborhood meeting. Members of the organizing committee, along with the organizer, circulate around the neighborhood in teams, knocking on doors to invite people to the meeting. At the same time the organizer helps the organizing committee members plan the meeting, so that the "indigenous leaders" can take the lead role. Fifth is the meeting itself. Run by organizing committee members, the meeting revolves around presenting the issue, asking neighbors to join subcommittees, electing temporary officers, and paying dues to run the campaign on the issue. Sixth is the collective social action—some kind of "creative confrontation" that is organized by the membership. It is vital that this action be winnable, i.e., that it be small enough and have enough potential for success that people will feel good and want to continue with the organization. The action might be, for example, a demonstration or a letter writing campaign. The last step in this process is the evaluation of the campaign so far, in which all members assess what went well and want didn't—as a way to ascertain next steps. "The process . . . is continual," explains Gary Delgado: "Research—action—reflection—research" and so on (89). The goal for ACORN, then, is threefold: to construct a viable neighborhood organization, to win an issue that could benefit the people involved, and "to construct . . . an alternative view of social reality" (Delgado, *Organizing* 75).

While the traditional ACORN model as depicted here might seem fairly rigid, contradicting, some would claim, the primary rule of organizing—"everything is local"—it does represent one of the key components of a social action model: replicability, i.e., moving beyond the single-issue, single-neighborhood campaign to broaden the concept of empowerment beyond a single group in a single locality. For most social action groups, the idea that there are common root causes which lead to specific problems or issues in a particular site is an overriding theme. Safety might be the issue in one place, adequate low-income housing might be the issue in another, and furniture might be the motivating force in the third; but social action proponents believe that all these issues are tied together because of their similar starting point: that "there's a tremendous maldistribution of wealth and power" in our county (Cantor), that those groups who have money generally have the power, and that those groups who have little money do not. If low- and moderate-income groups can wage campaigns on issues that concern them, believe these organizers, then they can begin to recognize how these issues are tied together, eventually coming to understand the need for an overriding change in the status quo. According to Dan Cantor, a former ACORN organizer, "This is an intensely political effort in a sense, [and] I don't mean electoral. ACORN does not believe you can solve these problems one neighborhood at a time forever. So you need to look at things more broadly." If groups are looking more broadly in similar ways across the country, the chance for real change to take place is heightened dramatically.

This notion of a replicable model has certain implications for what community organizing might look like in this orientation. First, the roles played by those who participate are fairly well defined. The organizer is an outsider, a professional hired to come in and work with a particular community in a specified way and then to move on. The community leaders are selected by the organizer who recognizes some kind of leadership potential and then trains those individuals in organizing strategies and techniques. The membership consists of people from the neighborhood who have a role which carries certain responsibilities: to participate on committees, to pay dues, to help keep the group going. Over and over across the country, ACORN chapters will have an element of similarity as these roles hold true.

Meredith Minkler begins her book *Community Organizing and Community Building for Health* by citing Mondros and Wilson's descriptions of community organizers as "conscious contrarians" (6). Conscious contrarians, she goes on to explain, can be identified by three characteristics: their different kind of world view in which social justice, rather than market justice, is at the foundation; their insistence on seeing a power analysis at the center of their work; and their deliberate choice of a career in which those two beliefs are at the center.

This depiction of community organizers as "conscious contrarians" strikes me as particularly true for those professional organizers who are a part of the social action orientation. Many organizers move from city to city and from organization to organization, always seeking a way to organize communities so that the underlying conditions which create inequality and injustice can change. Their strong sense that the world should be one in which justice can exist for all keeps them going; their belief that most of the world can be analyzed in terms of who has power and who does not informs everything they do. In part this constant movement of community organizers further necessitates the emphasis on a replicable model: organizers may come and go, but the structure of the organizing campaign remains the same.

At times, criticism is leveled at these professional community organizers on a number of levels: How can you possibly balance the needs of an individual neighborhood with that of a national organization? What happened to "starting with where the people are?" How can these organizers ever really understand what's going on in a particular community, since they stay for such a short time and then leave? An issue that's also raised for groups like ACORN: Since the organizers traditionally have been white, middle-class, college-degreed folks and the members traditionally have been working-class people of color, how does that affect the power relationships within the organization?

None of these have been easy questions for groups like ACORN to answer, although the questions themselves help the group's leaders think about the balances that must stay in the forefront of any organizer's mind. Most important for organizers is to develop a strong group of community leaders who are able to become the primary spokespersons in their communities and to continue the work once the organizer leaves. Dan believes, "A good organizer builds leadership, and leadership gets more comfortable over time. They do run their local groups . . . [and], yeah, they depend on their staff for lots of things and to me that's fine. It's a modern mass society. You can't . . . expect people to give up their jobs and go run community organizations. That's phony."

Leaders in the community, then, become very important in this model, and the development of those leaders is, in fact, one of the principal components of this orientation. Most social action organizers believe that "good leaders are not born, but are developed, usually by the organizers" or by some outside training (Delgado, *Organizing* 180). Thus numerous programs have developed around the country to help train community leaders in how to be effective: the Highlander Research and Education Center, the Industrial Areas Foundation, the Midwest Academy, and a host of others.[6] The Center for Third World Organizing (CTWO), for example, advertises its program as "the nation's premiere organizing center for activists of color," introducing community action training in a weeklong seminar that "provides hands-on training through discussions, role plays and field work." Among the issues covered: "the history of organizing, doorknocking training and field experience, identifying issues, political discussions on social change and principles of direct action" (CTWO 1998 Activist Training brochure).

In a social action mode, then, long-term change, the development of indigenous leaders, and a replicable model become the key elements. What defines the community, though, varies according to the signature style of the organization: for ACORN, obviously, a community is named by its geographic boundaries, but also by the common issues that affect that neighborhood. For another strong social action group, the Industrial Areas Foundation, community is a congregation-based entity. Present-day IAF chapters, the legacy of Saul Alinsky's work, still follow much of his initial structure: multiple congregations committed to a citizen's project headed by various church leaders representing these congregations. Originally arising from the Catholic church, today's IAF has expanded to include a number of religions—from Baptists to Muslims. Still other groups organize around issues of race, class, and gender, focusing on common issues that affect them as members of traditionally disempowered groups.

Tactics used by social action organizers are generally highly political, based on the kinds of strategic thinking Andy Buchsbaum spoke of in the last section. However, some community organizers also recognize the importance of another approach to change and empowerment—what Larry McNeil calls "the soft arts of organizing." The West Coast director of the IAF, McNeil recounts the kinds of hard arts that he and his organization certainly use, those elements generally seen as the mainstay of community organizing tactics: "recruitment, focused actions, disciplined meetings, institutional dues, carefully crafted strategies, issue victories, skillful use of political levers" (18). McNeil suggests that these elements are not sufficient to create an organization that truly achieves its named goals: to share power with as many people as possible in a democratic way, and to bring into the circle the stories and voices of those whose words have not been heard before. Organizing, for McNeil, is more than just problem solving or change making; instead, he sees it as "the active unearthing of people's individual stories, the collective examination of those stories in light of our shared story, and the opportunity to write new endings to both our individual and collective stories" (19). In order to achieve the kind of power this definition implies, he calls on organizations to focus some on the soft arts of organizing: active listening, active empathy, thoughtfulness, and ritual. He contends that the way to approach the hard arts is through the soft:

> If you want more member units in the organization, ask the question: How are we treating the members we already have? Are we at the center of their interests? . . . If you want more money, ask the question: Do we know members' stories? How many people have their story at stake in our collective strategies? How many people have participated in the discussions about money? If you want more leaders, ask the question: What are we doing with the leaders we have? Are they challenged, engaged, growing? (22)

For McNeil and others, while it is easy to get caught up in the tactics and strategies of a successful campaign, any change in the power structure has to begin with the power wielded within a community organization itself—and the attention paid to the soft arts will keep an organizer aware of the group that he or she serves.

Advocacy Orientation

You're just sitting down to dinner when the doorbell rings. Leaving the family and your rapidly cooling lasagna, you open the door to a college-aged woman holding a clipboard. "Hi," she says. "My name is Sarah Morgan. I'm here with the Public Interest Research Group in Michigan, the environmental and consumer watchdog group. We're best known for stopping some of the state's worst water polluters."[7] You sigh, hold open the door and listen to the rest of her rap.

"We're here tonight to stop toxic pollution. There are hundreds of toxic waste sites in Michigan. Chemicals leaking from these dumps are known to cause cancer, birth defects, and other really serious health problems. Instead of doing something about that, Congress is threatening to gut the laws that clean up toxic waste.

"So, we're working to make sure that polluters clean up the dumps and pay the bill. Congress is on the verge of letting polluters off the hook. That's why we need your support tonight."

She hands you a clipboard with a sheet attached, half-filled with the signatures of your neighbors, indicating their support of PIRGIM's efforts to defend the environment, protect national wildlife, and expose consumer rip-offs, and then she points out the place for you to add your name, phone number, and address. As you take the pen to sign up, she continues, "The best way to show your support for this campaign is by joining as a member. Membership gives us the financial and political support we need."

Wearily reaching for your checkbook as you smell your lasagna in the other room, you ask, "How much?" and make out a check. The door shuts, and you return to your dinner—a new member of this grassroots organization.

At its crudest level, this is the image of the advocacy strain of community organizing with which most of us are familiar. Advocacy, seen in this light, seems to consist of door-to-door salespeople, preying on guilty liberals, asking them for money to advance the cause. Such an impression leads some community organizers to question whether or not an advocacy stance is even a viable part of the community organizing picture, caught up, as it seems to be, in soliciting new members, but lacking a true commitment of time and responsibility by those members. Advocacy, for many community organizers, seems too easy; members have to do very little in order to be more than a nominal part of the group—an appealing proposition to some busy citizens, but an attitude which causes dismay for some longtime organizers. "Advocacy," complains Dan Cantor, "has replaced organizing for a lot of people."

Its growing popularity alone, though, seems a reason to look at an advocacy orientation and to spend some time thinking about how it fits into the complete matrix of approaches to community organizing. Advocacy groups are a large part of the movement toward change in our country as huge numbers of people come together around a single cause and a single organization, thus enabling these organizations to carry the clout to create changes in public policy. For that reason alone, it's worth understanding how advocacy groups—like PIRG or Sierra Club or Greenpeace or National Wildlife Federation—work, and how they fit into the overall picture of community organizing.

So what exactly is an advocacy approach and how does it fit with these other orientations? Simply put, an advocacy group advocates on behalf of others, i.e., on behalf of that large group of people who sign petitions, pay dues, and join up as members. Taking their cue from Saul Alinsky that "numbers count," these advocacy groups see large numbers as the key component: Groups like Sierra Club or Common Cause are able to argue to legislators and other policymakers that they should be heard because of the many, many people they represent who support a particular position, evidenced by the long lists of signatures on a petition in support of a bottle bill or physician-assisted suicide or preservation of certain wetland areas.

Thus, the notion of community for an advocacy group is quite different from that of other orientations; in this orientation, the parameters of community cross neighborhood, racial, ethnic, gender and socioeconomic lines. The community becomes, simply, those people who sign on, who generally are "people already sympathetic to your cause," according to Andy Buchsbaum. Because of the emphasis on gaining large numbers, the canvassers who go door-to-door to ask for dues and signatures try to cover thirty to forty houses per night. Thus, they often don't have time to convince people who are opposed to the issue under consideration; they merely hope to activate interest in those people already predisposed to sign on. The idea, Andy explains, "is to get big numbers fast."

While there is no one way advocacy groups gain their members, certain procedures are fairly standard. In some groups, canvassers go door-to-door, handing out general literature about the organization, talking briefly about a specific issue on which the organization is currently campaigning (generally a piece of legislation or a policy matter), and soliciting the citizen's support: always by asking for a contribution and often by asking the person to sign a petition in support of the group's stance. Other groups use different techniques: direct mail campaigns, telephone canvasses, or petition drives mounted from high-traffic locations around a town or city. Whatever the technique, the basic charge is the same: to sign on as many members as possible in a short period of time.

For some people this notion of advocacy leads to the charge that it's merely "membership without responsibility"—that, although members pay dues, they have little say in the day-to-day running of the organization, little input into the issues that form the basis of the campaign being waged. Barbara Israel describes the advocacy model she sees from her public health perspective:

> [Health educators] have access to information. They do the re-
> search, and they advocate for policy change. . . . It's the notion of
> advocating on other people's behalf. So there is a constituency,
> but often the constituency isn't involved on a day-to-day basis.
> Rarely do they come together to meet; rather, they provide funds.

Traditionally, an advocacy group is set up in a fairly hierarchical way: a staff who serve in the role of organizers whose job is both to research and become familiar with issues and to train the door-to-door or telephone canvassers in both the facts of the issues and techniques for signing up members, and canvassers who make actual contact with citizens, signing on new members and updating old members. Advocacy organizations also usually rely on a board of directors, comprised of folks who generally are elected from the membership. The board works with the staff in selecting the issues which will become the focus of a campaign; whether an organization is more staff-driven or board-driven depends on what Andy Buchsbaum calls "an accident of institutional history." Generally, though, a distinguishing characteristic of the advocacy orientation is that the issue selection is not done by the membership as a whole; instead, people sign on either because of the reputation of the group or because they see the merit of the preselected issue.

Some organizations do work to create more of a grassroots feeling among their members. Andy explains PIRGIM's decision to use a door-to-door canvass as its primary mode of soliciting membership: "We've always said that 70–80 percent of canvassing is political as opposed to fund-raising. Even though you're out there getting money for your organization, getting members for your organization, the political part is getting people to sign petitions, getting people to agree to do things, finding people for an activist list." Thus, groups like the PIRGs sometimes ask the newly signed-on members to call a legislator or sign a preprinted postcard the organization will then deliver to the member's legislator. In addition, they'll hand out information sheets, helping to raise the new member's awareness about certain issues: for example, a "Congressional Scorecard" which tallies the neighborhood legislator's support of issues targeted by the organization or a fact sheet which talks about laws under attack and why repeal of these laws would affect people. The PIRGs specifically invite new members to get involved in other ways, asking them to

- Join our e-mail activist network,
- Write, call, or e-mail your legislator on a PIRGIM-backed bill,
- Attend a local meeting with your legislator,
- Write a letter to the editor of your local newspaper about environmental or consumer protection issues, or
- Organize a meeting in your community with other PIRG members to discuss how to make an impact on issues you care about. (PIRGIM membership brochure, 1998)

The canvassers also keep a lookout for those people who seem especially interested in the issue they are canvassing on. These names then get placed on an "activist list" that's sometimes used to set up district meetings between these group members and congressional or state legislators.

Empowerment in the advocacy orientation centers on the organization itself rather than on its individual members. Unlike some other orientations, in which long-term, large-scale empowerment of the community members is the ultimate goal, in the advocacy strand the focus remains on adding to the clout of the organization as a whole. Once the organization gains that clout, it's better able to move its agenda forward. Andy Buchsbaum explains, "Power building is measured in terms of the power of the organization. The more powerful it is, the more it can get done. And the organization's power is measured by financial resources, staff resources (that is, numbers and seniority), media access, and the ability to activate grassroots members." In other words, the voice of any particular advocacy group carries weight because of its large number of members, its ability to get the media to cover a story it pitches, its ability to get its members to sign petitions or make phone calls—in short, its ability to call on its many members and use those numbers to push its agenda. Once a group gains a certain reputation because of these factors, its very presence on an issue is sometimes enough to make legislators take pause.

Clearly, then, the best way to make legislators take pause is to impress them with numbers—to demonstrate to them the number of voting citizens who support a particular cause. Advocacy groups often wage petition campaigns in which they present to a decision maker a stack of signed pages, attesting to strong public support for a particular stand. Another common tactic is what's known as a "postcard campaign." Canvassers ask new members to sign preprinted postcards which urge legislators to support or oppose a certain bill, for example. After gathering thousands of these postcards across an extended geographic area, staff members will deliver large bags of these notes to a legislator's office, coinciding with a press conference they have planned, and culminating with an effective photo opportunity of pouring out the bags of postcards on the legislator's desk.

A planned postcard event like this with its attached photo opportunity is one of many tactics that advocacy groups use to wage a strong media campaign. Strategic use of media is one of those skills experienced organizers have honed over the years, as they concentrate on using the media both to reach large numbers of citizens about a particular issue and to influence legislators—in fact, by *intentionally* using the media's ability to reach the public as one effective way to sway decision makers. But getting positive media coverage is a tricky subject, in part because of the many factors "beyond the story" that influence not only whether an issue will make it into a newspaper or onto the six o'clock news, but also how it will be covered.

One factor in whether or not an issue will be covered is its "media appeal." According to Andy Buchsbaum, the press is sometimes most interested in environmental organizations when they present themselves as the little guy up against the big corporate giants. He explains how media coverage changed for PIRGIM after they successfully won a large statewide campaign to make companies (rather than citizens) pay for their pollution, when their campaign to create a Polluter Pay law was passed by the Michigan legislature.

> The media stopped looking at the environmental groups as kind of these naive, idealistic amateurs, the Davids taking on the Goliaths, and began looking at environmental groups being in themselves professional, sophisticated organizations—in which case, a lot of our media appeal dried up.

In other words, as the "story" of PIRGIM changed, the media lost interest, and, as Andy explains, until another appealing story replaces it the media coverage for his group in particular and for environmental groups in general suffers.

Many of those skilled in the use of media, then, stress the importance of consciously framing their story in a way that will appeal to the media—and not relying on the media to be the ones who craft the story. A number of organizers in the public health arena have turned to what they call media advocacy, "a tactic for community groups to communicate their own story in their own words to promote social change. It is a hybrid tool combining advocacy approaches with the strategic and innovative use of media to better *pressure* decision-makers to support changes" (Wallack 340).

In his essay "Media Advocacy: A Strategy for Empowering People and Communities," Lawrence Wallack contends that media advocacy goes beyond merely providing information to the public through the eyes or words of a reporter; rather, it is "the strategic use of mass media to advance a social or public policy initiative . . . to reframe and shape public discussion" (342). He sees, then, that it is not enough to merely give the media information for a story; if change is the goal, community organizing groups need to take charge of how their story is presented to the media, thus shaping how it is further presented to the public.

Wallack proposes three functions for media advocacy, in order to raise the kind of public awareness that is essential for community groups:

1. Agenda Setting: Believing, along with scores of media analysts, that news events exist in large part because they are reported,

Wallack stresses that advocacy groups set the agenda of the issue they wish to be brought to light and use the media then to gain access to the public. Once the media spotlight shifts or fades, he explains, the issue likewise fades from the public's eye. Keeping the issues alive, then, is a necessary role for advocacy groups.

2. Framing the Problem and Shaping the Debate: While it is relatively easy to get reporters to cover a story, it is much harder to get them to cover it in a particular way; thus, Wallack believes advocacy groups must frame the problem for the media, "hold[ing] the spotlight on the issue and focus[ing] on 'upstream' causes" (344). In other words, many reporters may be content to let the obvious answers drive the way an issue is reported; media advocacy strategists argue for framing the issue in a particular way so that the root causes or larger aspects are exposed, to push reporters to see the problem in its larger social context and not in a narrow, obvious way.

3. Advancing Policy: Wallack also stresses the importance of advancing "a social or public initiative(s) as a primary approach to the problem" (344). By offering specific ways of looking at the problem that place the issue in a larger context and suggesting certain solutions to the problem as part of its media pitch, a group can continue to frame its presentation to the public—influencing policy itself in ways that the group has predetermined. Wallack explains,

> The most important work of media advocacy is really done in the planning stage before calling the media. Advocates need to know how they will advance their approach, what symbols to use, what issues to link it with, what voices to provide and what messages to communicate. Strategies can then be developed to frame for access and frame for content. (349)

Other community organizers agree that their role in *how* an issue will be covered is of great importance. For many, the notion of strategic thinking enters again here, as organizers consider the nitty-gritty of how to make sympathetic coverage a reality. Should an organizer, for example, rely on sending out a news release to all the media outlets in an area or should he or she target the story to one reporter? Should a group aim toward electronic or print coverage? Are certain days of the week better than others to plan a news event? Are certain sections of the paper better targets than others?

Again, Andy Buchsbaum explains his take on this, using the example of a landfill which is leaking pollutants to show some of the complexity of these decisions:

> Do we hold a news conference or do we leak it to one reporter? That's a difficult decision to make . . . if it's a difficult story, if it's one that's not easily accessible, if the problems with [the story] require some digging, if it's a more narrative story. The advantage if you give it to one reporter and you've got somebody in mind—you have a relationship with him and you know he'll do a good job, then you can get a really good story on this landfill and it will be featured high. It might be featured in a "Living" section, which more people read. And so, you can get a more complete picture of the problem. If you do it in a news release and a news conference, you can get TV, radio, . . . but you'll get thirty seconds. They're not going to do a complete job on the story. The print media won't go in-depth because TV and radio will have it first . . . yet you'll get much broader coverage. So it's a question of breadth versus intensity. And the tricky part is how to maximize each.

Mixing and Phasing through These Orientations

So what does all this have to do with teachers? Can an exposure to these orientations really help us in the matter at hand: the misinformation and mischaracterization of our practices and our theories in the public debate? Can a look at these specifics of community organizing help us imagine what we as teachers and teacher educators might actually be able to do to help reclaim our voices in that debate and to reset the boundaries of the discussion? I think so, especially as it helps us conceive more broadly how change happens and how ordinary people—neighbors, moms, even teachers—can be the ones to make it happen.

What is central to these orientations, I think, and what is of concern to teachers, is less the specific definition of each and more the extended vision that community organizing as a whole gives us of what it means to "be political." As I look back over the chapter, certain ideas seem vital:

- communities are the center of change;
- strong communities can be built around a common concern;
- shared stories can be the basis of community building and, ultimately, of change;
- becoming knowledgeable about an issue is the first step toward effecting change;
- thinking strategically about an issue is necessary to effect change;
- those people who are knowledgeable and passionate about certain issues are the ones who are most likely to make change happen.

Following these ideas, it makes sense to me that teachers are the natural choice to lead the charge for change. Teachers—who already are centrally located within the community, who are knowledgeable about the issues that matter, who understand the importance of parental concerns and the power of parents' and students' stories—are well poised to become change agents. Teachers can become "local heroes," the "regular" people who can "lead a pretty normal life and be active in social change."

As I study the five orientations, though, what also becomes clear to me is this: While teachers are urged these days to become more and more "political," the focus seems to be on one particular way of doing so: Teachers continually are being asked these days to write letters to the editor, learn the ins and outs of various legislative acts, call congressional representatives, write op-ed pieces, and so on—actions I see now as firmly situated in the mobilizing orientation. Thinking back to the essentials of these orientations, I recognize mobilizing as only one of many approaches to community organizing. And while I understand and value the important goals that can be achieved through that approach, I now know its limitations. The mobilizing approach relies on the short-term solution: fixing the legislation, blocking an action by the board of education, preventing the passage of an election issue. When done well, it can be incredibly effective in reaching those goals. But I believe that the goals of a mobilizing approach are not the only goals we should be striving toward, and I worry that a focus only on the mobilizing orientation limits our long-term effectiveness at creating lasting change.

What I realize now is that we need so much more. If I think about change from a community organizing point of view, I can see that we need bits and pieces of all these orientations. We need the education component, so that we can find ways to educate the public about the big picture of literacy instruction, moving beyond the small pieces that seem to be popularized in the press (inventive spelling or choice in reading). As those who practice the education orientation stress, we need to build a community by educating people, and we need to realize that the mere act of that education can lead to individuals thinking about issues differently—a vital step in any reform effort. We need, as well, the social work approach of planning/development, so that we can *hear* the desires of parents and begin to work with them at a local level, to see if their understandings of their children's needs might mesh with our understanding of best practices in literacy instruction. We desperately need their voices in this process, so that we can learn from them and so that we can build a community which sees itself as collaborative and not in conflict. We also need social action, so that we can focus on the big battle of who has the power to tell the stories of the classroom and who does not, so that we can work toward the empowerment of teachers and parents whose voices have not been heard in the public debate, and so that we can find a way to do this for the long term—and beyond the specific issues. And we certainly need advocacy, so that the beliefs of the large numbers of teachers might be represented more fully on the national scene, by both English educators and by the unions and professional organizations. We need to think about how to make our existing organizations even more effective advocates—by finding ways to increase the number of teachers they represent and by discovering new and effective ways to gain the attention of policymakers.

Thus what I've come to believe (along with Rothman and numerous community organizers) is that we shouldn't be sticking to just one orientation, but rather should be mixing and phasing among them: mixing what seems appropriate from the various orientations and phasing from one to another, depending on the stage of the project. I've learned that organizers are aware always that what works in a given situation does so because of the context of the local circumstances: what particular approaches are appropriate at a given time, in a given place, for a particular group of people; what kind of perspective or training the local leadership has toward its mission; what kind of organizing strategies might be most palatable for the community members. In a certain place, in a certain time, with a certain group, an "in-your-face" action might work well; in another community, a soft approach might be essential. As Barbara Israel succinctly captured it, "In my sort of eclectic approach to the world, I think we need all of it."

What is striking to me in these orientations is the sea of possibilities they offer us for thinking about how we might reach out to others in creative and effective ways, beyond the discussion of specific tactics which seems to overwhelm the current look at how teachers might become more action-oriented. These multiple, overlapping orientations allow for the teacher who might know it is her job to take more action but always feels guilty because she is simply unable to don the kind of public role that a mobilizing orientation seems to her to demand, the teacher for whom an approach of working closely with the parents in her class in both an education and social planning mode might seem more feasible and be equally effective. This multiplicity of approaches also allows for the teacher who has the skills and motivation to become an advocate for others, who will stand up and represent the views of her peers on a state and national level; it allows for the teacher whose school district seems to be moving in all the right directions and whose parents seem satisfied today, but who wisely decides to educate those around her in anticipation of a day when that might not be so.

Seeing community organizing in all its glory with its wide variations and burgeoning possibilities allows for our various contexts, our various personalities, and our various community needs. But underlying this vastness is some common ground, particularly in how these community organizers go about their day-to-day work. What I've discovered as I've studied community organizations and organizers is that despite the differences, there are great similarities in the steps they follow to get the job done. In the next chapter, I'll lay out a fairly broad model of what I've noticed about what organizers actually do—a model I've developed while keeping in mind an image of teachers as potential community organizers. My rationale is this: if we look at community organizing in a step-by-step way (knowing, of course, that this kind of simplistic look reduces a lot of the complexities), we might be able to figure out an approach for teachers to take in order to mesh a community organizing stance into their own outreach programs. By doing so, we might be able to move past the incidental, spontaneous, and often reactive responses in which most of us are currently mired. We might be able to create a sustained, consistent program of outreach, one that takes a lesson from the replicability stance of social action coupled with the "everything is local" rule that drives most organizing campaigns.

Notes

1. For a more complete history of the community organizing movement, see, among others, Delgado's *Beyond the Politics of Place*, Minkler and Wallerstein's "Improving Health through Community Organization and Community Building: A Health Education Perspective," and Garvin and Cox's "A History of Community Organizing Since the Civil War, with Special Reference to Oppressed Communities."

2. For more on a feminist approach to community organizing, see Bradshaw, Soifer, and Gutierrez; Hyde; and Weil.

3. For more on the work of DELTA, see Hope and Timmel's multivolume series entitled *Training for Transformation: A Handbook for Community Workers.*

4. Those familiar with community organizing in the areas of social work and public health will notice I have combined here what many see as two separate orientations: social planning and community development. Although I recognize the distinctions between these models, for the purposes of this discussion I will try to talk about them as a kind of continuum within a single model. For more on the distinctions, see Rothman.

5. See, for example, *Leadership Handbook on Hazardous Waste: Organization, Foundation of Our Future* by Lois Gibbs and Will Collette, *Ralph Nader Presents a Citizens' Guide to Lobbying* by Marc Caplan, *Taking Action: Working Together for Positive Change* by Elizabeth Amer and Constance Mungall, *Guerrilla P.R.: How You Can Wage an Effective Publicity Campaign Without Going Broke* by Michael Levine, and many more.

6. For a fairly comprehensive listing of organizing training centers, see Appendix B in Delgado's *Beyond the Politics of Place*, although it's important to note that the kinds of training these centers do vary greatly, from education to planning/development to mobilization to social action . . . and everything in between.

7. This rap is taken from a PIRGIM handout to its canvassers, entitled "Environmental Defense Campaign Standard Presentation."

4 Teachers *Are* Organizers: Tacit Knowledge and New Techniques

Maybe we're not the next Norma Raes or Candy Lightners; Ralph Nader and Lois Gibbs probably don't have to worry too much about us unseating them as gurus of community organizing. But as teachers—caring, committed teachers who are concerned about those children we encounter every day—we do have a lot in common with these folks. As I have been researching and writing about community organizing over the past couple of years, I have been struck over and over by the similarities between teachers and organizers. Looking back over the anecdotes and responses of the organizers from the last chapter, I once again see these commonalties so clearly: Both teachers and organizers stress the importance of building a community, whether it's with students or neighbors; both teachers and organizers actively try to develop leaders out of their communities; both realize that the best-functioning group actually would be one that could eventually function without them; and both reject complacency and seek change as the natural end of their efforts. Teachers use certain organizing skills every day with their classrooms as they bring together diverse groups of students, in particular those skills McNeil named as the "soft arts" of organizing: listening, empathy, thoughtfulness, and ritual. When I read Don Graves's depictions of sitting close to a student and asking her to "tell me more," or John Gaughan's heartfelt narrative of his transformation as a teacher as he's learned to trust his students, or Ralph Peterson's explanations of the need for rites, rituals, and ceremonies in the classroom, I hear echoes of community organizing.[1] And when I hear about the parties Cathy Gwizdala hosts for her multiage classroom students and the after-school writing club Karen Bailey offers her inner-city middle schoolers, and when I watch Kathleen Hayes-Parvin's sixth graders run a miniconference for my university methods students on writing workshop and writer's craft, I see the results of community organizing in the classroom. Good teachers, it seems to me, already do have the mindset necessary for transforming a group of kids into a functioning, united community, semester after semester, year after year—and they do so with a bagful of techniques that would make many a professional organizer jealous.

But teachers generally have not transferred this ability to the world outside the classroom—using these same organizing skills in order to work with the parents and surrounding communities, helping them become a community of learners who might reach the same level of understanding of classroom issues that their students have reached. And, of course, as I mentioned in Chapter 1, I realize this is no easy task. Teachers who are extremely comfortable in the classroom setting with their students sometimes freeze when they move beyond those walls to work with community members. Fear that parents will be critical or, perhaps worse, dismissive drives many teachers to isolate themselves from any but the most surface contacts with the parents of the students they teach.

But imagine, if you will, teachers who take the lessons of community organizing seriously, and who combine the skills they already possess with those that professional organizers use. Imagine having a cadre of teachers throughout the country, familiar with the ins and outs of a community organizing approach, who take on the challenge of entering the public conversation on education as an organizing task. These teachers could change the way in which curricular issues are depicted—as they mix and phase their way through educating, mobilizing, planning, acting, advocating—just as community organizers have changed the way the public feels on a plethora of issues. These teachers would understand the value of and strategies for educating the public about these issues in a *proactive* way, day in and day out, often in those communities in which everything seems to be going okay. In so doing, these teachers would prepare the way for challenges thrown at them when others disagree or propose roadblocks to curricular best practices; these teachers would know some specific strategies for response when this kind of opposition arises. Teachers who don the hats of community organizers would understand that there is a need to do this kind of work in a sustained way, rather than a spontaneous one, to develop a systematic approach, so that every year they can reach out in ways that are proven to work for organizers, no matter what their orientation, techniques that have a track record of helping to change peoples' minds.

Community organizing teaches me that in order for teachers to be able to do this, they must be knowledgeable in two ways: They must be knowledgeable, first, about the content of their message and, second, about the process they might use in order to advocate effectively for their stance. Recent books by strong voices in our field are available to help teachers with the first kind of knowledge, that is, to help them feel more confident about the kinds of best practice to which I refer throughout this book: such works as Regie Routman's *Literacy at the Crossroads*, Ken Goodman's *On Reading*, Connie Weaver's *Teaching Grammar in Context*, Zemelman and Daniels's *Best Practice*, and a host of others. These books can serve as a complement to the kinds of support networks that many teachers join to help them be able to articulate their knowledge, such as The National Writing Project, the Whole Language Umbrella, NCTE and its statewide affiliates, local study groups, and local curricular and standards efforts. As teachers participate in these groups and read professionally, they are able to become more confident in their knowledge of their practice. The understandings gleaned from these books and networks are vital for all teachers, as even those who are successful using certain practices in their classrooms are sometimes less aware of the rationale behind such practices. Teachers need to remember and reflect upon these connections between their practices and their underlying beliefs.

In this chapter, though, I want to focus on the second kind of knowledge, the process knowledge that teachers need to possess in order to make a community organizing approach work. When I think about the work of the teachers whose stories are told in Chapter 2, I recognize that they already possess considerable process knowledge about how to organize their own communities for change—what Berkowitz might call "latent skills." In stressing the need for social workers to become more like community organizers, Berkowitz insists, "The task is less one of learning new skills than of shaking loose latent skills that are already there" (*Community* 22). In a more recent book, an oral history of community leaders, he furthers this theme, explaining that in his analysis of how these leaders function, "There is hardly an operational technique cited by the participants . . . that's not in the catalogue of common sense" (*Local* 325). I think his point is particularly applicable to teachers. Teachers already own many of the skills necessary to be able to organize their communities, but they may not be aware of this tacit knowledge. My goal in this chapter, then, is first to help teachers bring that tacit knowledge to the surface and then to help them add new techniques to their repertoire, techniques which might be particularly appropriate for organizing the parent community. By giving a name to some of the techniques and by then situating them in a systematic model for change, I hope to give teachers a place to start if they choose to take on this approach to community building and reform—to become what I want to name *teacher-organizers*. Creating a replicable model of this sort can help teachers, I hope, uncover some specific ways to realize parent outreach as an ongoing task, one that goes beyond the parent conferences in the beginning of the year and an occasional letter home; it can help teachers see how such outreach might more effectively be a consistent part of a teaching program.

In this chapter, then, I will lay out a potential process model for teacher-organizing, gleaned from the work of community organizers, a model that weaves together five basic steps that most community organizing seem to follow in an ongoing, cyclical process:

1. establishing community/gaining entrée,
2. identifying purpose,
3. developing leaders,
4. taking action,
5. evaluating progress.

As I talk about each step, I'll first use some examples from community organizers: How do they, for example, establish community? develop leaders? evaluate progress? Then, I'll connect this to the work many teachers I know are already doing: How do teachers gain entrée with their parent communities? identify purpose? take action? Calling heavily upon the techniques of the teachers from Chapter 2, I want to show how some thoughtful teachers are already community organizers of a sort—but at the same time to stress that even their strong beginnings could benefit from a look at new strategies and from thinking about how to tie their piecemeal approaches into a consistent, sustainable whole.

As you read this chapter, then, think about these questions: What tacit knowledge do I already hold about teacher-organizing? Are there techniques that I am already using successfully? Are there ways to extend and expand those techniques? What new approaches offered here might enhance my practices? How can I turn my occasional stabs into a more effective whole?

1. Establishing Community/Gaining Entrée

Community organizing is nowhere without a community. And knowledge of what that community is—both for the members themselves and for the organizer—is of vital importance. Both groups need to understand who these people are, why they have come together, and what in their histories and current circumstances might unite them to be able to function in a positive and useful way. Whether the group comes together because of a shared interest in learning more about a subject or because they want to make an immediate change in their circumstances, the stories individuals bring to the table and their reasons for seeking community as an answer to their needs are important.

Further, while some communities seem naturally bonded because of a common need, the power of those individual stories cannot be denied. Organizers have to be aware of the balance between individual and community needs, even as they seek to help this group become more unified.

Many community organizers, particularly in the field of public health, believe that the balancing act between individual stories and community needs has gotten more and more difficult in recent years, in part because of the increasing lack of connections many folks feel within their neighborhood communities. In fact, for some community health practitioners, the old models of organizing, based on Rothman's orientation, for example, have given way to new models which specifically intertwine community *building* and community organizing, pointing out how the two connect and rely upon each other (see, for example, Minkler's *Community Organizing and Community Building for Health*). Marc Pilisuk, Joann McAllister, and Jack Rothman talk about the need in this day and age for community organizing to slow down some to allow for "building a sense of belonging to a caring community," the need, that is, for "a slower process of creating a web of continuing relationships so that people may indeed come together, share their supportive attentions and resources, and experience a sense of belonging to their community" (104). In particular, these authors and others argue, such an approach is necessary when there is not a strong community feeling at the beginning, which is more and more the case in neighborhoods in our current society.

However an organizer balances individual stories with community needs, community building, and community organizing, establishing her or his place within the community is a vital and complicated part of this first step. An organizer is part of, but separate from, the group in many cases; her or his ability to be accepted and wanted by the group is one key to the group's eventual success. In organizer lingo, this acceptance is known as "gaining entrée," a goal that all organizers must meet before the group can move forward.

For a number of organizers, this first step of establishing community and gaining entrée can be captured by a series of questions:

■ **Defining the community:** Who is a part of your community, i.e., what are its boundaries? Is this a geography-based community, bounded by certain features (streets, a river, a town line)? Is it an issue-based community (does one have to believe in a certain policy to be included)? Is it based on some other kinds of boundaries (e.g., race, gender, class, age)? Who is included and who is excluded? What are the reasons for inclusion or exclusion?

■ **Establishing its character:** What are the driving questions and needs of this community? What ties the members together as a community? What are the strengths and resources of this community? What problems exist for them as members of this community?

■ **Gaining entrée:** Are you as organizer a natural member (i.e., within the boundaries established) or an outsider? If you're an outsider, how can you become accepted by the group? What is your credibility? What can you bring to the group that they don't already have?

Every community organizer I've spoken with has thought hard about this stage, and each accomplishes its goals in a variety of ways. ACORN organizers, as I explained in the last chapter, identify a particular geographic neighborhood and then travel door-to-door, talking to people and learning about their needs and issues as members of a particular neighborhood. Renee Bayer, in her work in maternal/ child health, first brought together representatives of a number of groups to help identify the boundaries and issues of the community with whom she would eventually work. Some social work organizers send out surveys to people in the neighborhood to establish themselves and their group and to uncover needs. Many mobilizing groups start with a neighborhood meeting, initiated either by flyers in mailboxes or word of mouth. Tracey Easthope, in a recent campaign to raise awareness about medical waste incinerators, began with what she calls her "fishing expedition talk," an informational talk that she gave to hospital staff and various community groups about the dioxins and mercury contaminants contained in the medical incinerators, as she "fished" for interested people who might come on board to work for change. Despite these differences in style, the common approach in this step is to draw people together in some way so that they might begin the process of naming their own community.

The second part of this step, gaining entrée into a community, is directly tied to the credibility an organizer establishes, especially if he or she is an outsider to the community. Credibility can come from a number of sources: sometimes it is part and parcel of the position the organizer holds—as a social worker in a particular neighborhood or as a university employee who brings in grant money to work in a certain area, although, as Renee pointed out in the last chapter, at times that position might work against the organizer: A community used to university people coming in for a short period, gathering information in the name of change, and then withdrawing, might see a university employee as having a *lack* of credibility. Sometimes credibility is established through word of mouth: An organizer has proved herself or himself in other situations, and that endorsement comes through to the new group. Sometimes credibility emerges because of someone the organizer knows, perhaps a neighborhood leader or a person of some standing in the particular community. Sometimes credibility comes because of how the organizer conducts himself or herself from the very first contact with community members: as someone who listens, someone who encourages everyone to talk, someone who seems to care about the issues at hand. At a recent conference I attended on organizing in community health, one of the speakers, Meredith Minkler, shared a story of how she had established credibility in an unfamiliar community in which she wanted to start a project and for which she needed the help of some of the elders of the neighborhood. Realizing that she was not knowledgeable about some of the mores of this group, she asked others on her community board about how she could gain entrée into the community. She was told that when a newcomer comes to ask a favor of the older people in the neighborhood, she really should bring a homemade gift. This university researcher and organizer, who described herself as less than talented in the homemade gift department, spent many evenings making potpourris to give out on her initial home visits. At the first house, the elderly woman who opened the door, saw the gift, threw open her arms, and hugged Minkler! From the start, the university professor had shown her respect for the customs of the community, thus achieving credibility and entrée (Minkler, "Community-Based").

Examples from Teachers

- Hosting a picnic with parents and students
- Home visits
- Holding first-week "How are you doing?" conferences
- Sending home welcome letters

- Sending home a matrix of possibilities for parent involvement
- Inviting parents to join a reading/writing group
- Inviting parents to join a study group
- Inviting parents to come to an inservice program

As teachers begin to think about this important first step, the inclination might be to say the community is already defined, i.e., the members are parents of the students in a particular class, bonded together by their interest in their child's learning and their desire for their kids to succeed. But any teacher knows this is not as easy as it sounds. Parents bring a variety of experiences to the table, from their own schooling stories to their child's schooling thus far. They bring, as well, an intimate knowledge of their own child, knowledge they may feel has been ignored by the school. They bring certain perceptions of other parents in the classroom, again gleaned from their prior contact at a soccer game, on a playground, or at a school event. All of these individual experiences add up to a community whose members are as different as they are similar. A teacher-organizer might be able to set parameters for who or what constitutes a particular community in a fairly simplistic fashion (i.e., the parents in a particular class), but the challenge becomes how to help these people think of themselves as a community and perhaps even to build a community where one may not now exist.

A further issue for teachers is how to gain entrée into that parent community. For some parents, the sheer fact that the teacher is a teacher may be enough to establish credibility in the community; for others, who have had bad experiences with teachers, that role might be sufficient to limit the teacher's credibility. If teachers are serious about gaining entrée into the parent community, then, they need to establish themselves as people who want to learn about the strengths and resources of families as well as the needs—to establish themselves as people who want to learn *with* the families. Teachers need to engage families, as Shockley, Michalove, and Allen suggest, to establish "trust, shared goals, and genuine dialogue on a regular basis" in order to "to develop relationships with families where [they can] learn about what already [exists] in the families and connect that with the literacy classroom" (94–5).

In looking back to the stories of the teachers in Chapter 2, most of them used strategies that went a long way toward both gaining entrée and helping the group begin to define itself as a community. Carolyn Berge—the primary school multiage teacher—had in the past con-

ducted short home visits in the beginning of the year, merely to say hi
and to identify herself as the child's new teacher. Now, she holds a
picnic with all the families at the beginning of the school year.
Remember her words on this: "Parents love it, kids have a blast, and it's
a nice relaxed way for me to look like a real person. . . . [By the time they
leave] they have already a feeling that they are a community, . . . a
community of learners." In other words, part of her goal in this picnic is
to help parents come together in a social setting in order to begin to
know each other and to know her, thus both establishing her own
credibility as a person who cares about the children and hoping parents
will begin to define themselves as a community. Kathleen Hayes-
Parvin—the middle school teacher in the diverse, multiethnic setting—
also establishes herself as an approachable and caring teacher as she
meets with every parent in the first few weeks of the school year,
inviting and reinviting them until she meets with everyone. Kathleen
calls this contact "unbelievably important": "Because the next time you
call . . . you don't feel threatened by, 'Here I've never met this person,
and I'm calling to say something terribly negative about their child.'
You feel like, 'Hey, I've called this mom or dad, I've welcomed them to
our team, and now I'm calling for their help,' and they're much more
likely to do that for me." Again, she reaches out to the parents as
members of a team, a team that together can help ease the way for the
children.

　　This notion of welcoming parents onto the team and honoring
their knowledge of their children can happen in a number of ways, both
formally and informally. Carolyn structures her school day so that
students, upon entering, have a selection of "Smart Choices" that they
can pursue with little help from her. That purposeful arrangement of
time is done so that the parents who drop off their children can have a
chance to chat with her, while their children get right to work. As she
says, she wants parents to feel, "You can always come in." Carolyn,
Kathleen, and others always find an array of creative ways to invite
parents to become involved: Carolyn actually hands out a sheet with a
huge matrix of possibilities that allows for a variety of busy schedules
and are intended to help parents who can't volunteer during the school
day to feel a part of community. Kathleen pursues the unique talents
that some of her parents have. Some of them may not be able to help in
reading or writing workshop, she explains, but last year one mom
reupholstered the classroom couch and thus contributed to the community feeling.

Another teacher with whom I spoke, Sarah Lorenz, described the feeling of trust that exists at the small K–12 Christian school in which she teaches. In part, she believes that the trust arises from the parents' required presence at the school: single-parent families are asked to contribute ten hours of school service; dual-parent families, twenty hours. The parent involvement requirement can be satisfied in many ways, from collecting soup can labels (for a fund-raiser) or chaperoning a field trip to chairing a school event, working at a basketball game, or being a classroom aide. The point, according to Sarah, is that "From square one, parents have to be in the school." Once that happens, "parents know teachers" and each other, which she sees as key factors in creating a community feeling.

Other techniques for making this early contact to establish community and credibility emerge from the work of Julie King and from the parent study group established by Amy Pace and Ronda Meier. The letter Julie sends home to parents each year, explaining her program for language arts and inviting the parents to participate in that program, sets a sincere tone of welcome and invitation. Think about the kinds of early letters we send home to parents, often our first contact with them. Think about the persona we develop through the words we use in those letters and consider whether these letters are the kind which establish credibility for us as people who want to build a community with the parents of our students or if they instead serve the purpose of setting us up as rule maker. Consider whether the letters are invitational in nature, asking the parents to become part of the community of learners who have a role both with their own children and within the community of the class. For Ronda and Amy, too, the tone of the contacts they set up with parents in order to create the parent study group was important; using humor and welcoming language, they established themselves not as know-it-all teachers, but rather as co-learners who saw this project as a way for everyone to learn together.

Barbara Israel speaks of this need for community organizers to establish themselves as co-learners and compares the difficulty it poses for some health professionals to the difficulty it might pose for teachers. "[T]eachers, health professionals are trained as experts. They have the answers and they have the authority. . . . I think that makes it even more of a challenge. If you're not comfortable not being in control, you probably don't want to do community organizing." This point is one that teachers need to consider: Expertise creates a certain kind of credibility—but it is not the kind that will necessarily help much if your goal is to organize a community that values dialogue. For teachers—and organizers—to be successful in this step, they need to combine the kind of credibility that emerges from showing a strong knowledge base of the curricular issues (i.e., as Kathleen and Carolyn have done by creating parent libraries), with an openness to learning from the parents about their own issues and needs, their concerns about their children.

2. Identifying Purpose

The next step for community organizers is to work with their community to identify their purpose for coming together. Good organizers have learned a number of things about establishing purpose in a community group. First, the purpose must be true to the organizer's creed, "Start where the people are." The purpose needs to be something that the community itself identifies as important and something that they can buy into, preferably an issue that arises from the members. Even if the original impetus for the issue comes from the organizer herself (as with Tracey Easthope's medical waste incinerator campaign in which she brought the issue to the community), the definition of the specific goals should be reached in a consensus fashion by the group. The reasons, of course, are obvious: Community organizing relies on community building, and reaching common goals is a necessary step of building an organization that has any hopes for success.[2]

This need to build a community, though, can cause a tension in some organizing situations, as organizers recognize that problem definition, while extremely important, can't take forever. If a group of people has come together to create change and take action, too much time spent on establishing the purpose will result in some members dropping out. Obviously, people who perceive that too much time is being spent on problem identification, when they see toxic waste continuing to spew into their neighborhood, can get frustrated if the organizer spends meeting after meeting helping the group get to know each other and reach a consensus about the path they plan to take as a group. The organizer, then, needs to strike a balance based on the particular situation and the needs of the members: weighing the time spent in building the community and coming to agreement on the purpose versus moving forward to action steps.

Organizers also know that this need for many groups to move right to an action step can lead to their defining their purposes or goals in terms of solutions rather than problems or issues. Once this happens, the group can be placed in the position of putting on band-aids instead of getting at root causes. Barbara Israel explains,

> So often people identify problems [like] "lack of a basketball court
> for youth." Well, that's a solution; that's not the problem. People
> think you put "lack of" and that makes it a problem. . . . Well,
> what's really the problem here. That youth don't have time to
> interact with each other? they don't have a place to go? the schools
> aren't meeting their needs?. . . I've been in a number of situations
> when somebody will stand up and come up with a solution very
> early on and everybody's like, "That's great, let's do it." People
> jump on that idea of let's do it, but . . . you're putting the band-
> aid on the thing when you haven't yet decided on what the thing is.

In the long term, organizers know band-aid solutions don't last. The
dilemma for the organizer is to convince the community that while a
band-aid might be satisfying for the short term, it won't work over time;
good organizers often try to balance some immediate gratification for
the members on winnable issues with working on some long-term goals
that can effect real change.

This leads to another delicate balance for organizers and communities as they strive to define their purpose: A purpose must be big
enough and flexible enough that it can meet the diverse needs of the
group, but not so big or flexible that it leaves people with no direction.
Again, Barbara Israel offers advice:

> [At] the grassroots level, if the group's only working on one prob-
> lem, first of all you're going to lose a lot of people because that's
> not their issue. So, if you can do two or three issues, you're more
> likely to build different subsets . . . that can tap into their interests
> or energy. At the same time, you have to be careful. . . . How
> many balls can you have up in the air in one time?

Keeping people on board is vital in a community group; thus, if the
problem definition is perceived by some as ignoring their concerns,
they will not remain active. In addition, the purpose has to stand up to
ongoing assessment and change. As the group moves forward and
conditions change, the purpose may need to be reassessed. Too narrow
a focus may leave the group without a reason to go on, if it gets resolved
quickly and fails to address underlying problems.

Again, a list of questions sometimes helps the focus for the
organizer.

■ **Defining the purpose:** Is there a specific issue that is uniting
the group? Does everyone agree on the issue? Are there root causes
underlying the issue which need to be brought to light? Who has
brought up the issue: the organizer or the members? What are the
goals of the group? What does the group want to accomplish?

- **Anticipating problems:** Is there an opposition that the group needs to be aware of? Is the opposition's take on the problem significant in defining the group's take?

- **Allowing for change:** Is the purpose of the group too narrow to meet everyone's needs? Will the statement of purpose allow enough flexibility to meet diverse needs but be specific enough to keep the group from wandering aimlessly? Does the purpose allow for change as the conditions change?

Community organizers offer a number of ideas for how to help in the definition of a group's purpose, while at the same time building the community. As we saw in Chapter 3, many strategies are standard practice: listening hard to the concerns of the membership, creating a situation in which people feel comfortable talking about their issues and needs, and sitting back as an organizer so that other people's voices can be heard. Renee Bayer speaks about how important it is for an organizer to listen, "really listen, reflecting back what they say . . . [because] sometimes it takes people a while to put their thoughts together." She shares a recent example of sitting at a community meeting in which members of the community were coming together for one of the first times to talk about their experiences and needs in establishing a community health clinic. Each person sitting in the circle had a chance to introduce herself and to say something about what she thought the health clinic might accomplish. One woman, Bayer noticed, said one line and then became tearful and unable to talk. After everyone in the group had spoken, Renee raised her hand and asked the woman, "You can say no if you don't want to answer this, but can you talk about either raising kids in this neighborhood or what it's been like to work at this clinic?" As she responded to the first question, the words just began to pour out of her. "It was just listening to that voice," Renee recalls, knowing that this woman had something to say but maybe needed some more encouragement to make it happen.

Other organizers express the belief that if you've truly gained entrée into a community and if you take seriously the role of listening to people's concerns, you'll hear from a number of people about their issues. Some organizers see their role at that point as reflecting back what people have said and helping to make connections between people's ideas, saying for example, "I've heard from Bill over there that he's concerned about safety in the neighborhood. Cassandra has said that her concern is that teenagers don't seem to have any place to go. I'm wondering if these issues connect in any way for the rest of you?"

Beyond these important steps of listening, reflecting, and connecting, organizers often have some specific ideas on how to help members define their purpose. Barbara Israel speaks of having community members work from a "strength approach" and often asks community members to draw pictures of their community—the strengths and the problems—as well as a picture of what they envision as an ideal community. She suggests doing this in groups of three or four so that people have a chance to talk about what's good in their community.

> I think this is really helpful in giving people a lot more positive sense of who they are, who their community is, and the resources that are out there to try to solve some of the problems. . . . Continually referring back to, 'Oh, you mentioned churches [as a positive]' or 'you mentioned social networks' or 'you mentioned schools.' [Then the question becomes] how do you tap into those [positives] when it's time to start addressing problems.

In the book *Training for Transformation*, the authors adopt a Freirean approach in which they use "codes" or what they call "problem posing materials to stimulate discussion" (Hope and Timmel 1, 13). Like Freire's work, these codes present the drawing of a scene from the community which depicts some concrete experience that would be familiar to participants. Later, they ask members to divide into teams to write a bit about their perceptions of the vision and purpose of the group, circling key words from their writing, which lead to further discussion.

Examples from Teachers

- Asking parents to write about their concerns, needs, and interests
- Asking parents to draw about those concerns, needs, and interests
- Offering parents a matrix of choices for learning more about the curriculum
- Watching kids and parents carefully to identify key issues of concern
- Listening to parents in conferences and casual conversations
- Distributing "walking journals"

For teachers, this step of identifying purpose presents a number of dilemmas. Any overtly political statement of purpose like "getting the school to stop standardized testing" or "banning Phonics First in the school" is not only dangerous for teachers, but it also simply wouldn't fly with parents. Teachers are not the kind of community organizers who organize a community and then leave. Because teachers have an investment in the schools in which they work, they need to be certain they are not stepping on the toes of the teacher down the hall or the principal or the district curriculum director. Thus teachers who want to keep their jobs *and* be able to use the practices they are convinced work have to be careful of what they do and say. A subtle approach to identifying purpose, then, is a necessity in the sensitive world in which teachers move. Teachers might be wise to take a page from the education orientation to community organizing. Recall the focus of that orientation: a group of people coming together because of a common interest whose immediate goal is to learn together. Teachers might more comfortably see defining purpose in that way: as learning with and from parents the terms, the ideas, and the practices that are unclear or problematic for them. Asking parents to write or sketch something about the strengths of the reading program or writing program, as well as their questions or concerns about such programs may lead to the group's purpose becoming something like "learning about whole language" or "understanding multiage classrooms."

But first, of course, how do teachers move from the step of establishing community and credibility to actually putting together a group of parents who might talk about their purpose? How can teachers get all the parents in their class to come together as a solid community? Does a community organizing approach mean all kinds of extra meetings with these parents? And how might this help with the issues that the teacher sees are important (and which, in fact, are at the foundation of this book): helping to educate parents about curricular issues in education so that they can help teachers' voices be heard in the public conversation?

The teachers whose stories make up Chapter 2 have found some ways to start this process. Most obvious is the approach used by Ronda and Amy in setting up a parent study group. Multiple invitations went to all the parents in their class, asking them to come to a study group meeting; a small number responded at first, a number that grew a bit over the course of the year. Does that represent a failure because not every parent participated? I look back to community organizers to get an answer. Does every neighbor participate in an organizing effort to stop toxic waste? Did every neighbor in my community participate in our attempt to stop the building in our park? The answer, of course, is no—but those of us who did participate made a strong effort to keep others informed and to continue to invite them to be a part of our push.

Similarly, Amy and Ronda continued to invite all parents to come to their meetings, keeping them abreast of what had happened, sending the new readings to every parent in the class, so that new people could join without feeling behind.

Amy and Ronda tried hard to have the parents who did attend help define the purpose for the study group: asking them to identify the issues that concerned them, that they wanted to learn more about. And Amy and Ronda recall that this was difficult.

> *Ronda:* When we were asking them what they wanted to know more about, they couldn't really tell us. They couldn't really be definite about anything.
>
> *Amy:* Because they didn't have enough background knowledge about what to ask. [They'd say,] "Just tell us about reading." [We'd want to know,] "What about reading do you want to know?" And they didn't know what to ask.
>
> *Ronda:* They basically said, "We want to know what you do in your classrooms, so that when kids come home at the end of the day, we can understand what they're talking about.

Is this a contradiction of community organizing if the community members are not the ones who specifically define the purpose of the group? Is it a problem if Amy and Ronda come into the group with a purpose and ask community members to buy into it? Again, I turn back to community organizing for an answer. I recall Tracey Easthope's fishing expeditions, when she has an agenda—such as medical waste incinerators—and she brings that agenda into the community looking for interested participants. Similarly, teachers might walk into their parent communities with some general agendas (writing workshop, inquiry projects, whole language), offering those as possibilities to the parents and looking for takers. I think balance is again the key here: If teacher-organizers come in with a rigid agenda, the group is little more than a class in which the teacher acts in the role of professor and the parents are the students. If, instead, the teacher-organizer offers a general agenda and works with the parents to see if this meets their needs, finding ways for the group to reformulate the purpose until it does mesh with their concerns, then the teacher has kept within the spirit of community organizing. And as Minkler and Pies suggest, if organizers have done a good job in building and establishing the community and credibility, the purpose will often emerge as a joint concern: "[W]hen trust in the community has been demonstrated," they believe, "and when the immediate concerns of people have received primary attention, the organizer's original . . . concerns frequently then are seen by the community's members as having relevance for their lives" (122).

Carolyn, in her inservice nights, takes just that kind of approach: listing a number of possibilities for parents to consider and asking them to let her know what subjects they are most curious about. Teachers, I think, have enough experience to know right away some of the hot topics that concern parents; but they might, in addition, always be on the lookout for that moment in which an issue crops up that might serve as a uniting issue for parents in the class. Kathleen, for example, discovered one year a small group of African American girls who "were not producing anywhere near where I thought they could or should. I had gone through all of the . . . things I know in my little bag of tricks. . . . I made lots of parent contacts and I really wasn't happy with what I was seeing." Inspired by her recent reading of Barbieri's *Sounds from the Heart*, Kathleen invited the girls and their moms to sit down together and to think about some of the issues raised from that book, what she was noticing in class, what the girls and their parents were noticing. Although Kathleen admits, "this was only a one-time thing," the possibility for the development of a group with a particular purpose exists here: a group of African American parents and daughters looking at issues of impending adolescence and how those issues affect their school lives.

Another teacher I know began a parent/teacher writing group in which a small group of parents and teachers got together once a month in someone's home to share their writing and give each other feedback. Billed strictly as a writing group, this group nonetheless served the purpose of introducing the parents to the kinds of approaches to writing that the teacher practiced in his classroom: choosing one's own topic, prewriting and drafting, revision strategies, and peer responses.

In some cases, I know, teachers are simply unable to form a group outside the parameters of the classroom. Teachers with busy lives may not be able to offer outside inservices, writing groups, or study groups. Parents with busy lives may not be able to participate in any of these offerings. Can these teachers still use community organizing techniques to help pull the parents together so that they both feel more like a community and are more united in their understanding of best practices? I believe so, and, again, I turn to community organizing to look for an answer. In the advocacy orientation, you'll recall, members of the group do not attend meetings and participate directly in defining the purpose of the group. These members are represented by others, the leaders and organizers, who see part of their job as talking to the members to learn their interests and to help keep these members informed about current trends and ideas. I see this orientation as having a place in the world of classroom teachers. I think of several teachers I know who use "walking journals" to stay in tune with the needs of their parents. These teachers designate one or two notebooks as a place for parents to write about their interests and concerns about the schooling their children are receiving. These journals travel from parent to parent, with each new recipient reading the previous comments, responding if appropriate, and adding some of their own. The teacher enters the circle occasionally, reading and responding to what's been written. This process allows the teacher to keep a finger on the pulse of the needs and interests of the community, furthering her or his opportunity to share information about the classroom practices both through the journal and through subsequent mailings home that might speak to issues raised by the parents.

What is important in this step, I believe, is for a teacher-organizer to find a way to include as many parents as possible in identifying issues of concern or interest that they want to understand better. How that is done will be as varied as the multiple orientations of community organizing. Again, the basic principles of community organizing should serve as the guide: "Start where the people are" and "remember that everything is local."

3. Developing Leaders

As I mentioned in the last chapter, community leaders are a vital component in the community organizing mix. Community leaders, because they are members of the community, can be extremely effective in ways that organizers—especially outside organizers—cannot: inspiring friends and neighbors to join a group or having the kind of clout with a decision maker that only someone truly affected by a problem can have. Especially in those groups for whom long-term change is a major goal, developing strong community leadership is a priority; without members of the community who are determined to lead the group over time, long-term change is impossible.

Scads of material on developing leadership can be found in the literature on community organizing, most of it focusing on what some see as a community organizing truism: leaders lead, and organizers develop leaders. In this way of viewing leadership, "leaders are not born but developed, usually by organizers" (Delgado, *Organizing* 180). In its most traditional sense, the organizer's role is to determine who in the growing membership has the potential to be a leader and then to pluck that person from the masses and train him or her in the fine arts of leadership. For many of the social action groups in particular, learning how to identify and develop leaders is one of the most important skills an organizer can learn.

But even in groups in which this goal is less formalized, even in groups in which the organizer, too, is an indigenous member, this concept of developing leadership is key. Whether identification and training of leaders becomes a formal project or whether these leaders appear to emerge more naturally in a kind of self-selection process, I think it is important to consider both the characteristics of good leaders and the ways in which good leadership can be encouraged.

Gary Delgado believes that "leadership is not structural; it is a function" (*Organizing* 180); in other words, leadership in an organizing group is not a merely a position or a title but rather an action. Those who become leaders generally do so for a couple of reasons—either because they have a compelling interest in the *issue* at hand or because they have a compelling interest in the *process* involved in organizing a group of people. And according to the organizers with whom I spoke, both qualities are important: People who feel an issue deeply are likely to become good leaders because of that concern, but they also have to be able to move beyond that personal response in order to learn the process of how to move their concern into a priority issue for others. Beyond that, good leaders must be people whom "other people respect, listen to, go to for advice, and support" (Israel); they must be people who are "good listeners . . . good list keepers . . . with a sense of humor" (Cantor).

A number of organizers recognize the necessity of expanding the concept of leadership beyond the "natural leader" notion (that some people are just naturally born to be leaders) and beyond the rigid definition of who makes a good leader (the charismatic, well-spoken, hardworking group member). Most organizers today seem to recognize the necessity of trying to develop a number of leaders within a group, for several reasons. First, such an approach tries to take advantage of the various skills and talents present within a group (i.e., the articulate person, the writer, the artist, the one who can knock on doors easily and talk to people, the visionary, and so on.) In this way of thinking , each of the necessary jobs in a group is valued and labeled as an important element of leadership. Second, by developing a number of leaders, organizers hope to create a sense of collective ownership (i.e., the more people who feel responsibility for a group, the more solid the group will become). Third, organizers know that leaders often leave a group, either because they move away or because they just become burned out. And as Barbara Israel says, "[when] there's more emphasis placed on one leader and he or she disappears . . . then things fall apart."

One fascinating example of this multiple leadership occurred in an eleven-year battle by a group of citizens in the small town of Milan, Michigan, to keep a toxic waste dump from being built in their community. The original group of 13 members grew to over 1,000, with more than 4,000 people attending one public hearing. While the group relied on outside organizers for advice and support (specifically, Tracey Easthope's group The Ecology Center and Lois Gibbs's organization Center for Health, Environment and Justice), the leadership within the community developed and grew as various citizens took on different jobs. According to Hank Dertian, one of the citizen leaders, "What was really amazing was that we had people in the community who had all the skills we needed" (qtd. in Davey 7). This large group divided itself into several committees, each with specific functions and leaders which rotated over time: the technology/research committee, the membership committee, the public relations/media committee, the government affairs committee, and the events committee. The tech/research committee, for example, researched the facts of the potential hazardous facility and "fed the group facts, building a persuasive case against the dump" (Davey 8). They learned the facts and arguments about hazardous waste, becoming extremely skilled in the language of the opponent, so that they could wage both an information and a media campaign wisely and convincingly. This large membership and rotating leadership allowed the group to be able to continue for eleven years, until finally the company just gave up. Tracey Easthope, you may recall from the last chapter, credits the success of this group to its leadership model: "They have more leaders than any fight I've seen. . . . It's totally inspirational and I think it's because they had shared leadership."

So what does an organizer do to help develop this kind of committed leadership, finding and encouraging multiple leaders who will be enthusiastic and hardworking, who will be change agents and bulldogs in order to effect change? Answers seem to run the gamut from formalized leadership training to a kind of learning-by-doing, with a number of organizations stressing some of each. At one end, some organizers function in an immersion model in which the leaders learn by being immersed in their campaign, much like the Milan struggle. The organizers in this approach serve as a kind of advisor, both in steering the leaders toward the sources for accurate content information and in helping them learn the process for creating change. The PIRG model, for example, "has always been learning by doing," according to Andy Buchsbaum. "What typically happens is the leadership is developed by people doing work on particular issues and learning it. . . . The organizer, hopefully, doesn't do the work. The organizer helps [the leaders] do the work." Tracey Easthope describes her job in developing leaders as "talking them through the process of mounting a campaign," referring them to resource manuals and helping them learn "the menu of people to approach and the things to do." For other organizers, much of the process of leadership development involves modeling, demonstrating in all of their actions a way of group process that focuses on the skills of listening, reflecting back, encouraging discussion, connecting the ideas put forth so far—and then analyzing with the group the effectiveness of these strategies. Barbara Israel describes her role in working with a community of employees in an auto plant for six years as "more behind the scenes—encouraging, facilitating, talking about the issues": "[W]e spent a lot of time . . . processing with them what strategies we were taking, how we were going to find problems, how we were prioritizing problems, what next steps needed to be made, but it was all in the context of doing it, rather than sending people away for training." In a model like ACORN, the approach to developing leaders is a bit more formalized, as organizers actively seek leaders who will become members of the organizing committee and whom they then train to run neighborhood meetings: setting agendas, forming committees, making presentations, and so on. In the most formal setting, community leaders often attend a training program, offered by any of the numerous organizations mentioned in the last chapter, programs that—at their best—connect their training directly to the specific neighborhood issues. Barbara Israel, like many other organizers, sees a combination of approaches here as beneficial. "What I think is ideal," she explains, "is if people are participating in a [formal] training, [they can do it] with other people [from their community], and have an organizational base to go back to."

Other community organizers talk about the tensions they sometimes feel in turning over leadership to group members. While everyone I spoke with recognizes that this transfer of leadership is vital, sometimes organizers find it difficult to accomplish. Tracey laughs about some of the difficulties she's had with this:

> One thing that's clear, that wasn't clear to me in the beginning, is that . . . organizer's creed that says "put yourself out of a job". . . .

> I actually have trouble with this part of it. It's hard for me to know how much to give to people and how to make them autonomous. . . . My instinct is to help people as much as possible.

Renee Bayer explains that, for her, the problem was one of trusting perspectives that didn't always make sense to her and learning not to be judgmental:

> [I've learned] people's behavior always makes sense in some way or another. People consistently do things that make sense. So if you don't understand, it's not their problem. . . . It's your problem.
>
> But the other thing is just suspending judgment. . . . [W]e always want to make very quick judgments, especially as trained professionals. From our educational experience, we're supposed to be able to make very quick judgments.

She shares an example that helped her realize this, explaining her early work in Detroit when she was organizing with women on public assistance.

> *Renee:* What do I know about women's lives on welfare? I didn't know anything about it. Why would anyone use layaway [I thought]. You pay all this extra money to use layaway.
>
> *Cathy:* 'Cause you don't have enough money, right?
>
> *Renee:* Well, actually that's only a part of it. But the other part is that you get your check every two weeks or every month. You get a check and you have to spend your check. You aren't allowed to save enough of your checks, because then they'll stop giving you welfare. . . .Well, you don't have enough to buy a coat, but you have enough to put some money down each time. And you aren't allowed to save any of it. That's against the budgeting rules. So you put a little down each month, and in six months, by the time winter comes, you've got your coat. It makes tons of sense within their budget. For us, it makes no sense at all. So, it took me months to figure out that everything they do makes sense . . . within their world, [even if] I couldn't figure it out.

This new understanding has transferred for Renee into her work in developing leadership in groups, learning to trust other people's perspectives, to trust that leaders will step up.

> Something I literally do is sit on my hands. When I find myself taking too much of a leadership role that takes control of the situ-

ation or tries to move a situation a certain way, I literally will sit on my hands and I'll just lean forward. . . . I've started to limit myself to being able to talk three times in a meeting. And after three times I don't allow myself to talk anymore. . . . A lot of times I found myself putting things in, . . . if I'd just waited, there would have been other leadership that would have come along, and another voice that would have come along. My voice, the words I have to say, are rarely the most important, even though I think I'm going to say them just right.

Examples from Teachers

- Offering parent lending libraries
- Attaching teaching letters to student work
- Parent study group
- Parent newsletters
- Making casual suggestions to parents
- Providing forums for parent discussions
- Suggesting parents talk with each other
- Focusing on potential parent leaders for further conversations

What I learn from a community organizing approach to leadership is this: Organizers need community leaders, and part of their job is to help community members take on leadership roles, "so that the community is better able to organize itself in the future" (Pilisuk, McAllister, and Rothman 112). Organizers need to see this leadership development as a conscientious effort on their part, seeking and encouraging potential leaders in the group, as they help educate leaders in strategies for how to organize and to gain information about the focus issue.

How might this concept transfer to the work of teachers? When I think back to the anecdote which opens this book—Cathy Gwizdala's work with parents which led one parent to address the state board of education—I recognize that the development of parent leaders who can become vocal in the public setting is at the heart of my vision of proactive change. Parent leaders, who grow into an understanding of the content of the best practices under fire, who grow into an understanding of how to do something to share that content knowledge more widely, are a vital component for any reopening of the dialogue on public education. For teacher-organizers, then, figuring out ways to develop parent leaders is an important next step.

But again, this next step takes teachers into a delicate balancing act. While teacher-organizers might recognize the potential in the first half of this step—helping to develop parents' content knowledge—the second half—helping them learn strategies for organizing—presents some real dilemmas. First of all, most teachers are not that familiar themselves with organizing strategies (despite what they might learn from a book like this), and so the idea of sharing those untried acts with others when so much is at stake might seem overwhelming and even a bit arrogant. But even more important, teachers do occupy precarious positions in their schools when they start to think about themselves as community organizers. Is it really their job, as public employees, to help train parents in action steps which might implicitly or explicitly criticize certain school or district policies? What might be the consequences for teachers who begin to think in this way?

Becoming political is not an easy step for teachers, I know, but we might do well to think of teachers taking on these roles in almost a series of stages—stages that, like community organizing, depend so much on the contexts of the community. Some teachers, for example, might feel most comfortable in trying to educate all parents and letting leadership emerge from that group in a more casual, self-selecting way. In other words, parents who become informed about certain issues become leaders simply as they talk to other parents in line at the grocery store or at the soccer game. Other teachers might do the same kind of education for parents but be a little more directive in their approach, making casual suggestions to parents about what they might do with this newfound knowledge when they recognize a contradiction or conflict between the best practices they learn from the teacher and the policies they see being enacted at another level. For other teachers, a more straightforward political approach might make sense: becoming part of a concerted effort by parents and teachers to effect change by, for example, forming or participating in a reform group.

The key to making any of this work, however, is in offering parents a chance to learn about some of the issues they have indicated are important to them. Without this educational component, knowledgeable leaders who can spread the word to others will not exist. When I look to the examples of teachers with whom I have worked, I see them focusing on this aspect of parent outreach in some wonderful ways. Carolyn and Kathleen, for example, have put together libraries of books on teaching practices, generally offering to lend these books to parents, but specifically pulling out a volume when a particular parent asks a question. You may recall from Chapter 2 the occasion when Carolyn urged one parent who began to question her math program to check out a book entitled *Maths in the Mind* (Baker and Baker). This mother, a university-level mathematician, had what Carolyn called "strong opinions about the math program not being sufficient": "I could tell at conference time the mom was really nervous because she was going to blast it." So, Carolyn talked to the parent about her expertise in math, suggesting, "Maybe there's some way you can come in . . . to have some of these kids who desperately need it to work with you." This parent read the book, began to see how it might be used with kids, and began to volunteer in the classroom, trying out some of what she read.

Another excellent example of parent education comes from the teaching letters Kathleen has developed. Again, as I explained in Chapter 2, Kathleen uses teaching letters after she's finished a unit and students have produced an anthology of their work such as poetry or memoir. In the letter she sent home about the poetry the students had just completed, for example, Kathleen explained to parents some of what the kids had done in their writing, offering them instruction in some of the nuances of the work:

> Look for detail, alliteration, line breaks, the use of threes, and using old words in new ways. Our writing has greater impact in part because we're learning to use vivid verbs and pare down unnecessary words. Watch for the use of the five senses in our poems. And just as published authors do, we're writing about things that really matter to us.

In that short passage, Kathleen has taught parents so much about what she values in poetry writing: subjects that matter, great attention to word choice, detail. What I also notice is what she *doesn't* stress—rhyme, metaphor, iambic pentameter, and lofty subjects—all the elements that I was taught and evaluated on in my futile attempts to write poetry as a student, and which were probably the elements familiar to those parents who recall similar attempts. This kind of teaching letter gives parents a new way to think about poetry, a new language with which to talk about it, and teaches them what is valued in this way of education.

Further, you'll recall, Kathleen asks parents to respond to the poetry, again teaching them about a kind of response that does not look at spelling or grammar: "Please take a minute to respond to us. What did you notice, wonder, feel, what surprised you or connected to your own experience, what reminded you of another poem." Again, Kathleen teaches the parents about response, setting the stage for them for the kinds of authentic assessments teachers use with children in this new way of teaching. Kathleen then sends this anthology home with a parent whom she knows will respond generously and enthusiastically, making use of a parent who has already shown leadership potential and having that parent model for others a kind of response. As the book makes its way to the other parents, they are learning so much about the ways of teaching that are valued in that classroom.

Other teachers are using similar ways to educate parents about their teaching approaches and, in so doing, trying to find parent leaders. Amy and Ronda base their parent study group on this concept, introducing parents to many of the issues which are central in the controversies about best practices, through reading, discussion, and hands-on practice. These parents become familiar with the concepts, as they begin to grasp the terminology connected with certain ways of teaching. As Judy Kelley, the language arts consultant for that school district who attended one of the group meetings, told me one day, "Once these parents started making whole language jokes, I knew Amy and Ronda had gotten somewhere." Julie tries to help parents understand the language and the concepts behind it through the work of her students. As they create a newsletter about their classroom including articles with titles like "Conferences 'R' Us," "Mini Lessons," "Writing In Literary Logs," and "Come Sit in the Author's Chair," these middle schoolers are able to instruct their parents about the ins and outs of their classroom, introducing them to concepts which may be unfamiliar, but which become clear through the students' own language.

Cathy Gwizdala is one teacher who also makes use of less formal measures to help educate parents and find potential leaders. She talks about the social occasions—at school events, waiting for the bus for field trips, running into a parent at the grocery store—as a time for a little informal education. In her view, parents who are unable—for whatever reason—to be a part of any formal measures, still want to talk and learn about their children. Often these casual conversations about what's happening in the classroom can have a great impact.

Clearly, the ability of these teachers to educate parents is grounded in their own knowledge, both of best practices in general and of how those practices translate in their own classrooms. These teachers have read thoughtfully, reflected carefully about their own teaching, and articulated first for themselves their underlying beliefs about why they teach in the way they do. For these teachers, coming to understand where they stand has been vital, as it helps them gain confidence in expressing their views to others.

As the teachers begin to articulate this knowledge to others, some parents become natural leaders merely as they talk with others in a spontaneous way. Remember Andy Buchsbaum's mention of the "gossip factor"; some organizers believe that if one-third of a closed community has access to certain information, then the other two-thirds will hear about it. As parents talk to each other about what they've learned, new understandings about curricular issues spread. Even if a teacher has been able to reach only a small percentage of her classroom parents, what they have discovered about their children's learning will expand outward. (As teachers, we all know this is true; think about how *misinformation* spreads through our classrooms and schools, and consider what might happen with well-articulated information.)

What teachers need to consider, though, is how they might make this spreading of knowledge a more-than-incidental next step. What could teacher organizers do to help parents take on a leadership role in more concrete ways? As a first step, I believe teachers can begin to make casual suggestions, just as Amy and Ronda suggested that the parents in their study group might want to attend the meeting in which the school was considering creating a multiage strand for all grade levels. There was no "training" the parents in what to say at that meeting or suggesting that there was a party line to follow, but the parents, newly knowledgeable about certain practices, naturally assumed a leadership role: answering questions posed by other parents and sharing examples of how a multiage classroom worked from their own experiences and the experiences of their children. Similarly, when Carolyn's parents approached her after being confused by the school's proposed policy on enrichment and recognizing how opposed it was to what they had learned about kids' learning from their experiences with her, she suggested they might want to share that with the principal and the school improvement team. This approach of making casual suggestions to parents at that "teachable moment" is a bit more formalized than the incidental approach, but still allows teachers who feel uncomfortable taking a more obvious political stand to work toward developing parent leaders.

Cathy Gwizdala took on an even more formalized approach recently when she asked parents and children to come to a local board of education meeting to share with board members the benefits of her pilot multiage classroom. For Cathy, the stakes were high: Her program had been approved on a short-term basis, and convincing the board of its value mattered greatly. Because she had worked throughout the year to help educate parents and children about *why* she was teaching in particular ways, and because parents began to understand the connections between those ways of teaching and their children's success, these parents and students were enthusiastic about addressing the board—and were able to be convincing in their remarks.

Beyond that, some teachers will be able to be even more concrete, attempting to formalize this leadership development through existing and some newly-created outlets. Consider, for example, the role a teacher-organizer might play on a PTO or a school improvement team. A teacher who sees her role in those settings as one who can continue to educate parents about certain curricular issues also might be able to work with those parents in thinking about how to formally transfer that knowledge outward. A teacher who is already serving on a curriculum development committee might think about how to expand that committee to include a parent education and organizing component. Teachers who are involved in local affiliates of NCTE or National Writing Project sites might consider using those organizations as jumping-off points for starting parent/teacher study groups whose goal might be more directly political.

4. Taking Action

Taking action is not the same thing as creating change. Change, whether it's short-term or long-term, is connected to empowerment and relies upon all the stages I've talked about so far: establishing community and gaining entrée, establishing purpose, and developing leadership. In a community organizing way of thinking, taking action is merely one step in that overall goal of creating change. Action steps alone, in other words, without the other components, won't lead to change in any significant way.

That's not to downplay the importance of taking action. Without action steps, change can only go so far. "Knowledge and information alone, without effective advocacy techniques, will not win," says Alex Sagady, an environmental activist and organizer. For community organizers, action steps are an important element of a full-fledged campaign, and over time a number of groups have developed a bagful of techniques, some tried-and-true methods of taking action in their communities.

But before organizations can shift into figuring out the appropriate action steps for their campaign, they first need to consider what they mean by change, as well as the connection between change and action. Change can take many forms, from *inner-directed personal change* to *outer-directed public change*. As I mentioned in Chapter 3, change might entail an individual's new way of thinking on an issue, or it might entail changing the minds of other people. If the change is public in nature, it might result from *incidental actions*—members of the group talking to their friends and neighbors and putting forth publicly another point of view; it might also be part of a *prearranged action*—a deliberately structured event or series of events designed to change the minds of either a few specific people (like policymakers) or of a large group (the voters in a particular area).

In the traditional Saul Alinsky type of community organizing, change revolved around large-scale events in which a large number of community members would rally against a particular policy by directly confronting a policymaker on the issue. Large numbers and fed up people were the keys here; oftentimes the legislator, faced with the vehement crowd, would agree to make certain changes in policy.

Organizations see taking action a bit differently these days, allowing for that confrontational approach, but also seeing the need for a number of other approaches to reach large groups of people. Barbara Israel explains that the approach toward action depends quite heavily on the context of the community, the style that will seem comfortable to the members and will be effective with those whose minds one is trying to change: "There are times within the Alinsky model that you would so alienate the power structure you're not going to be accomplishing anything, and you can alienate the community members. . . . [Some groups] have been socialized to think they can't do anything. To come in and say we're going to do an Alinsky style action—they're going to alienate themselves." Again, for Barbara, this is where the idea of mixing and phasing comes in, as organizations see the action step as arising most appropriately out of "where the people are" at the moment, moving in and out of each orientation's notion of change depending on the context of the situation. If one is working with a group of people, for example, for whom collective action is a totally foreign concept because of their feeling that they have no control over change, then an education orientation is the place to start—"not just consciousness-raising about the problem and the source of the problem, but consciousness-raising about who they are, [about] power, and the ability or inability to bring about change."

Whatever the notion of change fits in with the needs and context of a particular community, the action steps that follow must be part and parcel of an overall approach. Sherry and Lipschultz, for example, explain that an action

> must be designed and implemented in a manner which (1) enhances the leadership and advocacy capabilities of the program participants, (2) develops their identification with and accountability to their constituent group, and (3) promotes a network

among individuals within and outside [the group] who have common concerns. (210)

In other words, actions are not a separate entity, but rather part of a cycle of change. Effective actions will not only move the group toward a particular change but also will do so in a way that helps to continually develop and empower the group.

So, where does a group start in developing an action plan? Again, certain questions seem significant to ask:

- What is the comfort zone of the community group? What kind of action fits within their understanding of change? What are the strengths and resources within the community group to carry out the action?

- What are the needs of the group? What kinds of change do they need to accomplish to order to feel successful?

- Is the change desired easily definable? Or is it a large-scale change that might be broken down into several action steps?

- Is the action winnable? If not, what can you hope to accomplish by mounting the action?

- Is there an opposition? If so, how can the group anticipate the moves the opposition will take?

Selecting and Cutting the Issue

For some organizers, developing an action plan begins with *selecting and cutting the issue*. As Lee Staples explains, "In community organizing, issue campaigns are both ends and means. Organizations are formed as vehicles to address issues, and the issues that they are created to resolve help the organizations grow and flourish. . . . Good issue campaigns [therefore] should have the twin goals of winning a victory and producing organizational mileage while doing so" (175). Selecting an issue on which to mount action steps is different, though, from defining purpose. Andy Buchsbaum explains the difference in this way:

> Your message is not the same as your purpose. Instead it's the communication of your purpose. For example, our group had the purpose of passing an environmental cleanup bond. Our message could go in a couple of ways. Is it that passing this bond will clean up all our environmental problems? Or is it that passing the bond is the taxpayers' down payment only, that the polluters still will need to do their fair share? When you cut it differently, your tactics will be different.

In other words, cutting an issue is part of an organization's strategic thinking process, as the group attempts to figure out the best way to reach a large number of people and to attempt to convince them of a certain point of view. Cutting an issue may include, among other things, identifying any opposition and considering thoughtfully how they might respond to an issue. Staples suggests that this consideration include "an analysis of potential (or actual) opposition, what is needed to overcome it, and who has the power to make the decisions necessary to produce an organizational victory" (190). Cutting an issue might also include identifying certain handles or hooks that a group might use to draw attention to its cause, such as those "teachable moments" which might help the group capture the public's attention.

Andy Buchsbaum describes one of the handles used by a number of advocacy groups—a postcard campaign. As mentioned in the last chapter, advocacy groups who use this approach typically have members sign preprinted postcards to be delivered to legislators, protesting certain actions or urging passage of certain bills. The usual next step is to stage a media event which centers on the ceremonial dumping of these huge masses of postcards on the desk of the policymaker. Andy recounts one occasion which captures the power of this kind of handle, both for winning a particular issue and for gaining power for the organization:

> The PIRGs and some other groups, led by the PIRGs, tried to generate a million postcards in defense of environmental statutes that are on the books but that the Republican congress was trying to roll back. So, Stop the Rollback was the campaign. While PIRG has got more full-time advocates on this issue than any other group in Washington, nobody was making a dent. [Eventually] they generated over a million postcards, . . . had a news conference to announce this, and then they delivered them to the people who needed to get them. Within hours, the PIRG director in Washington . . . was not only in demand by the media, but also by top legislative offices. He was at some reception and Clinton came up and asked to be introduced to him because of the postcards.

Choosing Appropriate Tactics

Finding a handle not only helps in cutting the issue but also overlaps into a consideration of the tactics that might fit a particular course of action. Again, as a group decides on the kinds of tactics it wants to use, it must think about the comfort level of the members and the anticipated response of others in the community (including those people who may be charged with making a decision on the issue). According to Si Kahn, author of *Organizing: A Guide for Grassroots Leaders*, a good tactic must have at least these eight characteristics:

- A good tactic must be winnable;
- A good tactic affects a lot of people;
- A good tactic unites people;
- A good tactic involves people;
- A good tactic is strongly felt;
- A good tactic is simple;
- A good tactic builds the organization;
- A good tactic is fun. (195–7)

A number of existing books provide excellent discussions of the many, many possible tactics that organizing groups might use.[3] Actions range from the kind of large-scale, in-your-face approaches of groups like Greenpeace (as activists steer small boats into the paths of whalers to try to prevent illegal or unethical fishing practices) and various practitioners of civil disobedience (whose tactics might range from hunger strikes to takeovers of buildings) to more low-key actions that might be more commonly undertaken by community groups. Among those more low-key actions, ones that I think would be more applicable to teacher-organizers, I've noticed that most tactics fall into one of four overlapping groups:

Kinds of Tactics

1. Action or educational events

2. Shared information

3. Media work
   - Creating necessary contacts
   - Creating media events
   - Writing to the media
   - Keeping watch over the media

4. Direct contact with elected decision makers

1. **Actions or educational events** usually focus on some kind of large scale occurrence that will help bring attention to the cause and educate others: workshops on a topic, rallies or gatherings, public contests or demonstrations. Examples might include a rock concert to raise money and awareness of the plight of homeless people in the community; a workshop for interested community members on recycling, including a demonstration on composting; a contest to name a bird that's just made the endangered species list; a rally filled with speakers and entertainment to protest nuclear arms.

The key to these events is the combination of entertainment and education: Large numbers of people may come for the entertainment but get a dose of the education at the same time.

2. **Shared information**—whether face-to-face or in other forms—is another viable tactic for action. This type of action might involve knocking on doors and distributing information on a flyer; it might involve using telephone trees to reach a large number of people; it might involve setting up in a public place and distributing information or asking people to sign a petition to support a cause. It might involve preparing "fact sheets," easily understandable lists of facts that help those less familiar with an issue come to understand it easily and clearly. It might also involve what I've been calling incidental contact, such as talking to a neighbor or colleague at a spontaneous moment—or even talking to that stranger sitting next to you on the plane.

3. The third kind of action step—**media work**—is a bit more complex and seems to fall into a few categories: (1) creating the necessary contacts and background with the media so that your group becomes the one they will call when they need a comment; (2) creating media events; (3) writing to the media on specific issues; and (4) keeping an eye and ear on the media so that you can respond appropriately to stories they have published that your group disagrees with.

The first kind of media work—creating the necessary contacts—is a sort of proactive response to any issue and involves calling an editorial page editor or beat reporter (whatever beat your issue falls under), for example, talking about your group and its goals and letting them know the expertise that you hold. Such a first contact is important for a couple of reasons: First, it lets these reporters and editors know the expertise your group holds on an issue; the hope is that when the issue comes up at some point, they will know who to contact for a comment. Second, if the issue becomes one about which the publication or station will run an editorial, the editors have heard from you personally and may use that information in making their decision about which side to support. Again, being certain of your facts and information is vitally important at this stage; the more credibility you gain with the media, the more they will rely on the information you share with them.

The second kind of media work centers on creating media events. These kinds of actions are necessary once a campaign has begun and your group wants to reach as many people as possible. Media events range from that dumping of thousands of postcards on a legislator's desk to demonstrating dangers of certain children's toys the month before Christmas. According to Marc Caplan, media events must be action-oriented (i.e., something must happen, not just be reported), must include a positive call for action, must be timely, and, if you want television coverage, must be visual. Calls to the various media outlets, including a news release about the event, are necessary to assure coverage. News releases, many organizers have told me, must be carefully written, sounding exactly as you'd want them to sound once printed in a newspaper, since many times, if no reporter covers your actual event, a newspaper might simply reprint your release as you've given it to them.

The third approach to the media—writing letters to the editor—is a common and powerful action step. Some groups host letter-writing days, in which all members of the group come together for an afternoon and write letters to various news outlets. Andy Buchsbaum talks about the three kinds of letters you might write: a letter of support in response to a positive editorial, a letter of concern about something not being covered, and a letter of rebuttal to a story or to another letter to the editor. On this last type, he offers some good advice: "Since letters to the editor are a highly read section of the paper, make sure that if your letter is in response to an article in the paper, you don't repeat the argument of the story, thereby giving more play to the [original] argument with which you disagree. Instead, mention only that *your* letter is in response and make your argument the crux of the piece."

In addition to letters to the editor and news releases, organizations may want to try to get pieces placed in the Living or Features sections of their newspapers, again because these are highly read sections of the paper. The kinds of articles placed here are more slice-of-life stories, stories about people and occurrences, rather than specific media-created events or actions. Again, proactive contact with a beat reporter is essential here; if the reporter already knows you and your interests, your alerting him or her to a newsworthy story is more likely to be successful.

The last kind of media action is a kind of reactive response—making sure the information reported by the media is accurate. Nancy Amidei in her article "How to Be an Advocate in Bad Times," talks about forming "truth squads," whose job is to keep an eye and ear on the media and refuse to let them get away with reporting "wild charges" and half-truths. She suggests dividing a community group up (i.e., the newspaper group, the radio group, the TV news group), arming them with good information, and having them monitor the media—and always calling in to correct misinformation. "You will not always get into print, but a point will be made with the editors all the same," she says (108–9). In my own experience with trying to stop the construction of the building in the park across the street, our group noticed that any time misinformation made it into a news story (and all community organizations need to realize that is the norm for reporting) and our spokesperson called the reporter to correct a misunderstanding—and did so in a gracious way—the next article that went in seemed more accurate and actually more sympathetic to our side.

4. A fourth kind of tactic involves **direct contact with elected decision makers**, such as legislators or school board members. Because these people rely on the will of the public for reelection, certain strategies generally affect them more immediately: those that involve large numbers of people and those that are attached in some way to media coverage. Thus, while an individual letter to your congressional representative may not carry much clout, a large number of letters, postcards, or faxes—all relaying similar information—may carry weight. Thus, a number of community groups push for letter-writing campaigns in which sample letters or postcards are distributed to a large number of people; as a result, those who want to respond to an issue but who feel they don't have the time or the expertise to create their own letter can merely copy the original and sign their names. In similar fashion, phone campaigns in which members of a group are provided with a basic script from which to talk are also effective. Legislators generally tally the number of people in favor of and opposed to specific legislation, based on the phone calls and letters.

Also effective with decision makers is an action directed toward them which has media coverage attached: inviting a legislator whose stances match your group's to be part of an educational event to give the legislator some positive feedback, effective testimony by members of your group at a public meeting which has media coverage, or staging a media event in a legislator's office (such as the postcard campaigns). Citizens can be extremely effective lobbyists, especially if they are given a little training in how to do it (see Figure 1).

Do's

1. Be prompt for your appointment (or a little early).

2. The legislator may be late; be prepared to wait, and don't mention it if the legislator or his or her aide is late.

3. Dress professionally.

4. At least one person on your team should bring in a notepad and pen.

5. Identify yourself to the receptionist in the office, giving your name, who you represent, and the time of your appointment.

6. Be polite and friendly at all times, even if the person you talk to is hostile or rude.

7. Ask lots of questions, rather than making statements (e.g., Have you heard of PIRGIM? Are you familiar with the legislation?).

8. Listen carefully to what the legislator says. Our goal is to gather information, not just to impart it. Did the legislator say he or she supports the legislation, or did he or she merely imply support?

9. Answer questions directly; don't evade them or try to explain your answer before you make it. If possible, start every answer with a "Yes," "No," or "I don't know."

10. Say "I don't know, but I'll find out and get back to you" if you don't know an answer.

11. Write on a notepad any questions the legislator has that require follow-up.

12. Thank the legislator for his or her time.

13. After you leave the office, immediately write down the legislator's response and questions, and what you think the legislator's main concerns were. Write these down in as much detail as possible so we can go over them when you return to the office.

Don'ts

1. Don't simply give a presentation. Questions from the legislator are good; encourage them. Try to get a dialogue going with the legislator; try to raise his or her concern about the issue.

2. Don't answer a question if you're not sure of the answer. Your credibility, as well as PIRGIM's, depends on accuracy.

3. Don't try to pin down the legislator too much. If the legislator evades your questions on supporting the bills, try one follow-up question, and then go on to the other areas you want to cover.

4. Don't threaten or confront the legislator, even if she or he is obnoxious or rude. Our role is to give the legislator information on the issue, the bills, and his or her constituents' concerns. It is up to the individual legislator to evaluate that information.

Figure 1: Do's and don'ts of lobbying (from a Public Interest Research Group in Michigan [PIRGIM] handout written by Andy Buchsbaum and given to student and citizen members).

Examples from Teachers

- Spontaneous action
  - Parents talking to parents
  - Parents talking at board meetings, PTO meetings
- Educational events
  - Student-led conferencing
  - Parent inservices
  - Student publishing parties
  - Poetry nights
  - Family literacy nights
- Shared information
  - Student anthologies
  - Teaching letters
  - Student work in public places
  - Web sites
- Media work
  - Letters to the editor
  - Making contact with the education reporter
  - Sending media releases (or having students write them)
  - Letter-writing days
  - Forming "truth squads"
- Legislative contact
  - Inviting legislators, board members to your classroom
  - Writing letters
  - Sending faxes
  - Making phone calls

For many teachers, this transition into taking action might seem to be a leap into the dark. While a number of educators feel comfortable with developing a community of students and even parents and helping those groups define their purpose, taking action seems to reek of "politics," a scary proposition to many teachers. Tactics for taking action may, at times, appear too complicated and too time-consuming for all but the most activist teachers. The challenge, then, becomes what busy teachers can do to take action steps which might integrate with their own teaching, making this step a *part of* rather than an *add-on*.

Dividing this step into some of the component parts I spoke of above might be one way to start, beginning with the strategic thinking involved in **selecting and cutting the issue**. If, for example, a group of teachers and parents decided that their purpose was to learn more about whole language and how it's used in the classroom, and if the group decides to take its knowledge and go more public, there are a number of ways they might cut the issue, each of which would send them in a slightly different direction. For example, the issue might be named and cut as (1) "Whole language works well with all kids," or as (2) "Phonics alone doesn't teach kids to read and write, but using phonics *in conjunction with* whole language approaches will teach kids the literacy they need," or as (3) "A true whole language program already includes phonetic strategies." Each cut of the issue implies differences in how to approach the public on it: ranging from providing evidence that whole language works to teach all kids, to showing how what's now known as a "balanced approach" works in the classroom, to conducting an education campaign that shows the various kinds of cueing strategies used in learning to read and explains how phonics fits as one of the strategies. Carolyn Berge, for example, when she offers a matrix of possibilities for parent workshops, puts across her literacy program this way: "Literacy: Reading and Writing, Speaking and Listening. For those interested in phonics, invented spelling, and how to respond to a child's writing when you can't read a word of it but know it must be wonderful!" This cut places the emphasis on the celebration of the child's writing, with an implication that phonics and invented spelling *both* play a part in developing literacy—a cut which speaks well to the parents in Carolyn's school.

Beyond cutting the issue, teachers like the ones I've been heavily quoting so far are using various tactics, many of them in conjunction with the parent groups with whom they are working. At the level of *spontaneous action*, think about Amy and Ronda's parent study group and their presence at the schoolwide parent meeting to consider a switch to a multiage school, and think about Carolyn's parents who approached the principal when they were unhappy with the way a new program was being shaped by the school improvement team. And even more examples of this happen every day, as parents take leadership positions and help inform others in their communities about best practices, just by taking the action step of talking to others in a casual way.

But teachers and groups of parents can and do move beyond these casual encounters, taking action by sponsoring *educational events* and by using *shared information*, *media contact*, and *legislative contact*. Among the kinds of *educational events* teachers create are the kinds of inservice nights Carolyn offers, evenings in which parents can get together to learn about topics on which they have requested additional information. And like a true educational event, Carolyn's inservices combine entertainment and information, as she asks the parents to write and to share their writing and then uses that as a basis for the explanations she offers (even giving them gold stars for their work!).

Similarly, Amy and Ronda combine entertainment and information in their parent study group evenings, recognizing the need for hands-on experiences for the parents: for example, asking them to start out with a traditional spelling test on the night they discuss alternative ways of spelling instruction, asking them to journal as they discuss ways of writing, and giving them time to play with various math manipulatives.

Other teachers I've talked with over the years use these educational events in very positive ways to educate a larger number of parents than their core group includes. Jennifer Walsh is one of many teachers who uses student-led conferencing as a way of bringing parents into the school for an evening to learn about their children's writing. Sue Kohfeldt is part of a growing corps of educators who publish children's writing in a class anthology and then initiate book-signing parties which bring parents and other community members into the school for an evening event. Other teachers plan poetry nights at school in which students read poetry in a coffeehouse atmosphere, family literacy nights where children and parents write family stories together, and even, in one case I know of, an Egypt museum in the school gym, which parents were invited to tour in order to see what the children had learned during their study of Egyptian history.

Many of these events bring the actual ways of teaching—the best practices—into the public eye, advertising, if you will, the kinds of products kids can create when immersed in certain curricular approaches. Proud parents who see this work begin to learn something about the kinds of teaching that go into these products. And as Phillip Schlechty, author of *Schools for the Twenty-First Century* insists, providing parents with this information is vital, because parents and community leaders "must have some product that will persuade them the schools are performing as they want them to perform. Until educators develop such products, test scores will continue to dominate the thinking of many outside the schools" (94). Simply by immersing parents in these kinds of educational events—events which are so beneficial to the students' learning—we can take a big step toward changing the mindset about what products count.

This kind of large-scale educational event can be coupled with what I've termed above as *shared information*: what in this context I see as getting the kids' work into the hands of parents and others in the community. When teachers like Kathleen send home anthologies of student work to parents, it accomplishes the goal of informing parents about the kinds of work their children are doing. When it's coupled with a teaching letter, it adds even more—helping the parents understand why certain skills are being stressed. Many teachers are beginning to move beyond sharing the information with just the classroom parents: using the public library as a repository for classroom anthologies or using the walls of a local hospital or other public building to hang students' writing, much as art teachers have done for years in displaying students' art to the community at large. Some teachers have taken classroom anthologies and distributed them around the community: to doctors' and dentists' offices and other spots where people flip through magazines as they wait for appointments. One school district I know has been creating an immense Web site on which they have placed both the writing curriculum and samples of student writing at each grade level, linked to suggestions for how to help one's child in his or her writing (such as writer's tricks, revision strategies, and ways to get started). All of these approaches are tactics that help larger numbers of people begin to see what is really going on in the schools, thus helping to make familiar what might be unfamiliar practices.

Media work is another area in which teachers can make headway. Making contact with the education reporter for the local newspaper, for example, and letting that reporter have access to some of your knowledge and classroom examples can help in both creating a story for the reporter and influencing how she or he might report other stories on education. In my own experience, simply calling the education reporter for our local paper and pitching the National Writing Project site which I direct resulted in a story in the Living section of the paper, complete with photographs of and quotes from the participating teachers. Sue Kohfeldt, whose students recently produced an anthology of their work, asked a student to call all the local papers in a twenty-mile radius to publicize an upcoming book-signing celebration; this resulted both in an announcement in several newspapers prior to the event and in coverage of the event itself in the Living section of two of these papers, complete with pictures. Other teachers I know have used press releases to announce events of this kind, even teaching the kids how to write them as both an experiment in a new genre of writing and to receive some press coverage. As certain teaching practices are legitimized by the positive slant given to them in these much-read sections of the paper, they begin to carry some familiarity and some clout. A community member who reads about how National Writing Project teacher consultants experience process writing themselves or how they publish an anthology of their own work becomes a bit familiar with those concepts and thus might respond more openly to the ideas when their own children are following these practices.

Teachers also have begun to write letters to the editor and even some weekly columns about educational events as part of their outreach programs. While this is still done on a somewhat individual basis, think how powerful it might be for a group of teachers to get together on one Saturday afternoon each semester and spend two hours writing letters to various newspapers, both local and national? Or to do this with a group of parents who are part of a study group? These sorts of afternoons might serve both as a kind of information sharing and as education (as teachers and parents consult with each other both on the best ways to phrase something and on the best kinds of information or anecdotes to prove a point). This kind of afternoon might make use of all three kinds of letters mentioned earlier: a positive letter about something reported in the paper, a letter of concern to report on something that has not been reported thus far in the paper, and a rebuttal to a story or editorial which misrepresented some educational issue.

Teachers might also want to form their own versions of "truth squads." What would happen if a group of teachers, committed to keeping tabs on media depictions of teaching practices divided up the media (such as newspapers, talk radio, television) in their community and called up in response to every mischaracterization they discovered? These kinds of calls need not be long or involved; they simply involve a practiced, almost scripted response:

> Hi, my name is _____. I teach _____ grade at _____ School. I (heard/read/saw) your story on _____, and I just want to provide you with a different perspective on it:

In like manner, teachers can begin the process of *responding to certain legislative proposals*. I know that the hardest part of this for most teachers is having the time to even know what the legislature is proposing until it is often too late. This is, in part, where an advocacy orientation comes into play. NCTE, the Whole Language Umbrella, the National Writing Project and other organizations are doing a good job now of letting people know what legislation is upcoming at a national level and providing teachers with phone and fax numbers of legislators and sample letters on how to respond to an issue. I know, from the perspective of an NWPer how effective that response to a legislator can be, as our lobbying efforts year after year seem to keep NWP funding in place even when many other kinds of educational funds are drying up. While this legislative campaign to keep NWP has a number of components (including some strategic efforts by James Gray, Richard

Sterling, Mary Ann Smith, and others at the top of the NWP organization), a large factor in its success has been the efforts of classroom teachers and NWP site directors. At the local level and in an ongoing fashion, a number of NWP sites invite legislators in to watch the teachers at work in the various institutes during the summer and in their classrooms during the school year as they demonstrate effective ways of teaching writing. Local sites also provide legislators with facts and figures as well as anecdotal evidence about the success of the project both locally and nationally. As the congressional vote about continued funding for the NWP approaches each year, teacher consultants and site directors mount a campaign of letters, phone calls, and faxes to their representatives, urging them to continue the funding and allow the good work of the NWP to continue. In addition, a number of NWPers attend a lobbying day each spring in Washington, D.C., talking with legislators and sharing with them their reasons for wanting NWP to continue. This multilevel campaign works well. Legislators continually express how impressed they are with the quality of NWP as a staff development model and as a way to improve student writing, and, most important, they can do so because of their familiarity with the project.

As teachers begin to take certain action steps with legislators and decision makers at a national level, this partnership with our representative groups is vital. At a local level, though, teachers can still make a dent, communicating, for example, with a local school board in a proactive way, sharing the work of students and explanations behind that work, and inviting board members to attend some of the educational events or just to come into the classroom. This proactive approach, coupled with specific response (such as testimony or letters) if the board is considering some sort of action, can help continue to inform and educate the board about issues of concern.

As I've portrayed it thus far, most of the work I have seen done at this action level has come from individual teachers' efforts and not from the work of a community organization. But as I think about the potential for a community group of parents and teachers to work together on these steps, I see some real progress. As I mentioned early on in this book, when Cathy Gwizdala's parent testified in front of the state board of education, the trustees listened in ways that they hadn't to the teachers who testified. Why could Cathy's parents testify so articulately? Because of the work she had done to educate and inform the parents in her community. They took action, because she took the time to create an environment where action steps could take place.

5. Evaluating Progress

Although I've placed evaluation as the last step in this model of community organizing, in reality it is a step that is integrated throughout the process. Community organizers are constantly evaluating their work: As they establish and define their communities, organizers look to assess the boundaries they've set up, asking whether or not they've been inclusive enough or how they might attract more members; as they define purpose, they work with community members to assess their own strengths and needs as a community; as they develop leaders, they assess their own process of selection and development, looking to see if others might join the ranks; as they take action, they assess the outcomes of their attempts, whether wins or losses, and look to the next steps they might take in the process.

And across the various orientations, the means of evaluation vary, from highly numerical assessments in which numbers count heavily to more qualitative assessments in which narrative and anecdotal accounts carry weight. In the social planning orientation, for example, evaluation might center on a follow-up form submitted to the group from a granting agency, an accounting, in many ways, of money well spent. In the advocacy orientation, a group may be evaluated by its board on a checklist of factors, evidenced by a series of numbers and percentages that constitute quantifiable measures of success: for example, its ability to gather new members, to gain access to the media, or to raise money. In a social action or mobilizing orientation, evaluation may center on the planned action: Did the group "win"? And if they did, how well did specific tactics work toward gaining that win? In an education orientation, the focus might be on the number of people educated or on the specific actions they have taken as a result of that education.

Whatever the orientation, evaluation is in most cases considered part of the cycle of change, and as such it takes the group back again to the beginning of the process. Gary Delgado, for example, talks about the ongoing process of creating change: "research—action—reflection—research" (*Organizing* 89). In other words, organizers use the results of their evaluation as a way to continually ask, "What next?"

For some community organizers, however, the whole issue of evaluation has become a sticky one. Assessment measures are often conducted by "outsiders," especially by grant agencies or boards that generally call for quantitative measures; even when they are conducted by insiders, the insiders are often the organizers or staff, leading to assessment measures that do not always call on the expertise and experiences of community members. Because of the participatory nature of the rest of the community organizing process, evaluation approaches which seem too top-down and too separate from the actual experiences and input of community members have, of late, received some criticism. A recent article by Chris M. Coombe speaks to this issue specifically for organizers in the field of public health, but his insights cross boundaries into other disciplines, I think.

In his article, Coombe explores the kinds of evaluation he usually sees in too many forms of community organizing—specifically, approaches which ignore the kinds of empowerment that community organizing is designed to create. He then critiques the traditional forms of evaluation he sees in public health at three levels. First, since many of the quantitative measures that are used focus on an "a priori hypotheses derived from outside the community," much potential knowledge is lost (293). In other words, many approaches to evaluation miss the mark by not asking the right questions and not asking them of the right people. Second, Coombe critiques the methods used in eliciting evaluative data. Because evaluators or evaluation strategies too often come from outside the community, community members are often left out, leaving them too much outside the process (294). Third, he believes that "[r]esults often are not applied to solving underlying problems and may indeed be used in ways that are harmful to the community"(293). In other words, certain findings derived from the evaluation process, because they are based on limited questions and thus cannot get at the whole story, may miss the boat in terms of what's really going on in the community. Coombe contends that such half-information can be harmful in a couple of ways: instead of a focus on action, the findings may lead merely to "further study," and, in some cases, misapplied findings might actually work against the people who originally came together to seek help.

Coombe calls for a different kind of evaluation—what has come to be known as empowerment evaluation in some fields—to create a more democratic and, ultimately, more directly useful kind of evaluation for community organizing. He traces its roots to traditions familiar to those of us who are teacher-researchers: action research, popular education (à la Freire), naturalistic inquiry, participatory research, and feminist research. In a nutshell, he conceives empowerment evaluation in contrast to traditional evaluation measures in this way:

> Breaking up the paradigm in which participants are passive ob-
> jects of study and researchers are the discoverers and creators of
> knowledge, empowerment evaluation establishes a spirit of col-
> laborative inquiry in which community members and evaluators
> work hand in hand. . . . [Empowerment evaluation] goes beyond
> collecting information and links knowing and doing through a
> cyclical process of *investigation, education,* and *action.* (297)

In other words, empowerment evaluation recognizes the voices and
responses of all participants and tries to build their understandings into
the whole process of change, from beginning to end.

Calling on the work of Fawcett, Coombe further lays out a series
of steps to create a process of empowerment evaluation:

> Participants determine where they are now (step one), where they
> would like to go (step two), and how to get there (step three).
> They monitor the journey to make sure that they are on track and
> making progress (step four). They collect and analyze new infor-
> mation along the way so that the project can adjust its course, if
> necessary, in response to changing conditions or unexpected re-
> sults (step five). Finally, they apply what they have learned to
> strengthen the organization and prepare for the next journey (step
> six). (299)

Examples from Teachers

- Asking parents to write in response to study groups,
  inservice nights
- Asking parents to respond to student portfolios, anthologies
- Asking parents to respond to choices for inservice nights,
  study group themes
- Evaluating how many parents are participating, and from
  what groups

For those of us who are teachers and who struggle with issues of
assessment and evaluation all the time, Coombe's charge seems a
familiar one. His musings are reminiscent, to me, of two important
movements in education: authentic assessment and teacher research.
Authentic assessment, of course, centers on the attempt to assess
students in a way that truly reflects the kind of work they are doing,
using real pieces of work, written for real audiences, in real situations.
Often, authentic assessment asks that student voices are incorporated
into the criteria for the assessment, and that the results of the assessment
are used immediately to help students improve in their work. Similarly,

teacher research involves an approach that is context-bound, calling on the voices of those who are the traditional research subjects and involving them in both the collection of information and the interpretation of results, so that such research becomes "researching *with* rather than researching *on*" (Fleischer 63). For teacher-researchers, a close look at a classroom or a teaching practice leads to action: Classroom practitioners take the results of their study and immediately try to put them into effect for the students in the classroom, rather than merely publishing their findings as a call for "further study."

Empowerment evaluation, then, seems to fit right into some of the best practices teachers already know of and use in their classrooms, practices that rely on three basic principles: evaluating throughout the process and not just at the end, involving participants in the assessment, and making use of the evaluation in an ongoing way to benefit those who participated in the study—not saving it for another time, another year. The teachers in Chapter 2 certainly follow these three principles in the evaluations they have done with their parents groups. Amy and Ronda, for example, made use of empowerment evaluation strategies as they constantly assessed the parents in their study group. Almost monthly, they invited the parents to write about their responses to the group itself and to what they were reading. From the beginning, when they asked parents why they joined the study group ("I had concerns about my nine-year-old's reading and wanted to learn how he was learning," or "To stay abreast on my child's education and understand the changes of teaching that have occurred since I went to school to better help my child"), they were able to ascertain the needs of parents and thus design readings and activities that would meet the needs. As the meetings progressed, they were able to discover if their sessions achieved what they had hoped. The following assessments from their session on spelling, in which the group looked at a student-centered approach (including invented spelling, various class activities, and individualized spelling programs) and began a discussion on the place of phonics within a whole language classroom, showed Amy and Ronda both that the parents were "getting it" and that they were feeling comfortable in the sessions:

> Towards the spelling, I learned or actually was reaffirmed that it's OK to look at my child's paper and look at the ideas. I'm somewhat of a perfectionist or from a traditionally spelled correctly background that I always *see* the misspelled words first. So I am reaffirmed, it's OK not to be on the spelling bee.

I enjoyed learning more of what goes on in the classroom—the approach and the methods used. As for spelling, I think that it will be interesting to see how this evolves and how the children's spelling improves.

I felt comfortable tonight. I was very safe, but I didn't feel like I had something to contribute. Thanks for inviting me.

Using these parent comments and taking time together to reflect on their experience has led Ronda and Amy to make further revisions in their approach for the next time they start up a parent study group.

Other teachers, too, rely upon parental assessment throughout their attempts at outreach. Carolyn, for example, assesses parents' needs in the beginning as she hands to them a list of possible inservice nights and asks them to indicate which, if any, would provide meaningful information to them. Julie uses evaluation strategies at the end of the year as she asks parents to respond not only to their children's portfolios but also to her, thus giving these adults the opportunity to raise questions as a result of what they learned from reading their child's work. Other teachers evaluate throughout, using walking journals, anthologies with parent response pages, and casual talk as a way to get feedback from parents about their responses to both the kinds of instruction that are going on and the education they are receiving about that instruction from these teachers.

As teacher organizers think seriously about developing a more sustained approach to organizing their communities, they may find even more ways to integrate parent participants into the evaluation process. Learning from the lessons of empowerment evaluation, teachers might invite parents not only to raise questions but also to be the ones who initiate the assessment process. What if, for example, a group of parents and teachers, concerned about the misuse of standardized tests in their district, came together to study the issue and raise other community members' awareness of it through a series of educational events, and then, to culminate their work, made a presentation to the board of education? An empowerment evaluation approach to assessing this campaign certainly would include an ongoing look at who was participating in the core group, along with constant rethinking by the members about how to increase both the number of participants and their representative groups; an empowerment evaluation approach would also entail looking continually at the kinds of information used to educate the members and making adjustments along the way to seek, for example, additional material in areas that might need more clarification or support; and such an approach would call for the group to look and relook at any actions taken, evaluating how and why they worked (or didn't), who they worked for, and what kinds of actions might reach more people.

The point is that the evaluation would be ongoing, would include as many people as possible both in seeking answers and in interpreting those responses, and would lead to change—ongoing change that continues to inform the next steps taken.

Where Do We Go Next?

I think it's clear from these numerous examples that teachers already follow many of the steps that community organizers would name as vital to their work. A number of teachers do focus on establishing and building a parent community; many set goals and purposes for their outreach programs; they strive to develop leadership among the parents; they envision and encourage taking action; they continually evaluate their progress. And their powerful results speak to the value of this kind of mindset: Parents become more knowledgeable about curricular practices and approaches, and teachers are more aware of the parents' concerns.

I think we can go much further, though. I think we can move from an approach that uses some of these steps on occasion to one that embodies these steps as a cyclical process, as part of a self-conscious and sustained program of outreach and partnership with parents and communities. Such an approach has the potential to create real change—in how teachers are viewed, in how teaching practices are accepted, in how parents and teachers might work together.

The question, of course, is how do we get there? How do we, as teachers and teacher educators, move toward this more sustained approach? In the next chapter, I'll explore some options—in particular for teacher educators and teacher leaders to use in helping move teachers to become teacher-organizers.

Notes

1. See, for example, Don Graves's *A Fresh Look at Writing* (and his many other works), John Gaughan's *Cultural Reflections: Critical Teaching and Learning in the English Classroom*, and Ralph Peterson's *Life in a Crowded Place: Making a Learning Community*.

2. Not all strands of community organizing stress consensus in the same way. The advocacy orientation, for example, because of its large numbers, cannot rely on a consensus approach.

3. For more information on tactics for teachers, see NCTE's packet titled *Shaping the Future of Education: A Guide to Political Advocacy for Educators and Administrators.*

5 Putting It All Together: Becoming a Teacher-Organizer

So, what do we do with all this information? How can a teacher take hold of this process model for community organizing and the examples from the various organizers and teachers provided in the last chapter and make them her or his own? How might she make use of all these bits and pieces and emerge with a sustained program of community building and community organizing that can help her reach out to the surrounding communities, that can help them think in new ways about the pedagogies she espouses? How can he do all that in a way that will recognize the local circumstances of his own school, his own classroom, his own parents? And, most of all, how can he or she do this proactively—before the occasions for battling back arise?

In this chapter I want to accomplish two things. First, I want to provide a few illustrations of what complete outreach programs might look like—and to do so in a contextualized way by beginning with some hypotheticals, each with its own unique contexts and circumstances, and then discussing the possibilities for outreach programs that these hypotheticals call to mind. Second, I want to discuss the transitional step. If we believe that community organizing has the potential to help us educate the public in order to provide an alternative explanation of "what's happening in education," what do we do next? How might we as teacher educators and teacher leaders help both novice and experienced teachers along the journey to become teacher-organizers?

Applying the Community Organizing Model

Let's start with a hypothetical—a scenario loosely based on the real experience of a teacher I know—in order to think through how a teacher-organizer might approach such a situation.

Parts of this chapter were previously published as "Advocating for Change: A New Education for New Teachers" in *English Education* 30 (May 1998): 78–100.

Scenario 1

Michael is a third-year middle school teacher who, inspired by his recent reading and participation in a National Writing Project summer workshop, wants to initiate a reading/writing workshop in his classroom. Excited by such ideas as choice in reading, young adult novels, linking reading with writing, and immersion in the reading/writing process, he is ready to jump into some new ways of teaching. The problem is this: He teaches in a fairly traditional school in which all of the other teachers seem to use grammar worksheets, sentence diagramming, and five-paragraph essay models as the basis of their composition instruction; they use whole-class reading based on an approved list of titles and questions at the end of the chapter as their reading program. Grading for these teachers is a matter of adding up points and assigning a number. Michael is concerned that the parents have come to expect these approaches as the way that their children are taught, and he is particularly worried about using the alternative means of assessment (such as portfolios) which he believes are appropriate to this way of teaching. He knows from experience that the parents expect to be able to call him on any given day to find out what numerical grade their child is getting at that particular moment. And he knows that once he adopts a portfolio system, he will not be able to tell them a specific grade on a specific day any more.

What could Michael do—proactively—to help parents understand and accept the changes he wants to make in his teaching? How might he become a teacher-organizer, using the techniques raised so far in this book, to help him gain support from the parent community for his pedagogy? Keeping in mind the process model for community organizing, I want to suggest some ways Michael might approach this situation.

First, of course, Michael needs to *identify his community* and determine a way to *gain entrée*. As a fairly new teacher, he does not yet have the benefit of a reputation of excellence with parents in this school, a reputation that would perhaps allow him a certain amount of leeway in his pedagogy because of the trust that's been established. And so his first concern must be to build some community with the parents on whom he wants to focus: Perhaps because he is a middle school teacher with, let's say, one hundred students, he may not want to concentrate on all the parents this first year. He might instead make a concerted effort with the parents from one class, while making sure to keep the other parents at least informed. Michael could choose a number of ways to start establishing that community: He probably will want to write a carefully worded letter to go home to every parent after the first day of class, in which he talks about his approaches and his rationale, letting them know what they should expect to see from their children in the way of homework and inviting them to participate in the workings of the class. He may want to offer them a matrix of choices for participation—from coming in to class and reading/writing with kids, to helping type final products, to building classroom bookshelves—making sure that his choices encourage participation from all kinds of parents, and not only those who already feel positively toward school or confident in their own literacy. If he has time, he may want to make phone calls to those twenty-five or thirty parents in the class on which he's focusing; as we've read about in previous pages, such phone calls really seem to make a difference in encouraging parents to come on board and establish a partnership with teachers.

Michael knows that the ways of teaching he's proposing are different from those of the other teachers in his school (and different from the ways he's taught in past years). And he does have an assumption about which part of this new teaching might be the hot button for the parents: his approach to assessment. In organizing lingo, he has *identified a purpose:* to help parents gain a better understanding of portfolio assessment and see its connection to these new ways of teaching. Experience tells him this is an area which will raise questions for parents, and thus it is a perfectly legitimate purpose for him to identify and begin with. Still, as a teacher-organizer, Michael needs to balance his perception of the identified issue with what the parents might raise as their own concerns. As a result, Michael would need to explore his parents' concerns, even as he lets them know that he realizes assessment issues might be of interest to them. Michael can do this in a number of ways: Through those phone calls home or through a response sheet attached to the letters he sends home, he can ask some questions, some that specifically focus on assessment, some that ask about other issues. Once he knows some of the questions his parents have, he can set up some opportunities for discussion: parent inservice evenings on such topics as "authentic assessment" or "process writing"; a study group in which they read together an article on portfolios or performance assessment and try out some hands-on approaches; a walking journal with an occasional article attached that provides, in accessible language, a way into these topics. What Michael chooses will depend, of course, on the interest of the parents and his own time commitments; what's important is that he continues to provide opportunities for talk and multiple invitations to the parents—not ending his outreach invitations at the end of September.

At the same time, Michael will need to provide more and more opportunities for parents to be immersed in ongoing practice and thus in the language of the classroom and of his pedagogy—specifically, in the language of assessment. At the start of each unit of study, he might inform parents through a newsletter about the components of his assessment program, explaining why he is using portfolios and asking for their input and help in specific ways, perhaps again offering a matrix of opportunities. Parents who themselves rely on portfolios (as photographers or architects or woodworkers) could be invited into the classroom to show their work—as a way to help both parents and students understand the breadth and usefulness of this kind of collection as an authentic means of assessment. As often as possible, he should invite parents to read and respond to student work (e.g., individual pieces, class anthologies), so that they can begin to see the components of good writing and how writing improves over multiple drafts, always helping them to learn how to respond through teaching letters. In order for parents to become familiar with actual student portfolios and to see both the gains the students are making in their writing and the ways they are able to reflect about their growth, he might either sponsor a portfolio night with students presenting their work to their parents or send portfolios home with a sheet for parental response.

As this is going on, Michael will probably begin to notice certain parents emerging naturally as leaders, parents who regularly come to an inservice or study group or who call often with questions. At this point, it is important for him to begin to work on *developing those leaders*—inviting them to take a more active role in reaching out to other parents. He might do this in a number of ways: asking them to be the first to respond to student portfolios and modeling the way for the rest of the parents, suggesting they bring along another parent or two to the next inservice or study group meeting, or wondering with them about ways to reach out to other parents, both to include more parents in the community that's been developing and to help more parents understand the ways of assessment that he's using. What's important for Michael, though, is to realize that all too often the parents who naturally emerge as leaders in a classroom are those who feel most comfortable in school settings—many times those who are well educated or who had positive experiences in their own schooling. As teachers, we often feel most comfortable with these parents, perhaps because of shared values or ease of conversation. Hard as it may be, we do need to find and develop parent leaders from other groups. At times this might require a teacher to reach out to other places—to other groups and individuals (such as an ESL parent group or parents of Title 1 children). It may also help to enlist the expertise of another teacher in the school (such as a counselor or a reading specialist) who has the ear of a specific group of parents and thus may help in establishing entrée into these groups and encouraging their participation.

In some ways, if Michael has accomplished all this, he's set the stage for the future: He's established and built a community, gained entrée into it, identified a purpose with the parents, and begun to develop leaders. Simply by accomplishing these things, he's helped in the step of *taking action*. Most likely, the parents involved have gained at least an open mind about the kinds of teaching and assessment Michael has undertaken. These parents are talking to other parents and helping to create a changed mindset among greater numbers of people than Michael will encounter in his own outreach. These parents are also primed for taking action if an issue should arise. Say, for example, given the current trend to deny "social promotion," the school administration is considering instituting a one-shot writing and reading exam that will determine if a child can pass into the next grade. Parents who have come to understand the value of authentic assessment and multiple looks at a child's progress over time will not automatically think this exam is a good idea. A teacher who fears what such an exam would do to his teaching practices (forcing, perhaps, a curriculum that focuses excessive time on "teaching for the test") has ready allies in his fight. While Michael would have to be very careful in how he approaches parents on this issue—he's untenured after all—being available to answer their questions and to provide them with articles which portray an alternative perspective—in short, simply having established the groundwork for an alternative discussion—may be the impetus that parents need to go forth on their own and state their displeasure. Recall Carolyn's parents and their disagreement with the school's proposed gifted and talented program, or Amy and Ronda's parents and their vocal presence at the meeting to discuss multiage classrooms. We can't, of course, guarantee that the parents who have been educated and organized in this fashion will step forward . . . but the chances are much better that they will.

Throughout all this, of course, Michael will be *assessing* his effectiveness as a teacher-organizer and the ways in which his parent organizing has been successful. He can do this numerically (counting the numbers of parents who have emerged as leaders or who have come to various out-of-school events or who have responded to their child's writing), or he can do it more qualitatively (reading the comments made by parents on portfolio responses and analyzing them in a number of ways, such as what those comments indicate about the parents' understanding of assessment and of students' writing). If his group has become a strong one and has taken outside action on its own, they might work together to assess their effectiveness as a group. Were they able to stop that one-shot assessment? Were their voices heard? What else would they need to do in order to be more effective in getting their message out?

Let's turn, for a moment, to a very different kind of scenario and do the same kind of analysis to determine how a community organizing approach would help a teacher. Again, the essence of this scenario is taken from the experiences of a real-life teacher (and is sure to have a familiar ring to many readers).

Scenario 2

Melissa is a longtime high school teacher in a small, rural town, a popular teacher who is much loved by parents and students alike. Melissa likes to say she's seen it all, watching principals, school boards, and teaching trends come and go over the years. She is, however, committed to certain principles in her own teaching, principles that haven't changed much over the years but that have been honed by her continual inquiry into best practices in language arts: choice, ownership, student inquiry, thoughtfulness. She accomplishes these in her eleventh-grade English class by using literature circles with student-selected novels, multigenre research papers with topics selected by the students, and frequent demonstrations by the students in which they share their knowledge with others, both the other students and herself. Her students consistently score well on state and national assessments; a large number of her students go on to two- and four-year colleges. While Melissa knows that most of her colleagues don't teach in the same ways she does, she doesn't believe in "creating converts" or "making waves." She merely closes her door and teaches as she wants to teach; so far, this has satisfied her various principals and colleagues. The latest school board election has her worried, though, for the first time in years. Running a campaign based on "Back to Basics," three new trustees were elected: one who has begun to home school her children because "whole language ruined" her oldest daughter, one who is pushing for charter schools because of the "lack of rigorous curriculum in public school," and one who seems to quietly support the other two but has made no public statements about her beliefs.

While Melissa is a teacher committed to many of the same teaching principles as Michael, their situations are quite different.

Melissa is an experienced teacher, one who has already gained the respect of her surrounding community. As an experienced teacher, she has years of proof that her ways of teaching work, and she has a parent community who, while they may not understand the theory or the specifics of her pedagogy, feel good about what she's done. Melissa also recognizes the presence of a potential "enemy"—or at least the presence of a new force which seems different and which she realizes may prevent her from doing the kinds of practices she is convinced work best for kids. This unease with the new board may be what will help Melissa get past her natural inclination to shut her door and get on with her work. She is concerned and knows that, while doing this will not be easy, she has to do something.

Melissa is primed to become a teacher-organizer and to do some proactive work before a reactive response to this new school board becomes necessary. She is already recognized as a positive figure among the parents in this small town; *the community, in some ways, is already established,* and *she has gained entrée.* Her reputation precedes her; the parents in this small community have experienced the gossip factor and already know before their kids walk into her classroom that she is one of the "good" teachers. The boundaries of her community, in other words, are set in part by this understanding of her as a respected teacher—and may encompass parents whose children have never even had her as a teacher. Melissa's charge, at this point, might be to draw upon this good reputation and educate the community by helping the parents become more knowledgeable about what she does to achieve this success with students and why she does it in certain ways. This charge shifts the boundaries of the core community a bit, as it moves from being a large number of parents with a sketchy but positive sense of her teaching to focusing on a fewer number of parents (for example, those parents whose children are in her classes this school year) who may be able to gain a more specific understanding of her teaching. The ways of creating this understanding that I've mentioned previously in this book and that Michael used would apply here: for example, newsletters home, study groups, and inservice nights for parents. Choosing one or two of these would be Melissa's first step.

As Melissa begins to work with these parents, *identifying the purpose* of her work becomes of key importance. How she cuts her message, in other words, will matter greatly, because of the potential for an opposition who may want to eliminate the kind of teaching she practices. As she analyzes the public statements of these new board members, she needs to use strategic thinking: to consider what lies behind those statements, what their fears might be, what she can anticipate they might do as a result of their beliefs. For example, she needs to think about what the board member whose daughter was "ruined by whole language" means by that statement. How does this board member define whole language? Is the phrase itself—*whole language*—a hot button for the board member, who has read those articles and listened to those talk radio hosts condemning whole language as destructive to both learning and our way of life? Does whole language conjure up for this trustee images of laissez-faire classrooms with no teacher intervention? What was her daughter's classroom like? And what do the other new members mean by "Back to Basics?" What are the core values that they see in that phrase? And what about the "lack of rigorous curriculum" statement? What does this member consider rigorous curriculum? Does it connect to canonical knowledge?

As she considers these statements and what lies behind them, she can begin to formulate the purpose and underlying message that she might have as she begins her organizing campaign. Will her purpose be to help parents understand that what she does in the classroom really is "Back to Basics," in other words, reclaiming and defining the term to show how her core values meet the most basic need of teaching kids to read and write? Or will her purpose be to oppose the board members' statements outright and help parents understand that the board members' take on pedagogy is not supported by the best of research and anecdotal evidence (of which she has plenty)? Or will her approach be more middle of the road, merely helping parents to see what she does in the classroom, find the language to name it and understand it on their own, thereby providing them with an alternative scenario?

Figuring out this cut on her purpose is going to be very important in Melissa's situation. Her parents are already satisfied; they may not yet see what she does as different from the approach favored by the board members (for whom they may even have voted), but if Melissa does not become actively involved in order to help her community understand, those differences may be defined in ways she does not like—by a board member. She also needs to be very aware of the feelings of the community members—an antagonistic approach to define herself as "right" (and by implication to define the trustees as "wrong") may backfire. She has gained entrée, but she is not immune to a community's potential shift in acceptance.

For Melissa, then, identifying purpose first for herself is key; then, as she works with the parent community to further define that purpose, she does so from a thoughtful position. Again, the kinds of activities Michael used would be appropriate at this point: getting feedback from parents about their concerns and issues through phone calls, discussions, or surveys. Keeping her message in mind as she seriously considers and connects the parents' issues will help as they, as a group, refine their joint purpose.

Developing leaders in this campaign will also be important. These parents will have to become quite knowledgeable about the curricular issues that may arise in the future—the kind of sketchy understanding and general goodwill that can suffice in some cases may not be enough here. As Melissa works with those parents who might naturally emerge as leaders, supplying them with articles supportive of her ways of teaching as well as multiple examples of student work, she may also try to target a few particular parents—those whom she knows have reputations in the community as thoughtful and respected people. If the board members decide to wage a negative campaign, she will need parents who can stand up and talk sensibly and knowledgeably about the issues at hand. In this case, a few hand-picked parents whom Melissa can talk to in depth, expressing her concerns, might be a wise choice.

Action in this case needs to be more than the kind of personal change that was sufficient for the parents in the Michael scenario. As a proactive measure, Melissa and her cadre of parents should go public, in ways that make sense to them. Parents who are active in Rotary or Kiwanis or other clubs, armed with samples of student writing, might sponsor an education night in which they (and even their children) could speak about the kinds of literacy instruction they want to see happening in schools. Parents who are dentists or doctors or who work in offices with waiting rooms might bring in copies of student-written anthologies for the patients, clients, and customers to read. Parents who know the editor of the newspaper might mention to him or her some of what is happening in the class (and others like it) and suggest coverage of a literacy night or a poetry reading or some other event the students are part of. The parent group might have an afternoon of letter writing in which they write to the newspaper or to all board members about their new understandings of literacy and their encouragement of these kinds of programs. In large part, this action should be like a public relations campaign—getting information out there about this kind of teaching and providing lots of products which represent it well.

The group has to make decisions, though. Obviously, they don't want to create backlash—to raise the new board members' hackles about something that hasn't arisen as an issue yet—but they want to achieve a background presence of positive thought about certain pedagogies. If the board members choose to become oppositional, then of course tactics would change, but at the juncture presented in this scenario, that low background hum of the value of certain practices is the goal. And Melissa in particular needs to be aware that in order to be truly effective, she needs simultaneously to be reaching out to other teachers and administrators, to reopen the door of her classroom and keep these colleagues informed. Melissa can't be a lone ranger here— such an approach would leave her open to accusations and resentment from other teachers whose practices may seem to be under attack by the stances she takes. As Denny Wolfe and Joseph Antinarella put forth in their book *Deciding to Lead: The English Teacher as Reformer*, "leading, attracting, and winning over . . . are the crucial goals for teachers interested in contributing to genuine school reform" (28).[1]

This approach needs to be constantly assessed, particularly because the parents and Melissa are walking a fine line here. One means of *assessment*, of course, is to watch the new board members: how they respond, what they say about the issues they've raised, what they propose as new measures for the schools. But I think there is more than the new board members' responses at stake. How the public reacts to this new information will, in most cases, affect the board's reactions (and will, of course, play a role in whether or not the board is reelected). So, as the group assesses how many community members they've reached, how many letters to the editor appear which are *not* penned by a member of the group, how the gossip factor seems to be going at the soccer games and in the grocery line, they will begin to get a sense of what the community is feeling on these issues.

Using Scenarios to Educate Teachers

As you consider my responses to the two scenarios presented above, it is likely that your responses will vary from mine. Perhaps your reading and analysis of the scenarios suggest different issues as the significant ones; perhaps you see alternative ways Melissa and Michael should approach their circumstances. You may raise questions about the actions I've advocated for these imaginary teachers, suggesting perhaps that Melissa should be more laid-back about her agenda in order to keep parents interested or that her very first goal should be to work with her colleagues in order to present a united front. Michael, you might think, needs to spend more time helping parents understand the rest of his teaching program; then assessment will follow naturally. And, in part, such varied readings are the point. Scenarios like these can be, should be, read in multiple ways—multiple responses to them can be equally "correct." It is for just this reason that community organizers regularly use scenarios as part of their training for new leaders: presenting realistic (or even real) situations, asking small groups to analyze the scenarios for their essential components, and then having them suggest what the characters in the scenarios might do to change the situation. As the small groups present their ideas to the group at large, multiple responses are offered, and the large group is able to discuss which approaches seem to be most feasible, which would get the best results, and what problems might arise from these approaches.

In like manner, teacher leaders who wish to expose teachers to a community organizing lens through which to view outreach might make good use of the scenario approach. Scenarios, such as the ones I've presented here, are easy to devise (unfortunately, in some ways—I just look around at the issues the teachers I know have to face every day, and I can come up with twenty scenarios in no time). And teachers who participate in a scenario-based workshop are able to learn to think like teacher-organizers in some creative and collaborative ways. Let me suggest for a moment one way to structure such a workshop, an approach that allows for multiple stages and which, ideally, should take place over several sessions.

Stage One

Hand out the process model for community organizing and discuss with teachers the essential components of each step. Using examples from the work of teachers you already know (or teachers mentioned in this book) to illustrate each step, ask the teachers what they have done themselves that might be illustrative of that particular component.

[The point of this, of course, is to get teachers to think about what they *already* do that might fit into the model. The feeling of "Oh, I already do some of that," goes a long way when asking them to try something which, at first, might seem overwhelming.]

Stage Two

1. Hand out a written copy of a scenario (either one you've created or one of the scenarios listed in this chapter) to teams of teachers.

2. Ask teachers to analyze the scenario, identifying the critical issues for the imaginary teacher and noting the context of that teacher's situation.

[This emphasis on context is very important. Most teachers—indeed, most people—have a tendency to see scenarios as either very like their own situations or completely different. For those who see the scenarios as very like, the solutions they come up with often say more about *their* context than about the context as presented. And, at this point, learning to see the issues of someone else's context is very important.]

3. Divide the teachers into teams and ask each team to discuss the scenario and make specific suggestions for what the imaginary teacher could do. Ask them to consider their suggestions through the lens of teacher-organizers: thinking about the five components of the model and how the imaginary teacher might create a complete approach to the situation in a step-by-step fashion.

4. Ask each team to share their ideas with the large group, leading to discussion about which approaches to organizing might work the best and why.

[These suggestions can and should be different. Listening to how others might approach the same situation is part of the point of this experiment—letting ourselves imagine a whole range of possibilities.]

Stage Three

1. Ask each teacher to compose a scenario which reflects some aspect of her or his own situation. Again, these scenarios should be written in narrative style and should try to reflect not just the problem but some of the flavor of the local context. Teachers might consider these questions:

- What are your concerns about your parents' and community's understanding of your pedagogy?

- What are the teaching practices that seem least understood by the community? that seem most problematic to the community?

- Has there been any opposition to your teaching practices, or teaching practices like yours, that you know of? If so, has that opposition come from individuals or members of a group?

- What are the circumstances of your context? Are you a novice or experienced teacher? How long have you been in this community? Do you also live in the community? How have you related to parents thus far? What are the most typical teaching practices in your school? Are your practices like or unlike those?

2. Have teachers work in teams to analyze each scenario. Teachers should identify the critical components of each situation and begin to apply the model to it. At this point, the teams' analyses should be as specific as possible, suggesting

detailed action steps the teacher might follow to implement a
sustained outreach program based on his or her needs.

3. Individual teachers should then have time to create some
of the documents necessary to implement their plan: writing
appropriate newsletters, creating a matrix of invitations for the
parents, composing teaching letters, devising a schedule for
when they can hold inservices or study groups, and so on. As
they create these artifacts, the team members and other participants in the large group can provide feedback, helping all
teachers create the most polished documents possible.

This scenario approach has proved to be beneficial for teachers
for a number of reasons. Starting with an imagined teacher in imagined
circumstances, it allows teachers to think through an organizing
approach in a low-risk way. Analyzing someone else's problem,
someone else's situation, is, in some ways, easier than analyzing one's
own: often, one can see issues more clearly and respond more honestly.
That created teacher is not there to say, "Oh, that wouldn't work,
because . . ."—a freeing kind of approach, I think, one that allows
teachers to imagine what they could do, if they had but world enough
and time. In addition, working on the first scenarios in a group allows
teachers to have the benefit of others' creative juices. Teachers begin to
share their experiences and ideas and create much more far-reaching
solutions than they can alone. As teachers begin to work on their own
scenarios, they do so then with a collection of possible ideas: those their
team came up with and those other teams thought up. If there's been
enough time in the workshop for the group to consider several
scenarios, then they also have the benefit of considering the connection
between contexts and action, seeing how the steps they might take in
their own situation depend so much on the details of their context:
while many scenarios might share some common steps toward change,
a boilerplate community action plan just won't work.

This scenario approach also assumes certain things, however. It
assumes that teachers are knowledgeable about their own reasons for
teaching in particular ways; it expects that they are able to articulate
their beliefs and their rationale for those beliefs to others succinctly yet
convincingly. And while I believe that most teachers are thoughtful
about their teaching, working diligently and imaginatively to help
children learn, I know that not all of them are as knowledgeable and
articulate as they need to be in this era of suspicion and distrust. English
educators and teacher leaders must see this community organizing
package, then, in slightly broader ways—beginning with helping
teachers get to the point of feeling knowledgeable, articulate, and able

to take on the leadership roles they will need to fulfill in order to make change happen. Thus the question becomes, What else can we do to help thoughtful and caring teachers get to that point?

Regie Routman talks extensively about this issue in her important book *Literacy at the Crossroads* and offers for teachers clear and concise sections on the "rhetoric and realities" of such practices as whole language, back-to-basics, phonics, and "other dilemmas." Ken Goodman similarly helps us separate the myth from the reality in his book *Phonics Phacts*, as do Zemelman and Daniels in *Best Practice* and Connie Weaver with her invaluable "Fact Sheets" found in *Teaching Grammar in Context*. Books like these give teachers some very specific answers to the question of *why* teach in particular ways, helping all of us articulate what may be tacit understandings. What I'd like to add to the ongoing discussion these books raise are some specific suggestions based on work I am doing with preservice and practicing teachers. My hope is that the suggestions will begin to offer at least one more way for teachers to consider what Knoblauch and Brannon call "the explosively simple question: Why do it this way?" (15).

Working with Preservice Teachers

"I Believe"

> Teachers have to be pragmatic; they have to be down-to-earth, but being down-to-earth without knowing the theoretical coordinates for the landscape is a good way to lose your sense of direction. We English teachers are given to recipe swapping—and that can be hazardous. In my ideal commonwealth . . . I would order the closing down of the Exercise Exchange; the NCTE would not be allowed to operate it unless they instituted a Theory Exchange. And you couldn't get the recipe unless you also went there.
>
> (Berthoff, *The Making of Meaning* 33–4)

This quote occupies a prominent spot in the syllabus I hand out to my English 308 (Teaching Secondary English) class each term. We begin the year, like many methods classes, by thinking hard about our own beliefs about teaching and learning, basing this process on our experiences as students, as teachers of others, as observers of classrooms. Following a number of short writing experiments familiar to most methods teachers ("Write about a teacher you really admire," "Write about your earliest memories of reading and writing," "What is your strongest memory of evaluation in high school?" and so on), we compose what I call "I believe" statements, that is, lists of personal beliefs about the teaching of English. We then try to connect the "I believe" statements to actual classroom practice, as we turn to reading lots of professional material written by practicing English teachers (Linda Rief, Nancie Atwell, and Michigan teachers collected in the *Michigan Literacy Consortium Journal*, among others) and watching lots of videos of classrooms in action. As we read and watch, we maintain a close focus on imagining what the "I believe" statements might be for those teachers, actually taking the time to write and talk about the generally unstated beliefs behind these teachers' practices. Eventually, students begin to see how beliefs relate to specific practices, even where there might be contradictions for these educators, and how the educators seem to have resolved them. As students then go back and revise their own "I believe" statements, they are more aware of their own contradictions, and thoughtful about which ones might be resolved, which ones can stand together in a classroom, and which ones might need more thought. At this point, students begin to add another column to their "I believe" statements: "If I believe x, then in my classroom I will try y"(or "my classroom will look like y"). Again, this reflection gives students practice in connecting theory with strategies, and looking to see how that cool exercise they saw done in some teacher's classroom may not fit in at all with what they believe about teaching and learning.

These statements become the center of everything we do in the class. When students eventually write lesson and unit plans, for example, they refer specifically to the beliefs they're trying to show in those lessons. When we have discussion about books or articles they've read, they immediately look to the author's underlying beliefs and try to make sense of them in terms of their own. What this specific and recurring look at beliefs does for the students, I think, is twofold: it constantly reminds them that thoughtful practices in English language arts classrooms are always based on a belief system about how kids learn literacy, and it starts them on the journey of identifying and articulating what those beliefs might be. They are able to say, "Linda Rief uses a workshop approach for a number of reasons. She believes that students learn best by x, y, and z; and so in her classroom she does it this way. In my own classroom, I believe students learn best by a, b, and c, and so in my classroom I will do it this way."

Reading Widely

When I began to compose these statements along with my students, I discovered a contradiction in my own teaching. While I believe my students best learn as they pursue topics of choice (and while I presented that as an important option for my students to think about for *their* teaching), I was stuck in the class text mode of teaching, with everyone reading the same chapters of the same text and using that reading as the basis of discussion. Lately, I've made a change so that after we read (fairly quickly) one text together, students select their own books and articles, reading at least thirty minutes every day and keeping track of their reading in a reader's log. Fifteen minutes before every class, I haul in a load of books on topics that have come up in class, and I bring in my growing collection of interesting articles filed according to topic ("revision," or "reader response," or "authentic assessment," and so on). The students skim through the materials while waiting for class to start (or after class), and we begin the day either with a book talk by me or with responses from students to my question, "Anybody read anything interesting?" Students are introduced to the journals in our field this way, to the presses that really speak to them, to Web sites and videos. Whenever a student brings in an article that she or he loved but that I don't know, I read it and ask for a copy for the file box. Students compose annotations for four books each term; we copy and share the annotations and thus we all walk away with strong summaries and recommendations for about one hundred books.

Again, this approach helps students to become more knowledgeable and articulate about their own beliefs and the beliefs of others in the field. They are reading much more than they ever did when I assigned a specific text, and they are making the books their own. Because they are responsible for informing their colleagues in the class about good books, rather than merely answering questions about a book we've all supposedly read, I've found that they read more thoughtfully, and they learn to articulate their newfound knowledge to others both in oral ways (though book talks) and in written ways (though the annotated bibliographies).

Reader's/Writer's Project

Another project I have introduced to students is the Reader's/Writer's Project, modeled after Linda Rief's project of the same name. The project immerses students in their own topic of interest, allowing them to explore an area of instruction in some depth and to become expert. Students are asked to pick a subject they want to know more about, such as literature circles, or multiple intelligences and the teaching of writing, or portfolio assessment (to name a few that were selected last term) and to research that subject in at least three different genres. We spend some time brainstorming what constitutes a genre, what genres might lead to more information than others, and what genres might complement each other well in order to lead to the most information. Last term, students came up with the possible genres of written materials, their own memories, interviews (with teachers or students), observations, Web sites, movies (both documentaries and feature films), classroom videos, and novels about education. We shared topics through whole class hand-outs and peer group meetings, so that those who had read or observed pertinent information on someone else's topic could offer resources.

Like Rief, I ask students to write up their understandings in three different genres, keeping in mind a specific purpose and audience for each, in part to allow them to experiment with writing in genres with which they are less comfortable and in part to get them to create some real documents that they might use in their teaching—as a way of introducing some of the advocacy strategies mentioned earlier. Again, we brainstorm possible genres and audiences, but each time I've done this, the idea of generating a piece directed toward the audience of parents comes up almost immediately. At this point I share with students some of the newsletters, introductory letters, teaching letters, and booklets produced by Carolyn Berge, Julie King, Kathleen Hayes-Parvin, Cathy Gwizdala, and others and begin a conversation about advocacy strategies and their importance. We talk about the media depiction of teachers and many of the curricular ideas I have introduced them to, and I stress that they might want to use this opportunity to create documents that would help them in advocating their positions to the communities in which they will teach. These preservice teachers respond immediately. Without my asking, they begin to bring in newspaper articles which provide very partial and generally unflattering explanations of some of the issues they have begun to study in depth. They share stories of what they've heard from parents and others in their communities and how they didn't know how to respond to certain arguments. They begin to talk about what they've learned and how they might respond now—and almost everyone chooses to practice that response for at least one of the genres of the Reader's/Writer's Project. Students immediately figure out how important this is—and that the language and information they will include depends upon on the audience they are writing for and the genre they have chosen. They begin to discuss how to be more articulate in the genre they have chosen, realizing what arguments may or may not work for particular people on particular occasions. (We are lucky to have a large number of parents as students at my university—last year over half my class; these folks do a wonderful job of offering peer critique for parent-directed pieces, explaining, for example, "This is too long; I'd never read it," or "This has too much jargon; until this term I would never have known what you meant.")

I also ask students to do two final things in the Reader's/Writer's Project, again adapted from Linda Rief. They write up a "process paper" which accompanies the three genre pieces, in which they explain what they did to lead to the final pieces, how their research went, what they discovered, and so on. I also ask them to do a final demonstration, usually a fifteen- to twenty-minute hands-on session, in which they share one aspect of what they learned. This forces them to develop their ideas in yet another genre—an oral mode—and to become very clear and articulate about their new expertise.

This project has been a powerful one for my students and me. Students have an opportunity to become immersed in a topic and to become fairly expert in it, to gain the depth of understanding necessary to exhibit some confidence. In my former methods classes, we only had time to talk about portfolios, for example, for a class or two, and the conversation inevitably became one of "how to set them up." Students could not see the range of possibilities for portfolios or even recognize the vast amount of information that exists about portfolios. They rarely got a chance to talk to teachers about portfolios if the teacher in their observation site (a site over which I have no control) did not use this approach, and they certainly did not spend a lot of time thinking about their own experiences with assessment in light of what they were learning. If they decided to use portfolios on their own when they began teaching, it would be with a very basic knowledge—and one that may not have stood up well to the questions or scrutiny of a parent or principal. In contrast, the students who complete a Reader's/Writer's Project know their topic thoroughly, understand how it connects to their own beliefs, and can explain it to others. And most of them begin to understand the kind of careful look they will have to do for future projects, in order to gain expertise in those. As they connect this project to their "I believe" statements and their wide reading, they recognize what they have to continue to do in order to be the kind of teacher who truly understands what she or he believes and how that translates into classroom practice.

Working with Experienced Teachers

Study Groups and Beyond

Ironically, experienced teachers all too often lose the support and camaraderie of like-minded professionals once they enter the schools. Busy schedules, large class sizes, and professional commitments that take them in a thousand directions all combine to place roadblocks in the way of caring and well-intentioned teachers who want to keep up the professional conversations that might help them continually reflect on and refine their practice. "Keeping up"—i.e., reading professional journals and books or attending conferences—often takes a backseat to other demands: the mandated inservice offered by the district, the required hours to get a master's degree but the dearth of classes offered by the local university that fit into the only available time slot, the IEP conferences, the chaperoning, the required coaching . . . the list goes on and on.

Those teachers, though, who have found the niches, who have found the time, who are able to continue their professional conversations, are much more able both to understand their practices and to articulate their understanding to themselves and others. A number of powerful teacher networks have emerged over the years: National Writing Project sites, various whole language groups (such as TAWL groups), and local and state affiliates of NCTE or IRA. More recently, a number of these organizations have pushed for teacher-developed study groups: a place for teachers to read carefully and widely and to connect that reading to their own classroom experiences. Typically, a study group is formed either around a topic (say, spelling development or writing workshop) or around a particular book. Teachers hear about these groups through word of mouth or by specific advertisement or invitation, and they self-select to participate. (This is in fact the first characteristic of successful study groups: Participants must join because they want to and not because they are mandated to; in my mind, it doesn't count as a study group when participation is required by one's school.) Prior to the meeting, teachers choose a manageable chunk of the chosen book or article related to the topic to read in preparation for the discussion. (Raising characteristic number two of a successful study group: The amount of reading must be doable; teachers who are already overwhelmed will drop out in a minute if the amount of reading becomes more than they can handle.) Teachers then begin to meet on a regular basis. I've known study groups who've met before school once a week for the whole school year to read one book; study groups that read an article or two for a monthly evening meeting; study groups that jigsaw articles or books, so that the participants read different but related pieces based on the same topics. (Bringing to mind characteristic number three: The group must determine the best times to meet and the best ways for discussion to occur. If the participants don't have ownership, the group won't continue on a long-term basis.)

As I discussed in the previous section on preservice teachers, this notion of reading widely on which study groups are based allows teachers to get a taste for the continuing professional conversation in the field. As they choose topics of particular interest to them, they are able to make some immediate connections to the problems that seem most vexing in their own classrooms by participating in a forum with others to help find solutions. The teachers with whom I have worked love study groups—in part because they provide both immediate support and the opportunity for long-term imagining.

What I want to suggest, though, is a slight twist to the study group concept, so that the participating teachers see themselves instead as part of an "inquiry group."[2] Such groups often adapt the typical study group format described above by beginning with a focus on their own backgrounds and beliefs. Teachers in an inquiry group, then, would compose the kinds of written reflections my preservice teachers write: thinking about their own backgrounds as readers and writers and what kinds of instruction worked for them; considering the experiences of some particular students they have taught over the years and what kinds of instruction worked for them; and reflecting on their own set of beliefs developed over years of experience and influenced by the reading they have done. Beginning in this way, teachers can approach the group reading a bit differently—quite consciously placing their own identified and articulated beliefs up against those of the author under consideration, looking for points of agreement and disagreement, trying to make sense of contradictions, and continually refining their own stances.

Building upon these background beliefs and the reading they're doing, inquiry groups can then look at their own specific classroom practices of the moment, practicing what Becky Sipe has called "soft teacher research"—that is, not a full-fledged attempt at studying a specific research question and gathering information in the classroom to answer that question, but rather trying out some "kid-watching," as Yetta Goodman would say, taking the time to watch the classroom practices and participants through the eyes of someone who is trying to learn more. As teachers do this, they begin necessarily to ask themselves some serious questions: Where does the practice mesh with my beliefs? Where is there dissonance? Teachers begin to seek connections among the three kinds of reading they're attempting: their reading of outside experts, their reading of their own sets of beliefs, and their reading of their own practice.

I think this shift from study group to inquiry group achieves an important goal I have in mind for developing teacher-organizers: to be able to articulate what we refer to as best practices (as defined by the published authors whose corpus of work is the subject of the study groups) and to specify how their own beliefs and practices connect with, extend, or vary from those practices. And the inquiry group itself—a collection of interested and caring professionals—can be a place for teachers to try out their beliefs and wonderings about their classrooms in a supportive environment, helping them to clarify before they go public.

From Teacher-Researcher to Teacher-Organizer

The most powerful means I know for teachers to reconsider and refine their own practice is for them to see themselves as teacher-researchers, as professionals who continually reevaluate their own classroom practices through close study and resulting action steps. Although so much has been written in the past decade about teacher research and its importance for the professional lives of teachers everywhere, Stillman's preface to *Reclaiming the Classroom: Teacher Research as an Agency for Change* (Goswami and Stillman) still strikes me as the best summary of what can happen when teachers begin to see themselves as teacher-researchers:

> 1. Their teaching is transformed in important ways: they become theorists, articulating their intentions, testing their assumptions, and finding connections with practice.

> 2. Their perceptions of themselves as writers and teachers are transformed. They step up their use of resources; they form networks; and professionally they become more active.

> 3. They become rich resources who can provide the profession with information it simply doesn't have. They can observe closely, over long periods of time, with special insights and knowledge. . . .

> 4. They become critical, responsive readers and users of current research, less apt to accept uncritically others' theories, less vulnerable to fads, and more authoritative in their assessment of curricula, methods, and materials.

5. They can study writing and learning and report their findings without spending large sums of money (although they must have support and recognition). . . .

6. They collaborate with their students to answer questions important to both, drawing on community resources in new and unexpected ways. . . .

Clearly, we know now that teachers who start to see themselves as teacher-researchers become more confident of their own knowledge and expertise and thus better able to explain that knowledge to others. Traditionally, teacher research has focused on sharing that knowledge with other educators: other teachers, principals, colleagues in the field. Teachers have been urged to publish, told that by sharing their findings with other colleagues, all of us in the field will gain much new knowledge: We'll have a series of stories to read and reflect on, and thereby gain a deep understanding of classrooms and students and teachers who are sometimes like and sometimes unlike us.

What I want to suggest is that as teacher-researchers become teacher-organizers, they begin to share those same findings beyond that audience of colleagues, that they find ways to communicate their newfound understandings with parents and the surrounding community. Certainly, the means of presentation might shift, but the spread of information outward could achieve at least these goals for teachers:

- they take on a new professional status in the community—as knowledgeable practitioners armed with their own research, they are now seen differently by others;

- they open a new kind of dialogue with parents and others by sharing with parents documented findings from their own classrooms which support certain best practices;

- they discover ways to transform their knowledge into language and formats that are appealing and understandable to others who are not in the field—centering that knowledge on the real lives of students.

Let me share with you an example in-process of how teacher-researchers might make the shift to teacher-organizers, an example based on a teacher research group with whom I am working at present. Ten teachers and I have been meeting for over a year now, as they take their first leaps into researching their own classrooms.[3] We began as most teacher research groups do: with teachers figuring out the wondering or question that kept pulling at them; situating that question in their own set of beliefs or values about classroom practice; learning various ways to research that question (through observations, interviews, surveys) and making sense of what they found (by immersing themselves in the information, trying out discourse analysis, searching for themes); and eventually discovering appropriate genres for representing their findings. It was at this point that the teachers began to consider the multiple audiences with whom they might want to share their work, based on discussions that evolved as I was getting feedback from them about my ongoing research for this book, which was then in progress. Most of them were struck by the argument and decided to expand their genres beyond the typical conference paper, article for publication, or inservice presentation for their school (all valuable and necessary outlets for this kind of work, I know and appreciate) in order to reach a wider audience of parents and others in the community. Terry Stout, for example, who has been researching her own writing workshop classroom and documenting how to increase her ninth-grade students' feelings of ownership and responsibility, has opted to write a series of columns for the PTO newsletter that goes home to all families in the school. As she describes her intentions,

> Parents are often unaware of what goes on in writing workshop classrooms; when they think of English they think of their high school teachers who solely corrected their spelling and grammar. There seems to be a certain attitude among them that says, "I suffered through endless sentence diagramming, so my children should have to also." The little information that they do get on process-based classrooms is skeptical and misleading, claiming that teachers are no longer concerned with the product and quality of a student's work, portraying portfolio assessment as little more than stuffing a child's best work in a folder and calling that assessment. My goal is to educate parents through a series of articles, highlighting best practices in the teaching of writing, particularly how they correlate with the state's content standards for the teaching of writing. My articles will focus on the following issues as they relate to current best practices in teaching English: student choice in reading and writing, authentic assessment, and what research says about teaching spelling and grammar.

Karen Watts's research has focused on how to help her students do a better job with their own self assessment, helping them move from making superficial judgments about the pieces of writing they submit for the classroom anthology and their portfolios to more considered assessments of their own work. One offshoot of her research is to create a handbook for parents so that they can begin to help students in this process. She writes,

> A classroom during writing workshop is not a quiet place. Students read aloud to themselves and to others; they conference

with the teacher and each other. It is a time to interact. In *The Art of Teaching Writing*, Lucy Calkins asks, "If we want our children to be lifelong writers, doesn't this mean that we need to encourage them to create these same richly interactive conditions in their homes and neighborhoods?" (506). Calkins says that it is not just a matter of valuing writing in the home, but that parents must engage their children in writing projects that are meaningful to the family. Students who have this kind of activity in the home, I believe, will be more likely to push themselves creatively in school and will understand the importance of selecting work that best represents themselves.

Toward this end, I will create a handbook for parents explaining how they can improve their children's perception of their writing at home. I will present them with what I believe to be the problem in student self-assessment and outline ways they can help at home. I will create an attractive, user-friendly handbook and distribute it to a select few parents whom I know to be concerned with their child's school performance to review and offer suggestions. Once the handbook meets these parents' approval, I will distribute it to all parents at November conferences.

Some ideas I have for this handbook include suggesting ways parents of older teens can demonstrate their pride in their child's work beyond the typical, and somewhat juvenile, refrigerator magnet. High school students have had elementary drawings and teachers' notes hung on the fridge for so many years that it is no longer special. My students will be producing attractive collections of their work that are worthy of sharing space in the magazine rack or bookcase. Parents may also have copies made of the collections to pass onto friends and family. These efforts will demonstrate to the teenage writer that their work is valued outside of the school setting. I will also suggest writing activities parents can share with their children, such as writing the family Christmas letter together, which have a meaningful and important purpose. It is my belief that once this has occurred in the home, students will be motivated to make subsequent class writing even better.

Another high school teacher, Jennifer Buehler, has been looking carefully at her students' responses and products in her ninth-grade English class, a class that has been devoted to choice reading—mostly of young adult novels. Convinced that this approach was working in general (she had some statistical proof that kids in her class read more and read a wider variety of texts), Jennifer decided to investigate what students were gaining from the experience, proceeding to conduct interviews, review students' literary logs, and distribute surveys. She has produced a booklet entitled *Making Lifelong Readers* that she now distributes to parents of all her incoming ninth graders in which she explains her philosophy toward reading instruction, paints a portrait in words of her classroom in action, and analyzes her students' responses to this way of teaching. She writes in the introduction,

> My goal is to establish a reading culture in the classroom where students will perceive themselves as people who choose to read, both inside and outside of school. Real-world readers surround themselves with books. They read often. They develop individual tastes and passions for particular books and authors. They talk to other readers. Through the reading culture in my classroom, I encourage students to develop lasting interests and habits as readers so they will want to continue their reading, even when it's no longer a class requirement.
>
> The following handbook is intended to show you a portrait of what happens in my reading workshop classroom. You will read about the behaviors that result when students are immersed in a reading culture, the conditions I create in the classroom to shape that culture, and the kinds of books students choose to read independently. I will present a few statistics that document what my students achieved in independent reading last year, and you will hear firsthand from individual students who became engaged as independent readers. Through their own words, you will find out what choice in reading can do to inspire and challenge high school students. Finally, I will show you some things I do to spark students as readers in the classroom, and what you can do at home to support your child's developing interests and habits in reading.

Other teachers in our group are creating newsletters or organizing inservice nights for parents, based on their research findings. At a recent meeting, these teacher-researchers even decided they want to get together one afternoon and have a letter-writing session, composing letters to the editor about their newfound knowledge of the classroom, confident in their ability as experts about their teaching practices and how those practices fit into the public debate on education.

What all these teacher-researchers have in common, I think, is both the desire and the knowledge to spread the word. They are confident in their knowledge about classroom practice because of their own immersion in their research. They feel able to articulate that knowledge and are committed to using their new understandings to help their students' learning and their own teaching. And they are aware that one important step in that process has to be informing parents—both to help parents understand why they are doing what they are doing (in part so they will be free to continue those practices) and to enlist the parents as partners in this enterprise. Teacher-researchers who expand their audience outwards have already made important steps toward becoming teacher-organizers.

Teachers Organizing for Change

Increasingly, as I work with both preservice and practicing teachers, I do so through this new lens: thinking about how to help them become knowledgeable, articulate teachers who are able to speak comfortably and convincingly about why they teach in the ways they do. I want these teachers to have more than the necessary skills and knowledge to reach their own students; I want them *to be able* to teach in the ways that reflect what we know about best practices in English language arts—to not be blocked from that enterprise because they are unable to explain why they are teaching in these ways. I want them to be able to explain to their colleagues, their administrators, and, most important, to the parents of their students. I want them to see the value of becoming proactive in their approaches, to be strategic thinkers who anticipate future reactions and who create structures to head off potential problems before they occur.

I believe community organizing offers us both a vision and a range of possibilities for how to do this. We teachers can be like Lois Gibbs or Candy Lightner; we can be like Tracey Easthope or Renee Bayer; we can be the kind of "local heroes" Bill Berkowitz honors in his book. As Ellen Cassedy, co-founder of 9to5, says, "The truth is that you can be a regular person and lead a pretty normal life and be active in social change" (qtd. in Berkowitz, *Local* 310). We teachers are regular people, leading pretty normal lives, but, too often, instead of being local heroes, we wait for a mythical somebody to come along and lead the charge. What community organizing teaches me is this: that we—as ordinary and regular as we are—can be that mythical someone.

And the truth is, we've seen what happens when we don't actively get involved, and it is not a pretty sight. We become a character in a story about education that has been authored by somebody else, somebody who doesn't have the knowledge, the experience, or, all too often, the compassion that we have toward all the kids we welcome into our teaching and learning communities. We become a stereotype, our teaching methods reduced to a generalization which omits the passion and the rationale, the successes and the challenges. We become placed at the mercy of local school boards, state and national legislatures, and the media—whose understanding of our role in the story too often is limited at best, and intentionally misleading at worst. Thus, we become part of the myth of "what's wrong with education today," a pervasive myth that becomes the sole informing story for too many citizens, even those we think should know better.

In his book *The Dream of the Earth*, Thomas Berry talks about the problem of replacing old stories with new ones. "It's all a question of story," he begins. "We are in trouble just now because we do not have a good story. We are in between stories. The old story, the account of how the world came to be and how we fit into it, is no longer effective. Yet we have not learned the new story" (123). I've thought about this quote over the last few years, in part because I believe it speaks to the problem we are facing in education. I believe we are between stories about how education works in the changing world we inhabit. The old story is just not effective for far too many kids, but the public has not yet learned the new story, perhaps because we have not taken the opportunity to teach them. And we must take this failing seriously: We cannot expect the new story to just emerge by osmosis; and until it does emerge too many people will be mired in the old one, secure in their understanding of that story, lacking the language and the imagination to consider another way.

We teachers can author our own story. We can take the organizing skills we already possess as competent and caring teachers; we can add to those a continuing growth and understanding of why we do what we do; and we can top it off with a shifted focus and a beginning understanding of community organizing strategies as we go public. Teachers can do it, *are* doing it, must do it if we have any hope of changing the dismissive nature of the public conversation in which we seem to be stuck. As Mike Rose entreats us in the closing lines of his powerful opus *Possible Lives*,

> When public education itself is threatened, as it seems to be threatened now—by cynicism and retreat, by the cold rapture of the market, by thin measure and the loss of civic imagination—when this happens, we need to assemble what the classroom can teach us, articulate what we come to know, speak it loudly, hold it fast to the heart. (433)

Teachers are the only ones who can do this, who can author the story and spread the word of what is actually happening in classrooms for kids of all sizes and shapes, who can proudly and knowledgeably proclaim what we know is true. We not only have within us the power to create change, we have the responsibility to do so: one teacher, one classroom, one community at a time.

Notes

1. This issue of creating change among your colleagues and peers is a related but separate issue from the one I am arguing for here, and worthy of lengthy consideration. In addition to Wolfe and Antinarella's book, see David Wilson's *Attempting Change* and Bonnie Sunstein's *Composing a Culture*.

2. I am grateful to my colleagues Becky Sipe and Laura Roop for conversations which have helped me understand the great potential of inquiry groups.

3. I have learned so much from these teachers, who are energetic and wise beyond belief: Jennifer Buehler, Paige Webster, Cari Gittleson, Terry Stout, Dawn Putnam, Karen Watts, Jennifer Nicholson, Mary Martzolf, Sarah Lorenz, and Tesha Thomas.

Works Cited

Amer, Elizabeth, and Constance Mungall. *Taking Action: Working Together for Positive Change in Your Community.* Toronto: Self-Counsel, 1992.

Amidei, Nancy. "How to Be an Advocate in Bad Times." *Strategies of Community Organizing.* Ed. Jack Rothman and John E. Tropman. Itasca, IL: Peacock, 1987. 106–14.

Atwell, Nancie. *In the Middle: New Understandings About Writing, Reading, and Learning.* Portsmouth, NH: Boynton/Cook, 1998.

Baker, Ann, and Johnny Baker. *Maths in the Mind: A Process Approach to Mental Strategies.* Portsmouth, NH: Heinemann, 1991.

Barbieri, Maureen. *Sounds from the Heart: Learning to Listen to Girls.* Portsmouth, NH: Heinemann, 1995.

Bayer, Renee. Personal interview. 21 Jan. 1998.

Berge, Carolyn. Personal interview. 8 Nov. 1997.

Berkowitz, William. *Local Heroes.* Lexington, MA: Lexington, 1987.

———. *Community Impact: Creating Grassroots Change in Hard Times.* Cambridge, MA: Schenkman, 1982.

Berliner, David, and Bruce Biddle. *The Manufactured Crisis: Myth, Fraud, and the Attack on America's Public Schools.* Reading, MA: Addison Wesley, 1995.

Berry, Thomas. *The Dream of the Earth.* San Francisco: Sierra Club, 1990.

Berthoff, Ann. *The Making of Meaning: Metaphors, Models, and Maxims for Writing Teachers.* Upper Montclair, NJ: Boynton/Cook, 1981.

Bradshaw, C., S. Soifer, and L. Gutierrez. "Toward a Hybrid Model for Effective Organizing in Communities of Color." *Journal of Community Practice* 1 (1994): 25–41.

Bryant, Bunyan. *Environmental Advocacy: Concepts, Issues, and Dilemmas.* Ann Arbor, MI: Caddo Gap, 1990.

Buchsbaum, Andrew. Personal interview. 31 May 1998.

Buehler, Jennifer. "Making Lifelong Readers." Unpublished essay, 1998.

Calkins, Lucy. *The Art of Teaching Writing.* Portsmouth, NH: Heinemann, 1986.

Cantor, Daniel. Personal interview. 8 Jan. 1998.

Caplan, Marc. *Ralph Nader Presents a Citizens' Guide to Lobbying.* New York: Dembner, 1983.

Center for Third World Organizing. *1998 Activist Training.* Oakland, CA, 1998.

Chiles, N. "Ebonics Might Just Work Out." *Ann Arbor News* 7 June 1998: A15.

Coombe, Chris M. "Using Empowerment Evaluation in Community Organizing and Community-Based Health Initiatives." *Community Organizing and Community Building for Health*. Ed. Meredith Minkler. New Brunswick: Rutgers UP, 1997. 291–307.

Cortes, Ernesto. Interview with Dave Winans. *NEA Today* (May 1996): 7.

Davey, Elizabeth. "Victory in Augusta Township: Activists Defeat Toxic Dump Plans." *From the Ground Up: An Official Publication of the Ecology Center* April–May 1998: 6–9, 18.

Delgado, Gary. *Beyond the Politics of Place: New Directions in Community Organizing*. Berkeley: Chardon, 1997.

———. *Organizing the Movement: The Roots and Growth of ACORN*. Philadelphia: Temple UP, 1986.

Duff, C. "ABCeething: How Whole Language Became a Hot Potato in and out of Academia." *Wall Street Journal* 30 October 1996: A1.

Easthope, Tracey, Personal interview. 16 Feb. 1998.

Fawcett, S. B., et al. "Empowering Community Health Initiatives through Evaluation." *Empowerment Evaluation: Knowledge and Tools for Self-Assessment and Accountability*. Ed. David M. Fetterman, Shakeh J. Kaftarian, and Abraham Wandersman. Thousand Oaks, CA: Sage, 1996.

Flanagan, Anna. "Beleaguered Principal Faces More Charges, Delayed Hearings." *Council Chronicle* June 1994: 1+.

———. "Myers to Be Expert Witness for Fired Teacher." *Council Chronicle* Sept. 1996: 1+.

Fleischer, Cathy. *Composing Teacher Research: A Prosaic History*. Albany: State U of New York P, 1995.

Fleischer, Cathy, and Laura Roop. "Reaching Out to the Community: Teachers as Advocates." Michigan Reading Association Annual Conference. Grand Rapids, MI. Mar. 1996.

———. "Taking It to the Streets: Teachers as Advocates." Michigan Writing Projects Leadership Conference. E. Lansing, MI. Feb. 1996.

Fleischer, Cathy, Richard Koch, Jennifer Lewis, and Laura Roop. "Learning to Walk It, Not Just Talk It: Standards and Michigan's Demonstration Sites." *Language Arts* 73 (1996): 36–43.

Garvin, Charles D., and Fred M. Cox. "A History of Community Organizing Since the Civil War, with Special Reference to Oppressed Communities." *Strategies of Community Intervention: Macro Practice*. Ed. Jack Rothman, John L. Erlich, and John E. Tropman. 5th ed. Itasca, IL: Peacock, 1995. 64–98.

Gaughan, John. *Cultural Reflections: Critical Teaching and Learning in the English Classroom*. Portsmouth, NH: Boynton/Cook, 1997.

Gibbs, Lois. *Dying from Dioxin: A Citizen's Guide to Reclaiming our Health and Rebuilding Democracy.* Boston: South End, 1995.

Gibbs, Lois, and Will Collette. *Leadership Handbook on Hazardous Waste: Organization, Foundation of Our Future.* Arlington, VA: Citizens Clearinghouse for Hazardous Wastes, 1983.

Goodman, Kenneth. *On Reading: A Common-Sense Look at the Nature of Language and the Science of Reading.* Portsmouth, NH: Heinemann, 1996.

———. *Phonics Phacts.* Portsmouth, NH: Heinemann, 1993.

Goswami, Dixie, and Peter Stillman. *Reclaiming the Classroom: Teacher Research as an Agency for Change.* Upper Montclair, NJ: Boynton/Cook, 1987.

Graves, Donald. *A Fresh Look at Writing.* Portsmouth, NH: Heinemann, 1994.

Hayes-Parvin, Kathleen. Personal interview. 1 May 1997.

Hope, Anne, and Sally Timmel. *Training for Transformation: A Handbook for Community Workers.* Gweru, Zimbabwe: Mambo, 1987.

Hyde, C. "A Feminist Model for Macro Practice: Promises and Problems." *Health Affairs* 9 (1989): 145–182.

Israel, Barbara. Personal interview. 17 Mar. 1998.

Israel, Barbara, Amy J. Schulz, Edith A. Parker, and Adam B. Becker. "Review of Community-Based Research: Assessing Partnership Approaches to Improve Public Health." *Annual Review of Public Health* 19 (1998): 173–202.

Kahn, Si. *Organizing: A Guide for Grassroots Leaders.* New York: McGraw-Hill, 1982.

King, Julie. Personal interview. 27 Oct. 1997.

Knoblauch, C. H., and Lil Brannon. *Critical Teaching and the Idea of Literacy.* Portsmouth, NH: Boynton/Cook, 1993.

Leo, John. "The Answer Is 45 Cents." *U.S. News and World Report* 21 Apr. 1997: 14.

Levine, Michael. *Guerrilla P.R.: How You Can Wage an Effective Publicity Campaign—Without Going Broke.* New York: HarperBusiness, 1993.

Lightner, Candy, and Nancy Hathaway. *Giving Sorrow Words: How to Cope with Grief and Get on with Your Life.* New York: Warner, 1990.

Lorenz, Sarah. Personal interview. 27 May 1998.

McNeil, Larry. "The Soft Arts of Organizing." *Social Policy* 16 (Winter 1995): 16–22.

Meier, Ronda, and Amy Pace. Personal interview. 2 Feb. 1998.

Michigan Literacy Consortium Journal 30 (Winter 1997).

Minkler, Meredith. "Community-Based Research." Panel discussion in series sponsored by Center for Community Service and Learning. Ann Arbor, MI. 12 Mar. 1998.

Minkler, Meredith, ed. *Community Organizing and Community Building for Health.* New Brunswick, NJ: Rutgers UP, 1997.

Minkler, Meredith, and Cheri Pies. "Ethical Issues in Community Organization and Community Participation." *Community Organizing and Community Building for Health.* Ed. Meredith Minkler. New Brunswick, NJ: Rutgers UP, 1997. 120–138.

Minkler, Meredith, and Nina Wallerstein. "Improving Health through Community Organization and Community Building: A Health Education Perspective." *Community Organizing and Community Building for Health.* Ed. Meredith Minkler. New Brunswick, NJ: Rutgers UP, 1997. 30–52.

Peterson, Ralph. *Life in a Crowded Place: Making a Learning Community.* Portsmouth, NH: Heinemann, 1992.

Pilisuk, Marc, Joann McAllister, and Jack Rothman. "Social Change Professionals and Grassroots Organizing." *Community Organizing and Community Building for Health.* Ed. Meredith Minkler. New Brunswick, NJ: Rutgers UP, 1997. 103–119.

PIRGIM membership brochure. Ann Arbor: The Public Interest Research Group in Michigan, 1998.

Rief, Linda. *Seeking Diversity: Language Arts with Adolescents.* Portsmouth, NH: Heinemann, 1992.

Rose, Mike. *Possible Lives: The Promise of Public Education in America.* Boston: Houghton Mifflin, 1995.

Rothman, Jack. "Approaches to Community Intervention." *Strategies of Community Organization.* Ed. Jack Rothman, John Erlich, and John Tropman. Itasca, IL: F. E. Peacock , 1995. 26–63.

———. "Three Models of Community Organization Practice." *National Conference on Social Welfare, Social Work Practice, 1968: Selected Papers.* New York: Columbia UP, 1968.

Routman, Regie. *Literacy at the Crossroads: Crucial Talk about Reading, Writing and Other Teaching Dilemmas.* Portsmouth, NH: Heinemann, 1996.

Sagady, Alex. "Environmental Streetfighting." Unpublished pamphlet.

Schlechty, Phillip C. *Schools for the Twenty-First Century: Leadership Imperatives for Educational Reform.* San Francisco: Jossey-Bass, 1990.

Schön, Donald. *The Reflective Practitioner: How Professionals Think in Action.* New York: Basic, 1983.

Sherry, Susan, and Clair Lipschultz. "Consumer Education as a Community Activator." *Tactics and Techniques of Community Practice.* Ed. Fred Cox, John Erlich, Jack Rothman, and John Tropman. Itasca, IL: F. E. Peacock, 1984.

Shockley, Betty, Barbara Michalove, and JoBeth Allen. *Engaging Families: Connecting Home and School Literacy Communities.* Portsmouth, NH: Heinemann, 1995.

Staples, Lee. "Selecting and 'Cutting' the Issue." *Community Organizing and Community Building for Health.* Ed. Meredith Minkler. New Brunswick, NJ: Rutgers UP, 1997. 175–194.

Stout, Terry. Unpublished project proposal, 1998.

Sunstein, Bonnie. *Composing a Culture: Inside a Summer Writing Program with High School Teachers.* Portsmouth, NH: Boynton/Cook, 1994.

Swap, Susan M. *Developing Home-School Partnerships: From Concepts to Practice.* New York: Teachers College, 1993.

Taylor, Denny. *Beginning to Read and the Spin Doctors of Science: The Political Campaign to Change America's Mind about How Children Learn to Read.* Urbana, IL: NCTE, 1998.

Vopat, James. *The Parent Project: A Workshop Approach to Parent Involvement.* York, ME: Stenhouse, 1994.

Wallack, Lawrence. "Media Advocacy: A Strategy for Empowering People and Communities." *Community Organizing and Community Building for Health.* Ed. Meredith Minkler. New Brunswick, NJ: Rutgers UP, 1997. 339–352.

Wallerstein, Nina, Victoria Sanchez-Merki, and Lily Dow. "Freirean Praxis in Health Education and Community Organizing: A Case Study." *Community Organizing and Community Building for Health.* Ed. Meredith Minkler. New Brunswick, NJ: Rutgers UP, 1997. 195–215.

Walter, Cheryl. "Community Building Practice." *Community Organizing and Community Building for Health.* Ed. Meredith Minkler. New Brunswick, NJ: Rutgers UP, 1997. 68–87.

Watts, Karen. Unpublished project proposal, 1998.

Weaver, Constance. *Teaching Grammar in Context.* Portsmouth, NH: Boynton/ Cook, 1996.

Weil, M. "Women, Community and Organizing." *Feminist Visions for Social Work.* Ed. Nan Van Den Bergh and Lynn B. Cooper. Silver Spring, MD: National Association of Social Workers, 1986.

Wilson, David. *Attempting Change: Teachers Moving from Writing Project to Classroom Practice.* Portsmouth, NH: Boynton/Cook, 1994.

Wixson, Karen K., Charles W. Peters, and Sheila A. Potter. "The Case for Integrated Standards in English Language Arts. *Language Arts* 73 (Jan. 1996): 20–29.

Wolfe, Denny, and Joseph Antinarella. *Deciding to Lead: The English Teacher as Reformer.* Portsmouth, NH: Boynton/Cook/Heinemann, 1997.

Zemelman, Steven, Harvey Daniels, and Arthur Hyde. *Best Practice: New Standards for Teaching and Learning in America's Schools.* Portsmouth, NH: Heinemann, 1993.

Index

Author

Cathy Fleischer is professor of English language and literature at Eastern Michigan University, where she teaches courses in English education and literacy and directs the Eastern Michigan Writing Project. In addition to her outreach work with K–12 teachers, she serves on the school improvement team and volunteers weekly in her sons' classrooms at Northside Elementary School in Ann Arbor. She is the author of *Composing Teaching Research: A Prosaic History* and *Literacy and Democracy* (with David Schaafsma), as well as a number of articles about literacy and teacher research.

This book was typeset in Palatino and Helvetica by Electronic Imaging.
The typefaces used on the cover were Garamond, Industria Solid, and Officina Sans.
The book was printed on 60 lb. Lynx Opaque by Versa Press.